State, Society and Religious Engineering

The **Institute of Southeast Asian Studies (ISEAS)** was established as an autonomous organization in 1968. It is a regional centre dedicated to the study of socio-political, security and economic trends and developments in Southeast Asia and its wider geostrategic and economic environment. The Institute's research programmes are the Regional Economic Studies (RES, including ASEAN and APEC), Regional Strategic and Political Studies (RSPS), and Regional Social and Cultural Studies (RSCS).

ISEAS Publishing, an established academic press, has issued almost 2,000 books and journals. It is the largest scholarly publisher of research about Southeast Asia from within the region. ISEAS Publishing works with many other academic and trade publishers and distributors to disseminate important research and analyses from and about Southeast Asia to the rest of the world.

SECOND EDITION

State, Society and Religious Engineering

Towards a Reformist Buddhism in Singapore

KUAH-PEARCE KHUN ENG

ISEAS

INSTITUTE OF SOUTHEAST ASIAN STUDIES
SINGAPORE

This Second Edition published in Singapore in 2009 by
ISEAS Publishing
Institute of Southeast Asian Studies
30 Heng Mui Keng Terrace
Pasir Panjang
Singapore 119614
E-mail: publish@iseas.edu.sg
Website: <http://bookshop.iseas.edu.sg>

The responsibility for facts and opinions in this publication rests exclusively with the author and her interpretations do not necessarily reflect the views or the policy of the publisher or its supporters.

ISEAS Library Cataloguing-in-Publication Data

Kuah-Pearce Khun Eng.
   State, society, and religious engineering : towards a reformist Buddhism in Singapore / Kuah-Pearce Khun Eng.
   2nd ed.
   1.   Buddhism—Singapore.
   2.   Buddhism—Social aspects—Singapore.
   3.   Buddhism and state—Singapore.
BQ569 S6K95 2009   2009

ISBN 978-981-230-865-8 (soft cover)
ISBN 978-981-230-913-6 (PDF)

Photo Credit: The photograph used on the front cover, the Dragon Light Pagoda at Lian Shan Shuang Lin Monastery in Singapore, is taken by Jasmine P.R. Pearce, reproduced with her kind permission.

Typeset by International Typesetters Pte Ltd
Printed in Singapore by Utopia Press Pte Ltd

Contents

List of Diagrams

Note on Romanisation

Chinese terms and names are transliterated by the *Hanyu Pinyin* system in the text with a hyphen between each Chinese character. Commonly-used terms and names are romanised according to the original spelling that appeared in the texts. In Singapore, this is often romanised according to the Fujian (Hokkien) dialect [H], the most commonly-used dialect in Singapore. Those that appear as quotations are written as they are in the original texts, which are spelled according to the Wade-Giles system [WG]. There are also several Cantonese [C], Japanese [J] and Pali [P] words. A list of the romanised terms and names and their corresponding Chinese characters is provided in the glossary at the back of the book.

Preface to the Second Edition

Religion, since the beginning of human civilisation, has played a crucial role in all societies. Its metaphysical appeal continues to fulfil individuals' imagination and quest for an understanding of the unknown and the events that unfold before our eyes. Such a role has become even more significant with the dawn of the 21st century as societies have become more complicated and besieged by increasing wants both metaphysical and material in nature. As we move into the age of globalisation, fraught with relativism that challenges existing structures, institutions and ideologies, we are confronted with a multitude of behaviours and insatiable demands that expose the world as both rational and chaotic, moral and immoral, and compassionate and ruthless. Amidst these conflicting demands, individuals continue to cope with religious and spiritual imaginations.

So, where does religion stand on the global stage in the contemporary world? Since the 9/11 incident in 2001, the world has been looking at all types of religious activities, religious revivalism and religious renaissance in a cautious manner. Could religion lead to what Huntington (1996) viewed as "clashes of civilization" considered inevitable because of differing ideological underpinnings of the different religions within different socio-political cultures, or could it be as the old school of thought has argued that religion continues its journey into humanity, allowing for discursive understandings and shaping the moral underpinnings of each individual society.

While the impact of the 9/11 incident has made us re-examine religions on the global stage, cementing the link between religion and politics and religion and security issues, too much attention today has been paid to this set of relationships, often neglecting the other aspects of religion in the globalised world that we live in. The political and security issues confronting religious activities often make it to the front page of major newspapers. Attention is focussed on the Islamic extremist groups and their actions or would-be terrorist activities foiled by various governments in the world. At the same time, the violence between Buddhism and Hinduism has also made headlines in the news. Towards the end of 2007 and first half of 2008, attention was turned to Buddhism with the sudden assembly of monks in saffron robes taking to the streets in protest against authoritarian regimes with regard to religious freedom, human rights issues and political freedom in Myanmar and Tibet. Such high profile movements gained worldwide attention.

While such high profile actions made news, it is imperative for scholars and individuals within the communities to understand the root cause of such actions when religion and politics have become closely intertwined. At the same time, it is also imperative that the spiritual aspect which is the *raison d'être* is not neglected.

For the last three decades, Buddhism has gradually increased its influence on the global stage and with new converts from various parts of the world. In particular, Buddhism has experienced rapid development in America, Europe, and Australia, alongside its stronghold in the various Asian countries. At the same time, in Asia, Buddhism has also seen a rapid revival although in a different form that is more in tandem with the modern individual and youthful needs. From Japan to Southeast Asia, China and beyond, it is blooming. In Japan and Taiwan, various new Buddhist groups have emerged and taken root not only within their own society, but also in the western societies. Likewise in Southeast Asia, a new reformist wave has swept through countries such as Thailand, Vietnam, Myanmar, Malaysia, and Singapore as the elites seek to reform and modernise to suit modern Buddhism needs.

This book thus aims to fill a gap in the literature on the Sociology/Anthropology of Religion by attempting to understand the modern needs of Singapore Chinese. Their religious pursuits have resulted in the transformation of a folk-based syncretic Buddhism into a modern Reformist Buddhism in Singapore through self-introspection of the Reformist monks, nuns and lay Buddhists. At the same time, this book studies the state-society-religion relationship and why the Singapore state continues to view religion as playing a crucial socio-cultural role in Singapore's multi-ethnic society. As such, the state established stringent guidelines to engineer the direction of the major religions in Singapore. The Singapore state has actively used various policies to encourage the religious groups to become socially engaged.

Reformist Buddhism in Singapore has grown out of a syncretic Chinese religious tradition which is commonly called *Shenism* where the saying is "going into a temple, one must light a joss-stick". Amidst the syncretic practices, there is a large element of Mahayana Buddhism. In addition, there is also a Singhalese culturalised version of Theravada Buddhist tradition patronised by the small Singhalese community and the Peranakan Chinese in Singapore. Today, Reformist Buddhism has taken root in Singapore society as many relate to its scriptural-orientation, focus on meditation, and compassion-based type of activities.

Another important aspect in the global revivalism of religion is its humanistic role where religious institutions throughout the world have become socially-engaged in education, welfare work and relief efforts at home and abroad. Increasingly, transnationalising compassion and work associated with religious philanthropy have become an important arena within the global religious supermarket.

Reformist Buddhism in contemporary Singapore society is now broadly seen as a humanist and socially-engaged Buddhism that seeks to promote spiritualism and compassion to the wider population. Thus, individual Reformist Buddhists engage in spiritual pursuit at one level and humanist and socially-engaged acts such as the provision of educational and welfare activities and facilities at another level. In so doing, Reformist Buddhists in Singapore create a new niche for themselves by becoming active providers of compassion.

The challenge for Reformist Buddhism in Singapore today is to reinvent itself at regular intervals. It also needs to seek out new niches that are closely grounded to the community where adherents are socially engaged in activities that are within the understanding and interpretation of their religious duties. In so doing, Reformist

Buddhism will ensure that it continues to be relevant to the needs of its adherents and their community as it marches into the 21st century.

Kuah-Pearce Khun Eng
2009

Acknowledgements to the Second Edition

I am grateful to the Institute of Southeast Asian Studies, Singapore, for their support in publishing the second edition of this book.

In pursuing this research, I am indebted to different groups of people for their assistance. I am most grateful to my informants – the lay people, the monks and nuns – who have endured numerous rounds of interviews and shared their thoughts and ideas with me. I am especially grateful to some monks and nuns who have allowed me extensive stays in their temples and nunneries so I could experience the ascetic monastic lifestyle. Without their readiness and their openness to answer all my queries, it would have been very difficult to complete this book. I have also benefitted greatly from discussions and information provided by members of the Curriculum Development Institute of Singapore and the Ministry of Education while conducting research in Singapore. I would also like to acknowledge my colleagues and friends at Monash University and the University of Hong Kong for their support in this research.

My family has been the most important pillar of support. I am truly grateful to them for they have made it a joy to conduct this piece of research. This book is dedicated to my mother and late father. Needless to say, any shortcomings remain my sole responsibility.

I also wish to thank the following journals and publishers for their kind permission to reproduce portions of the following pieces that appear in this book:

(i) Taylor and Francis (Routledge Journal), "Maintaining Ethno-Religious Harmony in Singapore", *Journal of Contemporary Asia*, 1998, 28(1): 103-121 (reproduced in Chapter 4).

(ii) Blackwell Publishing (John Wiley and Sons Inc), "Buddhism, Moral Education and Nation-Building in Singapore", first appeared in *Pacific Viewpoint*, 1991, 32(1): 24-42 (reproduced in Chapter 6).

(iii) Taylor and Francis (Routledge Journal), "Confucian Ideology and Social Engineering in Singapore", *Journal of Contemporary Asia*, 1990, 20(3): 371-382 (reproduced in Chapter 6).

(iv) Institute of Southeast Asian Studies, (ISEAS) Singapore, "Delivering Welfare Services in Singapore: A Strategic Partnership between Buddhism and the State", in *Religious Diversity in Singapore*, edited by Lai Ah Eng, (Singapore: Institute of Southeast Asian Studies, 2008, pp. 505-523) (reproduced in Chapter 5).

Introduction

Religion plays an important role in the process of modernisation and social change in contemporary societies. Likewise, a changing socio-economic and socio-political environment has forced existing religions to change and cater to the modern needs of the people, the society and the state. This is particularly the case in a post-modernist era with the rise of religious movements and a revival in the various world religions such as Islam, Christianity, Buddhism and Hinduism.

RELIGIOUS CHANGE AND MODERNISATION

This book explores religious modernisation and change within the Singapore Chinese society. It will focus on how Chinese religious syncretism – Shenism – is being forced to change and adapt to the modern needs of society and state. It will examine the process of "Buddhicisation" of the Chinese religious syncretism and a movement towards Reformist Buddhism within the Chinese community where 65% of the Buddhists now regard themselves as Reformist Buddhists. In this process of religious modernisation and change, the agents responsible for transforming the religious landscape of the Singapore Chinese include the Singapore state, the Buddhist Sangha and the Reformist Buddhists within the Chinese community. On top of this, the Christians, particularly Christian fundamentalists, with their aggressive proselytisation and rapid conversion rate, serve as a catalyst to hasten religious change within the Chinese community.

In searching for an answer to understand the relationship between religious change and modernisation in Singapore, it is imperative for us to explore the process of modernisation. Early debates on modernisation focus on the role of colonialism, the emergence of a group of Western-trained modern elites and the acquisition of Western skills in bringing about political, social and economic changes in a country. Modernisation is often equated with Westernisation, and this modernising path continues to be taken for granted in many parts of Asia today (Lerner, 1958; Apter, 1965; and Alter, 1989). Among the politicians in Singapore, modernisation continues to be equated with Westernisation in the immediate years of independence up till the 1980s. Since the late 1980s, with the then Prime Minister, Lee Kuan Yew, at the forefront, there has been a push among the Asian countries for the Asian brand of modernisation culminating in the "Great Debates on Asian Values".

On the academic front, a group of scholars gathered to discuss the issue of "multiple modernities" in an attempt to understand the various paths of modernisation embarked upon by different countries in the world today. They argued that the early theories of modernisation prevalent in the 1950s were based on the Western notion of modernity and hence, were inaccurate. They argued that modernisation should not be equated with Westernisation and that many countries today while in the process of modernisation continue to retain their own cultural characteristics and indigenous ideologies (Eisenstadt, 2000: 1-29). Tu argued that the rise of "Confucian East Asia" spells out the importance of traditions and local knowledge of non-Western countries as imperative factors in understanding the modernising process of East Asia. He further saw the need to understand non-Western perceptions of the modern West in order for us to gain a balanced view of the various paths towards modernisation (Tu, 2000: 196). He argued that Confucianism and non-Western spiritual traditions could help shape the modernising process (Tu, 2000: 198). It is thus no surprise that political leaders such as Singapore's Lee Kuan Yew and Malaysia's Mahathir Mohamad advocated "Asian Values" for their citizens (Tu, 2000: 199-200). Another aspect of the debate focussed on the transnational linkages between Singapore and Malaysia and their Diaspora communities where movements between them would bring about knowledge that would help each country embark on a unique path towards modernisation (Tambiah, 2000: 163-194).

To a certain extent, religious modernisation followed the Western model of modernisation on the one hand as evident from the Reformist Buddhists, many of whom were Western-educated and brought with them Western ideas of modernisation. On the other hand, there were the counter-elites of Reformist Buddhism, as well as the government, who have pushed for an alternative path of modernisation. For the Reformist Buddhist counter-elites, they brought along their Chinese traditions while the Singapore government attempted to use religious traditions as part of the "Asian Values" system that it had advocated to the general population.

INVENTING A RELIGIOUS TRADITION – CHINESE RELIGIOUS SYNCRETISM

The first focus of this book is to discuss how Chinese religious syncretism was invented during the early colonial years and continued to be the main religious belief system of the Singapore Chinese until recent challenges by the Reformist Buddhists. The early Chinese migrated to colonial Singapore from the two provinces of Guangdong and Fujian during the 19th century and the early part of the 20th century. During the colonial years, selected deities and rituals were reproduced and aimed at recreating a familiar religious environment as was found in the villages of China, whence the migrants came. At the same time, other aspects of the religious rituals, including the deities, were invented to cater to the needs of these early migrants.

Shenism derives its religious ideology from an eclectic mix of the wider Chinese cosmology that includes Daoist understanding of the polarity of *yin* and *yang* and the five elements, Buddhist understanding of karma, death and rebirth, and selected Confucian values. It also includes the worshipping of various folk gods and deities. During the early years, the gods and deities were worshipped by individual migrants in the clan or dialect-based temples. Likewise, communal religious celebrations were conducted for the benefit of the community. Communal religious celebrations were significant in establishing the Chinese community as a social entity and reminded the migrants of the social links between their local and village communities. Ancestor worship and religious celebrations during the various festive seasons were especially important. Likewise, certain gods and deities such as the Heavenly Empress, *Tian-hou*, the War Hero, *Guan-Di*, and a local deity, *Da-bo-gong* provided emotional and psychological comfort to these migrants. All these gods and deities, together with the rituals performance, continue to play a significant role among the Singapore Chinese today.

Another salient feature of the Chinese religion lies in the performance of death rituals and the prevalence of ancestor worship. Death was common during the colonial period and, being away from the home village, the performance of one's last rites became crucial for most migrants. The fear that the souls of the dead might continue to wander was unacceptable. So the recreation of the death rituals became an essential part of life in the migrant community. Village monks and priests were engaged precisely for this purpose. Today, this continues to be an important preoccupation of the Singapore Chinese.

The tradition of performing rituals is also important in establishing the Chinese as one community vis-à-vis the other ethnic communities of Malays and Indians, thereby providing the Chinese with a distinctive identity.

STATE AND RELIGIOUS ENGINEERING

A second focus of this book is to explore the role of the modern state in religious engineering. The modern Singapore state has played a very active role in modernising the various religions in Singapore. Religion is seen as an important instrument in promoting nationalism and nation-building on the one hand, and is regarded as a sensitive element in maintaining its ethno-religious balance on the other hand.

Since independence in 1965, the Singapore state has consciously attempted to create a nation out of an ethnically-diverse population. In a sense, it attempted to create an imagined community where the population, despite their ethnic differences, would call itself a nation (Anderson, 1986). Here, the Singapore state looks upon itself as being responsible for creating a sense of Singapore nationalism by implementing a process of nation-building. Thus, this group of modernising elites under the leadership of Lee Kuan Yew, a by-product of colonialism, and have acquired Western skills were seen to challenge the traditional status quo and pushed for modernisation and urbanisation (Apter, 1965). At the same time, there was a desire by these elites to break down traditional primordial ties in favour of the nation-state ideology (Alter, 1989). The fact that the ethnic migrants did not have a concept of nation-state but nevertheless opted to become Singapore citizens after independence meant that a new political culture needed to be created and a political tradition needed to be invented for their consumption.

The People's Action Party (PAP) government has been active in all aspects of its citizens' lives – in work, family, education and religion (Quah, Chan, and Seah, 1985). Social engineering and rhetorical persuasion, such as campaigns, are used to educate the people into acceptable political and social ideologies and actions. Sometimes, the legislature is also used to ensure social compliance to the various policies and campaigns.

Related to this is the process of religious engineering. In this area, the Singapore state has expressed anxiety over the religious conflicts among its ethnic populations. This anxiety was founded in the colonial past when failure to manage religious and ethnic relations resulted in two racial riots – the Racial Riot of 1964 and the Maria Hertogh Incident of 1951 – and which spelled out the underlying tensions among the ethnic communities. As a result of these two racial riots, the state has been attempting to contain racial tension through the management of the religious composition of its population. It established the ethno-religious link – the CMIO-BDIHC model. CMIO refers to the four main state – recognised ethnic categories, mainly Chinese, Malay, Indian and Others. "Others" refers to all other ethnic groups that do not fit into the Chinese, Malay and Indian categories. BDHIC refers to the main religious groups that are officially recognised in Singapore, mainly Buddhism, Daoism, Islam, Hinduism and Christianity. The state sees each ethnic group as closely affiliated to one religion in a multi-racial and multi-religious Singapore. It also sees the various religious systems playing an important role in promoting indigenous religious values to the adherents, thereby facilitating the state's push for an Asian values system in Singapore. Furthermore, it encourages the various religious institutions to become involved in welfare work for its citizens, thereby restructuring religion into socially-productive units of the society. In so doing, it forces the religious institutions to play a more significant social role in society and thus redefining the social agenda of the religious institutions. The Singapore state is able to engineer religious change through exercising strong bureaucratic and legal control and the use of its legislative power.

PRIVATISATION AND SECULARISATION OF A PERSONAL BELIEF SYSTEM – REFORMIST BUDDHISM

A third focus of this book is to explore the role of religion in the life of modern individuals. Today, contemporary demands and needs have led to a reassessment of this system of religious belief - Shenism and its orthodox religious ideology and ritual contents. The modernisation of Shenism has greatly changed its religious content, although the basic structure of ideology and social structure remain as they were. The religious ideology embodies elements of Buddhism, Confucianism, Daoism and elements of folk beliefs. Chinese Shenist religious rituals consist of elaborate practices found in numerous communal and domestic religious celebrations. The outcome has been a separation of the religious belief into two separate systems: a system of rituals and a system of ideology. The first is a modernised and institutionalised form of Shenism that is increasingly being rationalised as part of the wider Chinese culture. The second is a strong movement towards Reformist Buddhism. With Reformist Buddhism, the traditional role of the monks and nuns as ritual specialists is regarded as inadequate. In the Buddhist monastic order today, also known as the Sangha, members are expected to be not only religious specialists but also to be knowledgeable in scriptures and involved in welfare work.

This change is necessary to cater to a new generation of local Chinese whose view of religion differs greatly from the early Chinese migrants. They are not only interested in the functional aspects of religion, but rather are intent on seeking solutions to their individualised religious needs and personalised spiritual fulfilment. As with other modern religious trends, they see their religious needs as personal, no longer tied to the religious needs of their families or community. Thus, religion, to many of them, is a personal quest for spiritualism.

Among the younger generation of Singapore Chinese, there is an increasing level of dissatisfaction with the existing Shenist ritual practices that they consider "meaningless", "irrational" and "superstitious" and thus there is an attempt to rationalise these Shenist practices. Weber argues that the higher the level of rationalisation, the higher the level of inner tension experienced by individuals, culminating with a "break" in the social structure (Weber, 1958). Depending on the level of tensions and the resolutions sought, a radical religious ethic can develop. This new religious ethic may follow one of two paths: one of mastery and the other of resignation. The path of mastery is called asceticism and that of resignation (i.e., leaving things to "fate" or "god's will") is called adjustment or mysticism. To Weber, it is the mastery over the worldly aspects of individual life and social conditions that is most favourable for the development of a new religious ethic. He saw Ascetic Protestantism as an attempt at mastery of the world in which "every man became a monk but lived out his 'monastic' commitments in secular callings in this world" (Weber, 1958). To a certain degree, what the Singapore Chinese, alias Reformist Buddhists, are trying to do is to embark on a process of religious rationalisation according to the path of mastery by pushing for a new religious ethic in Reformist Buddhism. This is especially so in the promotion of ascetic Reformist Buddhism where individual Reformist Buddhists become lay monks and nuns.

Religious change occurs at three levels: the individual, the society and the state. At the individual level, it involves an understanding of the individual ideological consciousness (Luckmann, 1967). Luckmann sees the establishment of a private religious sphere within the individual as the most significant religious change that has taken place in the 20th century (Luckmann, 1967: 101). This is why the Singapore Chinese are now increasingly attempting to refocus on individual spiritualism away from communal religious celebrations, where they see religion as a private domain and that it concerns their personal belief. Individual religious freedom becomes an important issue here and one can choose to believe in one or another religion. The communal-based ritual practices become less significant to them. Thus, Lenski (1963) identifies two types of religious involvement, associational and communal, and two types of religious orientation, doctrinal orthodoxy and devotionalism.

Another area that the Singapore Chinese, together with the Singapore state, have embarked upon is their attempt at religious secularisation. Secularisation is, first, a decline in religion where the previously-accepted doctrines and institutions lose their prestige and influence in which " traditional religious symbols and forms have lost force and appeals" (Yinger, 1957: 119). In the case of the Singapore Chinese, the Shenist ritual practice has lost its appeal among the younger Singapore Chinese where the "mystical and supernatural elements" are being replaced by "a demythologised, ethical rather than theological religion" (Glock and Stark, 1968: 116). In our case, the focus is on scriptural Reformist Buddhism.

Second, secularisation is seen as "conformity with this world where the religious group or the religiously-informed society turns its attention from the supernatural and becomes more and more interested in this world" (Shiner, 1967: 211). The Reformist Buddhist attempts to be relevant to this world by taking on welfare work and by introducing an alternative spiritual-cum-secular lifestyle package to its adherents. Likewise, secularisation is seen as a separation of the sacred from the profane. As a result of this separation, religion is confined to the sphere of private life. This process results in an inward-looking religion that has little or no influence on institutions or corporate action. As a result, religion has no appearance outside the sphere of religious group within a society (Shiner: 1967: 213). Fourth, secularisation is seen as "a transposition of religious beliefs and institutions where knowledge, patterns of behaviour and institutional arrangements which were once understood as grounded in divine power are transformed into phenomena of purely human creation and responsibility" (Shiner, 1967: 214). Secularisation therefore results in a completely "rational world society in which the phenomenon of the supernatural or even of mystery would play no part (Shiner, 1967: 216). Ideally, the Reformist Buddhists would like to eliminate the mythical and supernatural elements from both the Buddhist and Shenist practices.

At the individual level, it is possible to argue that a move towards Reformist Buddhism represents a trend towards a privatisation and secularisation of the Chinese religious system, "a process in which autonomous institutional ideologies replaced, within their domain, an overarching and transcendent universe of norms" (Luckmann, 1967: 101). In this case, the primary concern of the individual is towards personal spiritualism and self-enlightenment. Here the move is towards the establishment of a private religious sphere within the individual that is the most significant religious change that has taken place (Luckmann, 1967: 101).

At the societal level, there are changes within the religious institutions where there is a separation of the secular from the sacred activities. Here, there is a separation of the temple from the Sangha, resulting in each performing separate roles. Temples can perform both religious and secular duties while monks and nuns are increasingly being confined to their roles in the religious spheres or those duties that are closely related to the religious morality. Furthermore, institutional change also resulted in a high level of bureaucratisation of the temple and Sangha structure, restructuring both institutions into modern-day bureaucracy.

While modern society stresses rationality and claims that the moral orders based on religious ethics become invalid, Wilson argues that there is constantly a desire by society to rejuvenate traditional religious teachings and rituals to cope with a rational and impersonal modern social structure (Wilson, 1982). To a certain degree, while Shenist practices have undergone a process of rationalisation, many of the traditional rituals continue to be enacted in communal religious fairs, reflecting the durability of these rituals in face of modernisation.

Furthermore, Wilson also argues that many of these traditional religious ethics find their expression in sectarian movements, and are patronised by individuals on a voluntary basis (Wilson, 1982). The emergence of religious sects is part of religious change and modernisation. Throughout the world, sects emerge when traditional religious institutions fail to provide for the religious needs of the adherents. A religious sect is a group with the following characteristics. First, it has exclusive membership and does not admit dual allegiance. Second, it claims a monopoly of religious truth. Third, it is often a lay organisation. Fourth, it rejects the secular notion of the division of labour and denies special religious virtuosity to anyone except its own founders and leaders. Fifth, its membership is marked by voluntarism. Sixth, it exercises sanctions against its members. Seventh, it demands total allegiance. Finally, it is a protest group (Wilson, 1982: 91-92). To a certain degree, Reformist Buddhism is a response to the changing needs of the Singapore Chinese on the one hand, and to their disenchantment with and protest against the Shenist practices on the other hand. Furthermore, it can be seen also as a protest movement against the aggressive proselytisation embarked upon by the Christian groups and the increased conversion to Christianity.

Today, different groups of Reformist Buddhists have emerged. Although they differ significantly from Christian sects, some nevertheless have similar features, such as exclusive membership, a lay organisation, voluntary membership, absolute allegiance from their members and an ability to function as protest groups (Wilson, 1982: 91-92).

Reformist Buddhism for the Singapore Chinese is new yet familiar. It stresses heavily the scripture and the learning of Buddhist teachings, also known as the dharma. Thus, it represents a shift from Chinese syncretism to ideological Buddhist scriptural purity. Reformist Buddhism also carries with it a class dimension. It has great appeal among the educated middle class Chinese elite in Singapore, as well as among similar groups in America and Europe who are seeking an alternative religion that will answer their quest for religiosity.

STATE, SOCIETY AND RELIGION

A fourth focus of this book is to explore the relationship between society and state in this process of religious modernisation. The relationship between the Singapore state and the Chinese community in their efforts at religious modernisation is an interesting one. Each has its own reason and agenda for pushing ahead with modernisation, but because of converging interests they have been able to establish a working relationship and ensure a relatively smooth process of change. The state wants to restructure Chinese religious syncretism into a modern religion to fit into a modern image befitting a modern metropolis. This coincides with the aspirations of the Reformist Buddhists to transform Shenism into a modern rational religion. Both the state and the Reformist Buddhists see the provision of welfare services as an acceptable modern rational image for Reformist Buddhism. As such, the Reformist Buddhists have consciously created this welfare niche as part of its modernising image. Furthermore, the Reformist Buddhists, by working hand in hand with the state in promoting various social values, integrate themselves into the political culture of the state.

However, the Chinese are also restructuring Shenism and promoting Reformist Buddhism according to their internal communal needs. Buddhicisation has resulted in a movement towards Reformist Buddhism and an increased awareness of Buddhism among the Chinese population. At the same time, rationalisation of Shenism has resulted in the elimination of some of the magical practices at the individual level, but at the communal level, communal religious functions continue to be celebrated on a large-scale basis. These communal religious celebrations are fully recognised as part of Chinese culture by the rational secular Singapore state. For example, Hungry Ghost Festival, Qing-Ming Festival and the Chinese-style funeral rites are widely rationalised as distinctive hallmarks of the Chinese cultural identity instead of being seen merely as Chinese religious practices.

At the crux of the state involvement in religious engineering is its desire to separate politics and religion. The state argues that it needs to maintain religious neutrality to ensure that all religions are given equal status and rights, as enshrined in the Singapore Constitution. To ensure this is observed, it argues that all religious groups need to observe and consciously separate religion from politics. Furthermore, the roles of religion and religious institutions are clearly spelt out in the Maintenance of Religious Harmony Act of 1991. In this respect, the state has acted according to what it thinks is best for itself and its citizens. The dynamics of state, society and religion are played out in full in Singapore society. The perceived sensitivity of religion and religious relationships among the various groups has led the state to exercise its full power. Although the state is highly involved in religious engineering, it is cautious in its treatment of all religious groups so as to attain a stable equilibrium through various legislation and policies despite the inherent tension among the various ethno-religious groups.

Part of the aspirations and ideals of the state converge with those of the Reformist Buddhists. Both see the path towards Reformist Buddhism as the ultimate direction of religious modernisation. Because of this, the involvement of the state in religious engineering is received with enthusiasm by the reformers. These converging objectives of the state and the Reformist Buddhists serve to provide the socio-legal legitimacy for the reformation to take place without much tension between state and society on the one hand and between the reformers and the traditionalists on the other. Although there continues to be dissatisfaction among a small group of Chinese, they find little support within the rest of Chinese community.

In this process of religious engineering, it is possible to argue that the state has emerged once again, as in other social and economic fields, a Confucian paternal guardian exercising its moral authority and dictating the broad direction of religious modernisation within the wider society and the Chinese community. At the same time, it leaves the Chinese community to fill in the details of its religion.

RELIGIOUS GLOBALISATION

A final focus of this book is to explore briefly the impact of religious globalisation on the local Reformist Buddhist movement in Singapore. Since the 1980s, there has been a strong resurgence of religious revivalist movements throughout the world. In Asia, the United States, Europe, Africa and Latin America, these religious movements have gathered strength. For example, the emergence of the Christian-based Liberation Theology can be found in Latin America and parts of Asia. Likewise, in the Middle East and parts of Asia, the Islamic Dakwah Movements have gathered much momentum. A strongly-resurgent Buddhist Revivalist Movement can be found in Asia and America. And in the sub-continent of India, Hindu resurgence has occurred. The focus of religious revivalism is on the self-renewal of one's position and identity in a globalised world where rapid modernisation and modern communication technologies have resulted in a loss of identity and values. These movements have brought new meaning to the various religions found in the Asia Pacific countries that have been suffering from a decline in membership and are facing competition from Christian evangelists.

These pan-religious movements cut across political boundaries and have the effect of binding those of the same faith irrespective of their nationality. The globalisation of religious movements has been brought about as a result of the availability of information technology in an increasingly globalised world that has become more compressed in time and space. The influence of these religious movements on different groups of people has become more intense as knowledge has reinforced competition, until no community now is immune to this new wave of religious revivalism that has penetrated every part of the world. All these religious movements have sought to convert others to their faith through their numerous activities, some being more successful than others.

The process of globalisation within the social and religious spheres has led to the emergence of a global religious culture that can be transmitted almost instantaneously from one place to another, largely through the mass media and information technology. This information flow, which allows those possessing the information to have an edge over their competitors, also allows the formation of a global cultural and religious village where the information flow enables the formation of a network among people with similar cultural and religious values. In this way, a transnational community of the faithful is formed. To a certain extent, Anderson's concept of an "imagined community" is applicable here, where it is possible to speak of an imagined religious community of people who share the same faith in cyberspace but without real knowledge of those involved in the communication process. Religious knowledge can now be transmitted across the world via satellite, linking all the believers instantaneously in prayer, sermons, religious teachings and other ecumenical activities. Television evangelism has long become an established feature of the Judeo-Christian tradition, resulting in the formation of a powerful global Christian congregation. But other religious faiths have yet to make use of this modern technology to further their own religious base.

This process of religious globalisation results in a much closer and more intimate religious community irrespective of members' actual knowledge of each other. It has the effect of binding believers together in a shared belief system. It is also a powerful force in separating one religious community from the other, establishing a clear delineation between insiders and outsiders, between those who do not share the faith and those who do. As the Asian societies follow suit in religious modernisation and globalisation, Asian religions too, transform themselves into important global Islamic, Buddhist and Hindu movements. In this process of globalisation, they have attempted to shake off various cultural baggages – most important of all, the colonial baggage – and, at the same time, de-territorialise themselves to become a world religion.

METHODOLOGY

This research is based largely on the anthropological fieldwork method of participant-observation. Ethnographic interviews were conducted from 1985-86 and updated annually since then to gain insights into how the Chinese viewed their religion, its changes and the rise of Reformist Buddhism. A total of 250 Chinese of different age groups selected from people who were visiting various temples in Singapore were interviewed. A structured questionnaire was also issued to 260 Reformist Buddhists, selected from various Buddhist organisations, to gather their views. 126 members of the Sangha were also interviewed extensively concerning their attitudes, perceptions and religious roles. The interviews were conducted with the help of an open-ended questionnaire. Several representatives from the Ministry of Education and the Buddhist Studies Team at the Curriculum Development Institute of Singapore were also interviewed regarding their roles in shaping the Moral Education programme. Documented sources were used extensively to provide background information and further analyses of the subject. Most of the material used in this book comes from my doctoral dissertation while new materials have been added as events unfolded gradually in the last two decades.

OUTLINE OF THE BOOK

This book is divided into three parts.

The introduction provides an overview of religious change and modernisation. Using various conceptual ideas such as rationalisation, secularisation and privatisation, it looks at how individuals are involved in the process of understanding religious change and modernisation. It also explores the role of the state and the link between nation-building and religious engineering.

In Part One, Chapter 1 explores how the Chinese migrants established a community in Singapore and reproduced village religious syncretism, known as Shenism, in the colonial environment to cater to their early socio-religious needs. This chapter also discusses how these religious ideologies were constructed into a coherent whole by the Chinese themselves and how the various religious elements continued to be viewed as significant and were reproduced in the colonial context. Chapter 2 examines how the Singapore Chinese communicate and negotiate with their gods, deities, ancestors and spirits. It discusses the inter-communication processes between the Chinese and the religious deities and the numerous rituals and ceremonies that continue to play an important role in the life of the Chinese.

Part Two explores the relationship between the state and society in the engineering of religious change. Chapter 3 explores the separation of the temple and the Sangha as two separate entities as a result of the bureaucratisation process. It argues that the Singapore state is instrumental in bringing about a bureaucratic organisational structure within the religious sphere, subjecting the temple to modernising influences. It also explores the social history of the monks and nuns, their views on monastic life, the tensions between the orthodox Sangha and the Reformist Sangha, and their attempts at religious modernisation. Chapter 4 examines how the Singapore state views a significant link between ethnicity and religion and how it has established an ethno-religious framework and introduced the Maintenance of Religious Harmony Law to protect this link. It attempts to demarcate clearly the ethnic identity of its population through their religious identities. Chapter 5 explores the creation of modern temples and their involvement in charity and welfare. Through its land law and land policies, the state has engineered religious organisations to become part religious and part welfare institutions, where the care of the aged and the handicapped is now part of the temple functions. Chapter 6 looks at how religious values are promoted as desirable Asian values by the Singapore state and how they are incorporated into the schools' formal curriculum and become part of moral education. The state argues for the need to use traditional values to educate Singaporeans in the area of morality.

Part Three examines the emergence of Reformist Buddhism. Chapter 7 examines the rise of a group of Reformist Buddhists and its role in promoting Reformist Buddhism in Singapore. It also discusses how Reformist Buddhism is now offering an alternative spiritual lifestyle package to its adherents. Chapter 8 profiles the members and their religiosity. Chapter 9 examines the competing claims to modernity and class status between Buddhism and Christianity. It examines how Christianity has, through the years, become associated with modernity, rationality and upper class status. Because of this modern image, Christianity has been able to attract and convert a substantial number of Chinese into its faith. Reformist Buddhism is now contesting with Christianity in this exclusive claim to being modern and rational. The Conclusion reiterates the significance of religious modernisation within the Chinese community. It also projects into the future state of Reformist Buddhism as part of the global Buddhist movement where it is involved in global religious networking, so that, in this sense, religion moves individuals from local to global identity.

PART 1

Inventing a Religious Tradition

CHAPTER 1

Reinventing Chinese Syncretic Religion: Shenism

INTRODUCTION

Since the 19th century, the Chinese in Singapore have been practising what was commonly known as *bai shen*, literally "praying to the deities and gods". This is the traditional Chinese religious syncretism. It is non-institutional and individual-based and fulfills the functional, socio-psychological and religious needs of the practitioners. The complex and syncretic nature of Chinese religion has resulted in it being termed differently by different scholars. Tan refers to it simply as Chinese Religion (Tan, 1995: 139) while others such as Hu called it "Siniticism" to denote the indigenous Chinese belief system (Hu, 1969:32) and Elliot termed it Shenism (Elliot, 1955). Wee noted that majority of the Chinese in Singapore who called themselves Buddhists were in fact practising Chinese religion with Buddhist elements (Wee, 1976: 155-188). While there is a variation in the terms and labels for Chinese religious syncretism, I have chosen to use the term "Shenism" as expounded by Elliot, as the Chinese continue to use the term "bai-shen" when worshipping their gods and deities. The term "shen" is used to describe gods and deities within the Chinese religious syncretism.

The early migrants, particularly the women, were engaged in a process of cultural reinvention. In this process of cultural reinvention, invented traditions are seen as "traditions actually invented, constructed and formally instituted and those emerging in a less traceable manner within a brief and dateable period – a matter of a few years perhaps – and establishing themselves with great rapidity" (Hobsbawm and Ranger, 1983). By reproducing familiar gods and deities and adapting ritual practices to the local environment, as well as inventing new ones, the Singapore Chinese are constantly negotiating their religious needs within the Chinese cosmological boundary.

CHINESE COSMOLOGY AND COSMOGONY

The Chinese cosmogony and cosmological worldview is predominantly a synthesis of Daoist and Buddhist metaphysical ideas, with Confucianism providing the moral base. The extent to which these religious doctrines are intertwined and integrated constitutes the strength and uniqueness of the Chinese religious system (DeGroot, 1964, Weber, 1951, Yang, 1961). It is therefore possible to identify the Chinese cosmogonic and cosmological worldview as comprising the Daoist, Buddhist, Confucianist and Shenist universes (Diagram 1.1).

a) Daoist Universe

The Chinese call the origin of the universe the Great Beginning. The birth of the universe began with a void, from which the Great Breath, *Taiji* (太極) developed. This Great Breath, in turn, gathered momentum and spun till it split into two equal breaths. The two energy forces moved in separate directions, one downward and one upward, becoming earth and heaven, crystallising eventually as the *yin* and *yang* forces, respectively.

The *yin* and *yang* forces produced the five elements of fire, water, earth, wood and metal and they, in turn, governed the four seasons. Each of these elements was placed in a position so that they formed two perennial forces, one clockwise, which is the cycle of construction, and the other, anticlockwise which is the cycle of destruction. Together they constitute the cycle of life and death. All activities on earth, including the basic activities of living, agriculture, hunting and domestication, go through the process of life, death and the renewal of life and death. The positioning of these various forces are therefore instrumental for the orderly behaviour of activities on earth. A break from the correct positioning would bring about disastrous consequences, experienced as natural calamities and man-made hazards (Diagram 1.2).

In another context, the *yin* and *yang* forces are poles of darkness and light respectively. The element *yang* is the rule of heaven corresponding to the elements of light, fire, life, masculinity and movement. The element *yin*, on the other hand, represents the earth, darkness, water, death, femininity and stillness. As elements constituting nature and process, they affect the seasons and hence agricultural production. *Yin* and *yang* are also located within the body. The head contains the *yang* substances whereas the lower part of the body is imbued with the *yin* spirit of the earth. Their relationship is reflected in the stages of growth. A healthy child at birth is filled with *yang* energies. As he grows, the *yang* element grows with him. When he reaches maturity, the *yang* element is at its peak. After that, *yin* takes over to bring a decline in all faculties. Thus, at old age, the *yin* element is preponderant over the *yang*. Finally, at death, there is a complete take-over of the *yang* element by the *yin* and the process is complete. Death is thus seen as a separation of the *yin* and *yang* parts of an individual. Although men and women have both *yin* and *yang* elements, men have more *yang* elements and women have more *yin* elements (DeGroot, 1964,1:4).

Women and men thus constitute the polarity of these two basic energy forces of *yin* and *yang* respectively. The *yin* force is gentle whereas the *yang* force represents ferocity. The two forces should balance. *Yin* and *yang* are also poles of darkness and light, inaction and movement, death and growth, and evil and good. They are found in both animate and inanimate objects. Permeating the sequence of natural events as the cycles of the seasons and of day and night, and also human activities such as life and death, and the consciousness through senses and feelings, these energy forces work to achieve desired ends. The elements of *yin* and *yang* and the five elements are also found in the human body and govern the emotions and the senses of the individuals, producing a healthy or sickly person.

23

The dictates of these forces necessitate that we follow a specific course of action in order to harness them for positive ends and minimise the negative side of the scale. For all actions, there are two sides – the positive and the negative. The trick here is to attain a balance of the two forces. Too much of one or the other is counterproductive. But the balance is situational – at times, there is a need for more *yang* energy, at others, more *yin* energy is needed, but on normal occasions, the two need to be in balance (Diagram 1.3).

Life is therefore like a stage and the events associated with living constitute a social drama that needs to be played out according to a pre-set script. But the pre-set script only provides a sketch; the actual details await to be spelt out as the drama unfolds itself. While the broad outline is fixed from birth, it is possible for minor changes to be made to the details. The resulting attitude is one of acceptance and adjustment and at the same time, of hope, where one knows of the possibility of alterations, no matter how minuscule they may be. It can also be one of great despair when there is no alternative to one's negative pre-set broad script. With despair comes acceptance, but with great determination comes the will to change. Some embark on the first course while many refuse to surrender and pursue the alternative, having nothing to lose. This, to the Chinese, is destiny, *ming-yun*. This is why the Chinese resort to magic and divination and consult their gods and deities for help to change their destiny, whenever the occasion arises.

The interaction between the physical and the social worlds is also largely determined by the balancing of these two forces, which explains why the Chinese concern themselves as much with the physical as with the social worlds. The harmonious relationship between the two worlds can only come about with mutual respect. This is especially so with regard to human attitudes and actions towards the treatment of the physical environment.

Every tree, animal, bird, stone, river, mountain and path is part of the grand cosmological design and in each of them resides a spirit. Hence, like humans, they are sacred too. The sacredness of all things has to be respected in order that the cosmic balance is maintained.

Repeated patterns of disruption, their consequences and the resultant recovery have made the Chinese acutely aware of the need for action to combat both foreseen and unpredicted events. The general consensus is that while many of these events are the result of human folly, it is the incursion of the wrath of spiritual beings through human misdeeds that brings about disharmony to all. Magic, rituals and rites are therefore important components in the attempts to restore order and harmony.

In traditional Chinese society, the changing of seasons, and the shift from one agricultural cycle to the next were seen as major events. It was during transitional phases that rituals and rites were performed to appease gods and spirits alike and to ensure a smooth passage. Village communal religious fairs dotted the annual cycle, marking out these phases. The religious ceremonies included elaborate offerings of food and theatrical performances for the gods and spirits. They were offered for a bountiful harvest, and a smooth and peaceful year, as well as to ameliorate the effects of unfortunate events that had befallen. For the latter reason, the ceremonies were often conducted when the misfortune was at its height. Often special rituals were performed to specifically address the perceived cause of the misfortune. These were conducted on a large-scale basis, involving all in the community. It was not an uncommon practice for the religious personnel, either the Buddhist monks or Daoist priests, to lead the sacrificial offering and appeasement (Hsu, 1952). At the metaphysical level, the rites and rituals were their answer to the uncertain world that they faced. At the social level, they were significant for kinship and clan solidarity (Yang, 1961). In a good year, these rites and rituals took on a different meaning. Communal offerings were given in appreciation of the efforts of the spiritual beings for a smooth transition to a peaceful year. Religious and social events intermingled to produce an atmosphere of success and contentment. The rituals and rites performed on these occasions served to reinforce the moral values, embedded within the Confucian ideology, to promote a sense of optimism and hope, and to exemplify strict adherence to the socio-religious order.

Within the Chinese community in colonial Singapore, selected aspects of Daoist ideology and ritual were most popular.

The ritual practices included worshipping all the gods, goddesses and deities, and practising animism, divination, astrology, magic and exorcism. Legends, mythologies and folklore were all intermeshed together to form part of the folk religion. The Chinese migrants identified with them all. These practices provided the Chinese with one aspect of cosmology that helped them go about living with the known and unknown, the supernatural forces, the dead and the living. They helped to cushion them against the shock of uprooting from their villages and adapting to a foreign place. The unknown physical and supernatural environments were something that the Chinese migrants could not and did not want to take chances with. They had to ensure that they were adequately protected from harm of all sorts. It was only natural then that they asked their known gods, goddesses, deities and ancestors for protection. Likewise, rituals, rites, prayers, appeasement and sacrificial offerings to the local spirits were conducted in order that the men, women, children, animals and spirits could co-exist harmoniously in the land that they had chosen to come to work in. Rituals, rites and prayers were conducted periodically at Chinese communal religious celebrations. These were also important for the renewal of kinship and communal ties with the living, as well as with the spirits of the ancestors and of the land.

b) Confucian Universe

Confucianism has dominated Chinese social and political thought for over two millennia. The teachings were an important source for policy-making right up to the beginning of the Republican Era. Confucianism has been the pervasive ideology of the Chinese State since the Tang dynastic epoch and became the guiding philosophy of Chinese life, from the courtly people down to the peasants. It was translated into an elaborate religious and ritual system that was practised by all Chinese. The result was the emergence of numerous agrarian cults, including the Cults of Heaven and of the Ancestors, the worship of which was regarded as essential for maintaining the cosmic order.

At the philosophical level, Confucianism was most concerned with the ethical value system, the structure of the society, the state and human relationships. The state regarded Confucianism as an important ideology for social control and institutionalised it within the imperial system. It established the Cult of Confucius that subordinated all classes to the emperor, who claimed a divine origin (Yang, 1961). This ideology stressed absolute loyalty to one ruler, formalised patterns of behaviour, and enjoined strict observance of moral rules regarding chastity, filial piety and mourning rites (Wright, 1960:231). Confucian ideology was used by the imperial state to perpetuate the traditional class order comprising the scholar (*shi*), the peasant (*nong*), the artisan (*gong*), and the merchant (*shang*).

At the ethical level, everyone, especially the ruling elite, strove for social and ethical excellence, as expounded in the model of the Gentleman (*jun-zi*). In acquiring propriety, loyalty, filial piety, honesty and benevolence, the scholar-rulers correspondingly gained more *yang* substances, which were necessary to maintain worldly harmony (Weber, 1951:131-3). The combination of a Confucian ethical system with ritual practices allowed the Mandarin officials to be integrated into the political system.

The people too were expected to adhere to Confucian personal values. The five main Confucian values are loyalty, justice, benevolence, wisdom and propriety. The central teachings involved observing proper behaviour between subordinates and superiors, among friends, kinsmen, strangers and even enemies. Likewise, Chinese women were expected to uphold Confucian teachings and turn themselves into filial daughters, virtuous wives and compassionate mothers. Only when men and women observed their roles and rightful positions could there be peace and harmony within the family. These would generate loyalty and justice within society. In this way, Confucian ethics, which involved the acting out of social life in its proper manner, symbolised the attainment of the highest human virtue.

At the religious level, Confucianism was concerned with the origin of civilisation and the role of heaven. The peasant beliefs about *yin* and *yang*, nature, balance and fate became part of the Confucian ideology and manifested in the various rituals that the Chinese peasants observed.

Confucian ideology postulated a theological system where the emperor and the heavenly Jade emperor were responsible for the correct balance and proper continuance of the cosmic, the physical and the social orders. In addition, Confucianism also proposed a hierarchical moral social order, in which all – the emperor, the mandarins and the four classes – were bound to each other by their own specific duties for the good of all.

Confucian values were transmitted and reinforced through the migrants' daily social discourse and enculturated through formal Confucian education. From the mothers, the young children learnt how to conduct themselves within the domestic household. From the fathers, especially the sons, they were trained to deal with the public sphere of life. They were also taught Confucian rituals and values which explained Chinese attitudes, behaviour and action among themselves and, in Singapore, towards the colonial administration as well. Confucian loyalty dictated that they continued to look to China as their homeland and the emperor as their rightful ruler because of its stress on the source of origin, where cultural roots served to bind the Chinese migrants together as one people. It was this sense of imagining themselves as one group that provided the Chinese with a base from which they built their identity.

In a colonial setting, with their homeland far away and their emperor remote, their loyalty became localised. It was to the headmen (including the leaders of secret societies, and later the clan leaders) that the Chinese paid their allegiance. To a large degree, Chinese leaders and their social institutions became the surrogate substitutes for the emperor and the imperial kingdom they knew of.

Confucianism also stressed frugality and self-sufficiency. The pursuit of wealth was not only for the betterment of individuals but also for the whole community. Wealth generated from mercantile activities in the Straits Settlement was both for the improvement of the home villages, where remittances were expected, and for the general welfare of the Chinese community in Singapore. In Singapore, it was used to fund the numerous activities including communal religious functions and for Chinese education conducted by the clan associations. Gradually, the mercantile and working classes came to replace the *literati* as they sought status in a colonial society where the production of wealth was the *raison d'être*.

c) Buddhist Universe

Buddhism had a central doctrine pertaining to spiritual development. It answered questions on eschatology and theodicy. It had a religious doctrine supported by the Buddhist texts which expounded the *dharma*, a monastic order of monks and nuns, a pantheon of Buddhist deities and a plethora of religious prayers, rituals and rites. It had elaborately designed monasteries of enormous dimensions and small localised village temples.

The Buddhism practised by the Chinese was of the Mahayana tradition, which for the Chinese can be divided into two main types. For the literati, it meant abstract doctrinal Buddhism, and they focussed on the *dharma*. This was also the central focus of the monks in the big monasteries. However, the majority of the Chinese practised a ritual form of Buddhism, often known as "the little tradition". This was village Buddhism, and it was imbued with elements of magic, animism and folk beliefs.

Like the villagers of rural China, migrants to Singapore were attracted to the functional aspects of Buddhism. They were interested in the esoteric, the magical and the divine aspects of Buddhism, mixed with Daoist/Shenist practices. In short, it was the little tradition of Buddhism that was the key focus. Translated roughly, the rituals, rites and prayers were of central significance, for they helped to deal with the events that unfolded during the daily discourse. They were enormously popular among the migrants. Temple visits by individuals and communal religious functions had specific motives, either for personal or collective needs. It was this village Buddhism and its village temple structure that were reproduced in the colonial Singapore environment.

Buddhism, because of its focus on enlightenment, is especially relevant in the treatment of the dead and is also considered as a religion of the dead. The elaborate death rituals that grow out of it and the intensity with which they are conducted has earned the death rituals the name of *nam-mo*, chanting for the dead, among the Chinese in Singapore. It is this aspect that is the most significant and that gains the most attention. It is also this aspect that the young Chinese find quarrel with in present day Singapore.

Within the Buddhist universe, there exists a monastic order, the *Sangha*, that serves the needs of the people. In scriptural Buddhism, the primary concern of the Sangha was to impart the *dharma* to the general public, and in the big monasteries the primary aim was the pursuit of enlightenment; but this was not the case of the Sangha in village China or colonial Singapore. There, the primary aim of the monks and the nuns was to serve the ritual needs of the migrants, and they came to be identified as ritual experts. Increasingly, the monks and nuns came to serve the dead more than the living. During the early years, the clan associations recruited the monks and nuns. Much later, when monks arrived independently, servicing the ritual needs of the migrants and the dead became a strategy for survival. The reciprocal exchanges of religious services and monetary rewards between the monastic personnel and the lay Chinese became commoditised in a changing colonial social environment. In the end, ritual services were conducted for individuals for a sum of money.

d) Shenist Universe: A Religious Syncretism

Among the Chinese, there was little identification with either one of the three religious ideologies. That is why Soothill describes traditional Chinese religion as thus:

> While a few of the laity, devote themselves, some solely to Buddhism, some solely to Taoism and some to Confucianism, the great mass of the people have no prejudices and make no embarrassing distinction, they belong to none of the three

religions, or more correctly, they belong to all three. In other words, they are eclectic, and use whichever form best responds to the requirement of the occasion for which they use religion (Soothill, 1973: 13).

To the Chinese, their religious universe can be described as a "Shenist" universe where their main religious preoccupation is to "pray to gods *[shen]*". There is very little understanding of religious purity and they do not subscribe to any particular religious ideology. "Shen" refers to gods and deities and Shenism therefore consists of deities and ritual practices from Buddhism, Daoism, Confucianism and Chinese folk beliefs that are consciously selected and integrated together. The elaborate system of rites without a central theology or an organised priesthood was the Chinese peasant religion and it was this religious system that was reproduced in colonial Singapore.

Shenist Hierarchy of Gods and Deities

Within the Shenist hierarchy, all beings, gods, deities, ancestors and spirits are measured according to the following criteria: good virtues as in the Confucian ideal, supernatural power, specific roles they play and popularity. According to these criteria, at the top of the hierarchy, stood the omnipresent and omnipotent Heaven, *Tian*, also known as *Tian-Gong*. *Tian* is personified and represented as a supernatural being in the form of the Jade Emperor, *Yu-Huang-Da-Di*. This is followed by all the Buddhist deities such as Skyamuni Buddha, Amitabha Buddha and *Guan-Yin* whose roles and powers are fully recognised by the practitioners and are popular among them. Following this are the various folk deities, guardian gods and deified heroes. They include *Tian-Hou* (Heavenly Empress), *Kong-Zi* (Confucius) and *Guan-Di* (war hero). Below them are the local gods and deities such as *Da-Bo-Gong* (Grand Paternal Uncle), *Jiu-Wang-Ye* (Nine Emperor God), *San-Tai-Zi* (The Third Prince) and the lesser deities. They are followed by the ancestors. All these gods and deities reside in the heavenly plane of existence. This is followed

31

by beings from the spirit world. Within the spirit world, there is again a spirit hierarchy according to their status and power. At the apex of the spirit hierarchy is the guardian god of the underworld, the King of Hades (*Yan-Lo-Wang*), followed by his subordinates and the various categories of lesser spirits. At the bottom of the hierarchy are spirits that do not have a home, commonly called the wandering, lonely and hungry ghosts.

Within the Chinese society, communal and individual worships are common occurrence. Based on the Chinese knowledge of the status and position of the gods, deities and spirits in the religious hierarchy, the Chinese constructed a plethora of rituals and rites to provide offerings to their gods, deities and spirits. According to Ahern (1981), these gods, deities and spirits are stratified according to their power and wealth and the title they hold – a sort of class order. She points out that there was great similarity between the social structure of the human and the spirit worlds and that a social and bureaucratic hierarchy of the spiritual beings existed. She argues that there are three categories of spirits – gods, ancestors and ghosts – and that they reflect the three categories of government officials, kinsmen and strangers. These spirits are believed to have human-like qualities as they were formerly soldiers, scholars, doctors or paragons of virtues (Ahern, 1981: 1).

The gods and deities are also classified according to their domains of power, influence and popularity, and are seen as national, regional or localised gods and deities. In Singapore, this categorisation continues to be held by the Chinese community. Certain gods became more popular with the migrants and assumed higher status. *Tian-Hou*, also known commonly as *Ma-Zu*, protector of seafarers, *Guan-Di*, the War Hero and *Kong*-Zi, Confucius, are examples. The Buddhist Amitabha Buddha (*O-Mi-To-Fo*), the Goddess of Mercy (*Guan-Yin*) and the Guardian of the Netherworld (*Da-Shi-Ye*) are high status gods. Other deities and gods are patronised at the dialect level. These are localised deities and are confined to specific groups. The five major dialect-groups (Hokkien, Teochew, Cantonese, Hakka and Hainanese) have their own temples housing their favourite and revered deities. At the clan level, each clan has its own patron god, although many clan associations have opted for *Guan-Di* to be their guardian god.

All these represented exclusive claims of loyalty from the members at different levels. At the top, the system identified all Chinese migrants as part of the wider Chinese community. At the second level, it bound those who spoke similar dialects together, forging a dialect-based identity. Finally, the guardian god of the clan served a small and exclusive group of Chinese, marking them out from the other Chinese according to kinship ties, both real and imaginary, and according to surname and/or territorial groupings. It is in this way that the boundaries between insiders and outsiders were marked, boundaries that the Chinese jealously guarded. It is through the adoption of these exclusion strategies that the Chinese drew their interior boundaries.

As we move from the gods and spirits representing the wider Chinese community to those representing specific groups, their status becomes more parochial, as are their influence and popularity. However, at the more localised levels, certain gods and deities assume great popularity and hence high social status among the worshippers. It is not uncommon for these gods and deities to be appropriated by other groups and it is also common for different dialect groups to share a deity.

It is therefore possible to summarise Chinese cosmology and cosmogony in the following manner. There are three religious ideologies making up the three religious universes namely the Daoist, Confucian and Buddhist universes. Elements of these three religions are selected, together with the folk religion to form the Shenist universe. Within the Shenist universe, there is the Shenist religious hierarchy, which is again made up of elements from the Confucian, Buddhist and Daoist ideologies. While the Shenist universe and its hierarchy of gods, deities and spirits is the most understood and widely practised by majority of the Chinese, a small group of Chinese practice either the Daoist, Confucianist or Buddhist religions and uphold the universe associated with that particular religion.

DIAGRAM 1.1: TRADITIONAL CHINESE
RELIGIOUS SYNCRETISM – SHENISM

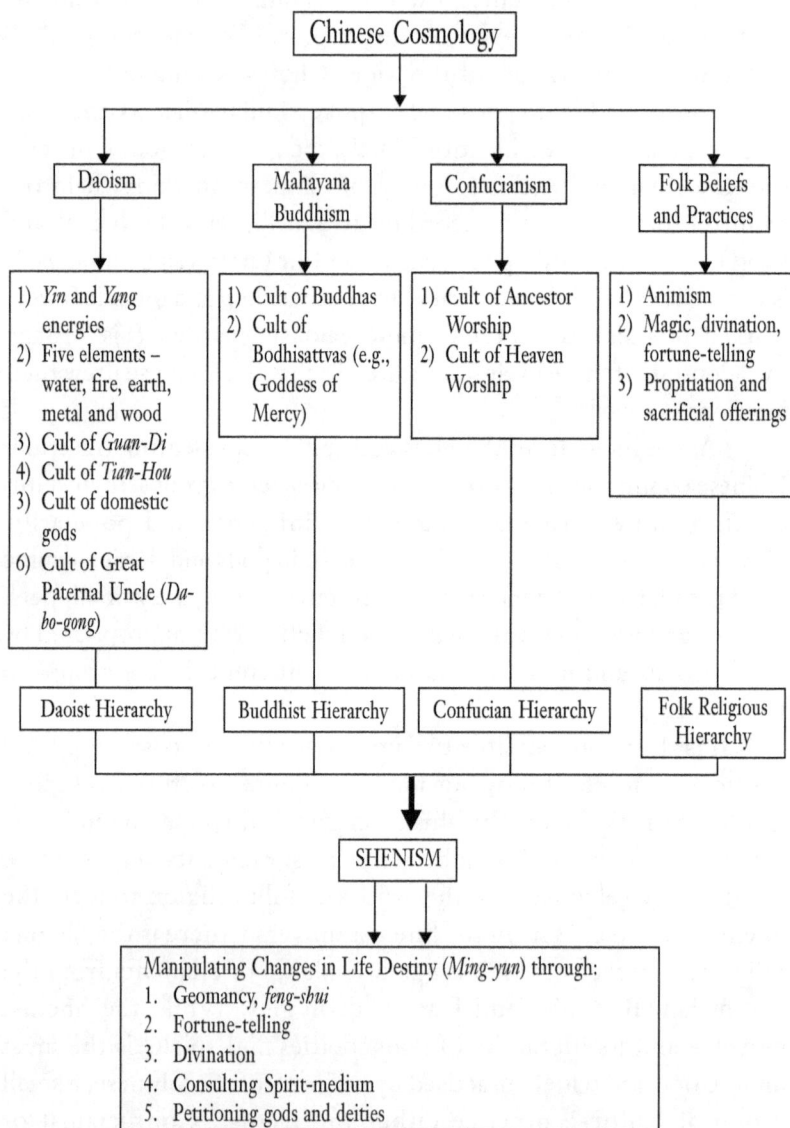

```
                        ┌─────────────────────┐
                        │  Chinese Cosmology  │
                        └─────────────────────┘
```

Daoism	Mahayana Buddhism	Confucianism	Folk Beliefs and Practices
1) *Yin* and *Yang* energies 2) Five elements – water, fire, earth, metal and wood 3) Cult of *Guan-Di* 4) Cult of *Tian-Hou* 3) Cult of domestic gods 6) Cult of Great Paternal Uncle (*Da-bo-gong*)	1) Cult of Buddhas 2) Cult of Bodhisattvas (e.g., Goddess of Mercy)	1) Cult of Ancestor Worship 2) Cult of Heaven Worship	1) Animism 2) Magic, divination, fortune-telling 3) Propitiation and sacrificial offerings
Daoist Hierarchy	Buddhist Hierarchy	Confucian Hierarchy	Folk Religious Hierarchy

```
                          ┌──────────┐
                          │ SHENISM  │
                          └──────────┘
```

Manipulating Changes in Life Destiny (*Ming-yun*) through:
1. Geomancy, *feng-shui*
2. Fortune-telling
3. Divination
4. Consulting Spirit-medium
5. Petitioning gods and deities

Source: Diagram by the author

DIAGRAM 1.2: THE GREAT BREATH (TAIJI)

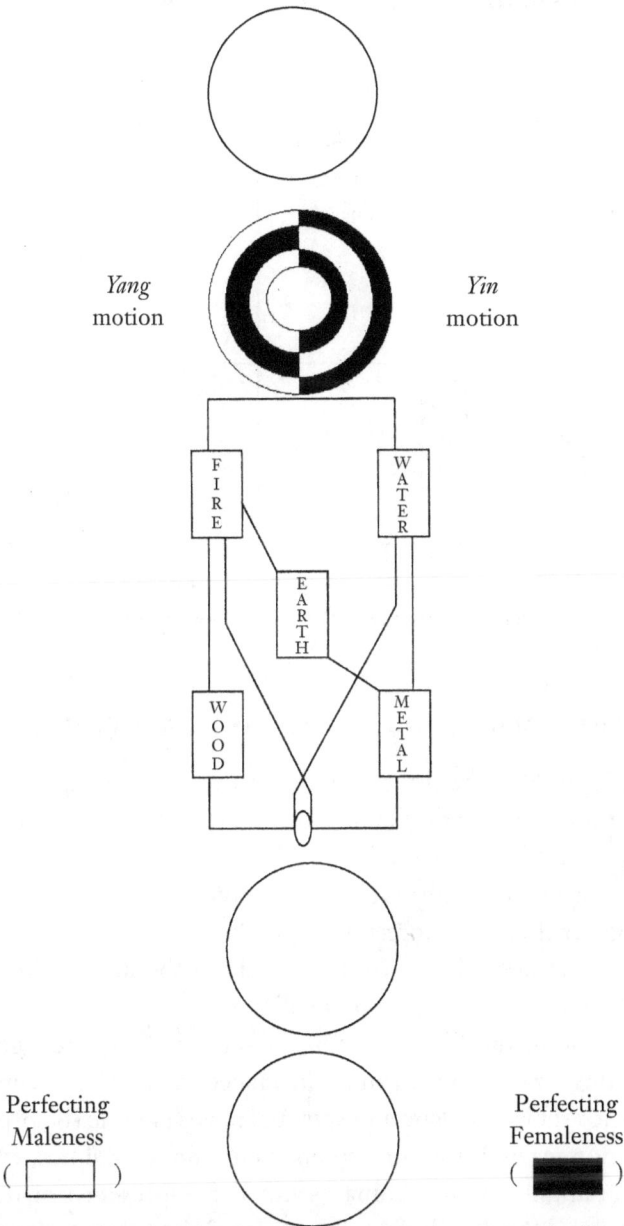

Yang motion

Yin motion

FIRE

WATER

EARTH

WOOD

METAL

Perfecting Maleness

Perfecting Femaleness

The myriad things in transformation and generation

Source: Adapted from Feuchtwang, S.D.R., 1974, An Anthropological Analysis of Chinese Geomancy, p. 34

DIAGRAM 1.3: YIN AND YANG ENERGIES
CORRESPONDING TO THE FOUR SEASONS

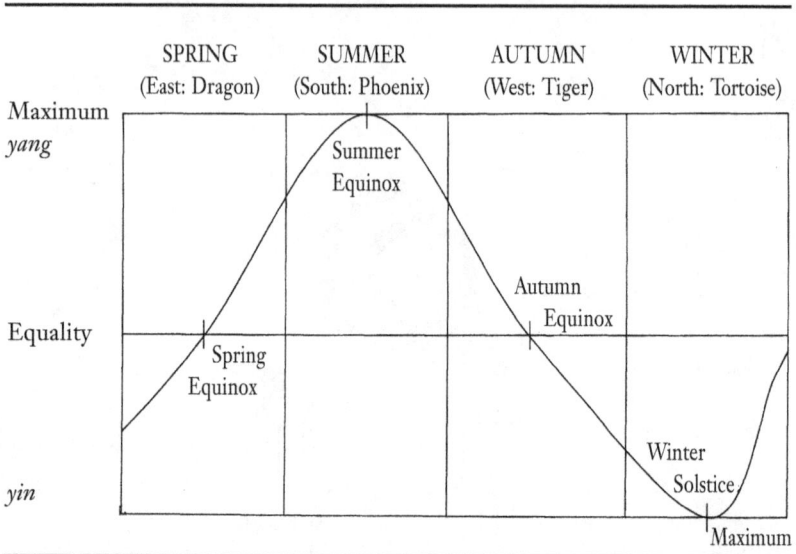

	SPRING (East: Dragon)	SUMMER (South: Phoenix)	AUTUMN (West: Tiger)	WINTER (North: Tortoise)
Maximum *yang*		Summer Equinox		
Equality	Spring Equinox		Autumn Equinox	
yin				Winter Solstice
				Maximum

Source: Adapted from Feuchtwang, S.D.R., 1974, An Anthropological Analysis of Chinese Geomancy, p. 37

REPRODUCING SHENISM IN SINGAPORE

Until the 1990s, Shenist rituals were the most popular religious practices found within the Chinese community. The collection of ritual practices included worshipping all the various gods, goddesses and deities; animism; supernaturalism; divination; fortune-telling; astrology; magic and exorcism. Legends, mythologies and folklore were all intermeshed to form part of the orthodox religious tenet. The Chinese identified with them all.

Almost all the Shenist elements – the beliefs, rites, gods and institutions – were adapted and reproduced by the Chinese migrants to cater for their mundane and spiritual needs and the socio-political and economic conditions in a colonial environment. Thus, while the basic paradigm for old China assumed the presence of the state (emperor and the mandarins), the lord and the peasant; the colonial paradigm assumed a migrant community with two social classes –

namely, the labouring and mercantile classes. It had to transform itself to suit this environment.

Another point to note here is that while there was religious continuity from village China to colonial Singapore, it was not a wholesale transference and reproduction. The poor would and did possess the basic cosmological and eschatological concepts of the Chinese religion. As noted above, their religious beliefs revolved around their understanding of the basic religious cosmology and their own ritual practices, including the knowledge of the *yin* and *yang* polarity, of death and ancestor worship, of the gods and deities, and of the ritual practices and communal religious festivals. Shenism was part of the wider Chinese culture, and it was this sense of belonging to Chinese culture that compelled the early migrants to attempt to recreate the ritually-appropriate forms of living and dying.

The uncertainties of a foreign environment led the migrants to hold on to their religious beliefs for protection. Although the need for readjustment to the environment compelled changes within the religious arena, on the whole, they managed to restructure and adapt old practices to a new environment. As the migrants lived in an urban colonial environment and worked as labourers, the types of protection needed differed from those of an agrarian society, so a different set of deities and gods came to be revered, since only the correctly-chosen deities could bring proper benefits.

Protection was needed to survive in a hostile tropical climate which, together with the lack of medical facilities, brought diseases and took the lives of many migrants. This was compounded by long hours of work and a poor diet. Many workers, such as rickshaw-pullers and port and plantation labourers, were unable to meet basic needs despite extreme hard work. Many also suffered from depression, resulting in many cases of suicide.[1] A common saying at that time was, "Out of ten who went overseas, four survived and only one made it rich".

Among the early migrants, religious life centred on communal worship, which was both religious and social. At the same time, the preoccupation with death and the desire to pay respect to one's ancestors in a foreign land also meant that communal ancestor worship became important for the predominantly male migrants. Temples were established and housed the desired deities sought by individuals to solve their problems.

Communal religious functions were celebrated on various occasions to gather the community together. The rituals of the New Year celebration were aimed at strengthening the moral values of optimism, harmony and goodwill. Likewise, the Qing-Ming festival cemented ties with dead kinsmen, and the Zhong-Yuan Festival also reminded the Chinese of their responsibilities towards the dead (Yang, 1961: 95). As Malinowski puts it, "Religion sets its stamp on the culturally valuable attitude and enforces it by public enactment" (Malinowski, 1954: 65). Below are some of the common deities and ritual practices that were communally and individually worshipped and carried out by the Chinese.

(i) Heaven: Tian and Religious Rationalisation of Social Events

Heaven worship is one of the most important ritual practices in Chinese syncretic religion. Heaven (*Tian*) and its representation constituted an integral aspect of Chinese cosmology. In Confucianism, *Tian* assumed both a prescriptive and descriptive role. It "manifests in and prescribes those behavioral forms that Confucius laid down as the basis for Ruist (Confucian) practice" (Eno, 1990: 85). *Tian* worship was also viewed as a ritual path towards sagehood. *Tian* was seen as an ethical arbiter, which prescribed moral values and punished immoral action (ibid: 87). In its prescriptive roles, *Tian* was seen as identical with the "Way" or "*Dao*" of Ruism and Daoism and legitimised political idealism, including the acceptance of political fatalism (ibid: 94) because *Tian* was also conceived of as an anthropomorphic ruling god, commonly known as the heavenly god, *Tian-Gong*. It was a pervading cosmic force, mystical and supernatural. As an anthropomorphic figure, it was identified with the Jade Emperor from whom the emperor derived his divine status. As a cosmic force, it held the cosmic balance, allowing all life forms to carry on in equilibrium. As the Jade Emperor, it assumed a form and was worshipped.

In traditional Chinese society, respect for *Tian* was absolute and remained unquestioned. The fate of the peasantry in face of an uncertain agrarian economy was tied to their trust in *Tian*. *Tian* would protect the peasants and their crops. In return, they were expected to perform sacrificial religious offerings to *Tian*. The faultless nature of *Tian* meant that imbalance in cosmic forces was often attributed to human action. Often, failure to perform the correct rites to *Tian* would bring about disasters to all. The consequence was poverty and hunger, the punishment for the failure to perform the correct rites; the magnitude of the disaster was a reflection of the degree of human folly. Disaster symbolised a period of moral bankruptcy of the leaders, the masses or both. When such disasters or misfortune happened, it was expected that all levels of people, from the elite to the masses, had to engage in propitiation and reassessment of their moral conduct (Yang, 1961: 150). The elite, especially officials of the imperial bureaucracy, were expected to perform the correct rites, but the masses too had to make their own sacrificial offerings (Hsiao, 1967: 221).

While this elite version of *Tian* was remote to the migrants, *Tian* took on a transcendental form and continued to feature prominently in the life of the Chinese migrants. As the Jade Emperor or *Tian-Gong*, it continued to dictate their social actions and moral conduct for it provided an explanation for the causation of all events. Sacrificial offerings were made to Heaven and many temples were constructed to house the Jade Emperor.

(ii) Ancestors and Ancestor Worship

According to popular Chinese belief, upon death, the *yin* part of the soul (*po*) returns to the soil while its *yang* part (*shen* or *hun*) wanders the earth. Death was thus not the cessation of life but merely the separation of the *yin* and *yang* spirits. Care therefore had to be taken over the disposal of the spiritual being. The *yang* energies could be harnessed for human benefit when captured and encapsulated in the ancestral tablet and worshipped as ancestors. The *yin* part, which represented an evil and malignant force, had to be propitiated to avert misfortunes. As the female sex embodied more *yin*, the death of a female member was seen as an extremely malignant event because her *yin* soul had to be cautiously propitiated. Family misfortunes, disharmony among clan members and ill health were interpreted to be, in part, the work of dead ancestors who because of neglect by their kinsmen, inflicted harm in order to gain attention to their own predicament. Herein laid the germ for the growth of the elaborate system of mourning rites (*sang-li*) and the cult of ancestor worship.[2]

According to the Daoist understanding of *yin* and *yang*, the rite of ancestor worship brought about the well-being of the worshippers. Confucian filial piety (*xiao*), on the other hand, required it as a duty. Funeral rites were viewed as an expression of gratitude towards ancestors and a reminder of cultural roots (Yang, 1961:44). The Confucianists saw them as a way of cultivating moral values, especially filial piety, and the familial sentiments concerning the relationship between the living and the dead. It was important for a son not only to serve his parents during life but also after their death. His filial piety would bind the living and the dead within the family and keep lineage structure intact. The mortuary rites, together with the expression of grief, were therefore formal acknowledgement of this relationship.

Death, funerary rites and ancestor worship occupied a central position in Chinese religious practice. The soul assumed two formless personalities, *hun* or *shen* and *po*, upon death, the *yin* part of the soul, *po*, returning to the soil and the *yang* part, *hun*, wandering on. One scholar has explained these entities in the following manner:

> ...the *chi*, breath, is the full manifestation of the *shen* and the *po* is the highest manifestation of the *kuei*. The union of the *kuei* and the *shen* is the highest of all tenets. Living beings are all sure to die and as they certainly return to the earth after their death, the soul which accompanies them thither is called *kuei*. But while the bones and flesh mulch in the ground and mysteriously become

earth of the fields, the *chi* issues forth and manifests itself as a shining Ming light (DeGroot, 1964, vol. 4: 4).

Thus, funerary rites were important in harnessing the *hun*, helping it to move to the heavenly realm while *po* was brought to the underworld. Funerary rites were performed to constrain the spirits from wandering around freely, lest they inflict harm on human beings. The *hun* of the dead occupied an important position within the wider social kinship structure; they had to be captured, contained within the ancestral tablet and revered, as they embodied the dead ancestors and continued to exert an influence on the living. The *po* had to be propitiated to prevent them from becoming hungry ghosts.

Death was considered a polluting event that had repercussions on the well-being of the family, including distant kin, if it was not taken care of in a ritually-correct manner. One view suggests that funeral rituals were performed to keep the spirit within the dead body during the initial stages of death, as separation prior to the ritualised expulsion from the community was thought to bring disaster (DeGroot, 1964: 8). Through proper rituals, the dead were transformed into benign ancestors; failure to care for them would lead to revenge and disaster for the family. The living could also harness the dead to their advantage through ritual propitiation, and by selecting and correctly arranging the geomancy of the tomb and burial site.

The death of an elder in a household required all members to participate in the mourning rites. The head of a family, lineage or clan was responsible for these rites. Participation by the extended group was necessary to provide moral support for the immediate family and to create a sense of solidarity. Ritual weeping, for example, an essential part of mourning, distinguished kinsmen from non-kinsmen, loyalty from disloyalty and insiders from outsiders (DeGroot, 1964: 37). Death also served to consolidate the extended family as a social group, bringing the individuals of a family into physical proximity and under obligation to participate in the funeral procession and the mourning feast. It also allowed for a demonstration of the status of the dead and the family, which were judged from the degree of elaboration of funeral decorations in the mourning hall, the lavishness of the feasts, the banner and the geomantic appropriateness of the burial site. The last was of utmost importance for the prosperity of future generations.[3]

Associated with death and funeral rites was ancestor worship, regarded as an important moral responsibility, especially for sons, but also for daughters. The dictates of Confucian moral order viewed ancestor worship as a means of cultivating moral values concerning relationships between the living. The relationship was viewed in the following manner:

> Funeral and sacrificial rites serve to inculcate benevolence and love. By attaining to a feeling of love one can perform the rites of mourning and sacrifice, while the perpetuation of the sacrifices of spring and autumn serves to express the longing of the mind. Now sacrifice consists in making offerings to the dead, how much more will there be so to the living. Therefore it is said that when the mourning and sacrificial rites are clearly understood, the people are filial. (Yang, 1961: 45).

Ancestor worship, with its elaborate rituals, also fulfills other important social functions. Yang sees it as a means of providing moral support for the family, creating a sense of solidarity and helping to ease the pressures of pain and suffering. It distinguishes outsiders from insiders, and kin from non-kin, allowing the people to identify themselves as belonging to one social group (clan or lineage). The elaborate ritual practices also reflect the social status of the family, as has been mentioned.

Within the village, ancestor worship at the clan level was a common practice. Members of a clan collectively built an ancestral hall or temple and maintained their own burial ground, relying on contributions from wealthy clansmen. This was a common practice in rural Fujian and Guangdong during the 19th century (Freedman, 1966: 118-154). Within the ancestral hall or temple, ancestral tablets of dead clansmen were arranged in rows in the main shrine hall, with the most central position being occupied by the tablet of the founding member, and others arranged genealogically around it. The ancestors were worshipped regularly and given offerings on festive occasions, such as the Chinese New Year and the harvest festivals, by the male clan members. The sacrifice was presided over by the clan head and other members performed acts of obeisance with the eldest going first. The sacrificial act more than any other symbolised the unity of the clan. At the rituals, group consciousness, loyalty and unity were verbally stressed.

Ancestor worship was also conducted within the family. In each household, a domestic altar displaying the ancestral tablet, together with household gods, was not uncommon among the rural peasantry. Sacrificial offerings of food were given on special occasions. On the other hand, in villages where the clan or lineage group was sufficiently wealthy, a memorial hall was constructed to house the tablets of all ancestors. Communal worshipping of the ancestors became a status symbol, reflecting on the wealth of the individual clan or lineage. It also served "as a visible representation of the long continuity of the clan and stood as a tangible reminder that not living members alone, but the roles of the living and the dead together, made up the lineage organisation" (Yang, 1961: 41). Ancestor worship, thus, had a binding effect, reinforcing identity through participation. (Freedman, 1966). Today, lineage ancestral houses in village China have being rebuilt for this purpose (Kuah, 2000: 139-172).

In colonial Singapore, the uncertain life experienced by the early migrants meant that early and premature death was always considered a real possibility. It is thus not an overstatement to say that the most important expression of migrant religiosity was in the rites of passage for the dead. As outlined above, the dead needed to be put to rest in a ritually-satisfactory manner to ensure peace for the living. The new migrants had even greater religious needs than their village counterparts to protect themselves against the dangers and uncertainties of their environment.

Apart from a few wealthy migrants who could afford to have the dead shipped back to the home village in China for burial, all the early migrants were buried locally. The religious ceremony and the recruitment of priests came about very early in the migration because of the need to cater for the dead in a ritually-satisfactory manner. As most of the deceased were single men, without near kinsmen and living in poverty, funeral rites did not have the aura of elaboration and solemnity that was befitting an ancestor. In many cases, the dead were "black haired youngsters and not the white-haired men" and therefore, according to Chinese custom, could not be given full rites. The lack of close kin in colonial Singapore also meant that the last rite was given by the clan or dialect association or the temple, and that the dead were without offspring and buried in a common cemetery of their own dialect group (Yen, 1986: 47 and 179). They were not revered as ancestors. For these single, unlamented men, a communal sacrificial offering was made once a year during the Hungry Ghost Festival.

The wealthy migrants who were buried locally had elaborate funeral services. Anticipating death, some wealthy migrants pre-selected a burial site with good geomancy (*feng-shui*). They were often leaders or substantial benefactors of their clan associations, in the memorial hall of which their ancestral tablets found a place. They were also worshipped in the households of their descendants.

Within the migrant community, ancestor worship on a communal basis was carried out twice a year to coincide with the spring and autumn festivals (Yen, 1986: 87). These were important celebrations for all the migrants, for apart from their intrinsic religious worth, they also provided a social location, real or imagined, for the often emotionally-dislocated individuals. A good and dutiful son was one who did not leave his roots and parents unattended. By migrating to a foreign land, many migrants were confronted with the dilemma of seeking a livelihood and fortune and being filial at the same time. The early migrants thus carried a deep sense of guilt because of their inability to perform the proper duties expected of them. Under such circumstances, it gave them great satisfaction to express their duty towards their ancestors and their immediate progenitors in the alien land.

Ancestor worship at the clan level also provided each group with an identity. Awareness of one's image and the clan became an important preoccupation, so that migrants from different areas and villages could differentiate themselves. Collective efforts were made by all to bind themselves together into coherent social units and to arouse the consciousness of their social duties towards each other as members of the same group. This latter point became relevant because of constant rivalries among the various clans. Ancestor worship was thus used not only to promote clan solidarity but also to promote inter-clan competition and conflict.

(iii) Cult of Guan-Di: A Frontier Deity

One of the most popular deities revered by the migrants was *Guan-Di*. *Guan-Di* was a deified hero, the status as a deity was given by the emperor to recognise his contributions to the wider community. Today, he is revered in Chinese communities throughout the world, including those in Taiwan, Singapore, Hong Kong, Malaysia, Australia and the United States.

Guan-Di, also known as *Guan Gong*, was the God of Martial Arts and War. He was believed to be a real person, *Guan Yu*, born in 160 A.D., a great warrior hero during the Three Kingdoms period. He was deified upon his death for his bravery and loyalty to the people and nation and is also known as the "God of Loyalty" (Wright, 1960: 53).

The popularity of *Guan-Di* among the lower stratum of Chinese society was linked to the Chinese understanding of social relations. The concept of sworn brotherhood adopted by the secret societies began with the legendary figures of *Guan Yu*, *Liu Bei* and *Zhang Fei* who had bonded themselves as sworn brothers and vowed to protect the country and people till death during the politically-tumultuous period of the Three Kingdoms, a period of internal revolts and external threats. Sworn brotherhood became a common phenomenon in colonial Singapore, especially among members of the various secret societies and/or the business community. Close friends, business associates and risk-takers would become sworn brothers, pledge loyalty to each other and provide assistance when the need arose, giving rise to the present-day social network commonly called *guanxi-wang*.

45

Guan Yu was awarded posthumous titles – ducal, princely and imperial – by Sung and Ming edicts, and from Yuan times on he became the official God of the Warriors. The Qing emperors ordered the construction of thousands of *Guan-Di* temples in his honour. In the midst of the struggle against the Taiping, he was elevated by a decree of the Qing government to boost the morale of the imperial army and was accorded the same status as Confucius (Wright, 1960: 174). From the *Guang-Xi* reign onwards, official committees of scholars compiled successive editions of his hagiography. These political moves were efforts "to indoctrinate the populace in loyalty and submission to authority" (Wright, 1960: 174).

In colonial Singapore, *Guan-Di* was a symbol of courage, devotion and loyalty. His picture was not only widely placed in the temples, often as a guardian god, but also in homes, businesses (*kongsi*), coolie houses and clan associations. He was much revered by members not only of the secret societies and businessmen, but also of the police in Chinese communities in Southeast Asia (Bloomfield, 1983: 213). As the migrants experienced but little cultural familiarity and had few local kin, it was natural to look to friends and fellow migrants for emotional and physical support, as it was important for the migrants to feel secure and to trust their fellowmen. Thus, *Guan-Di* was often used as a symbol to seal a sworn brotherhood and to establish a *guanxi* network. One of the earliest temples in Singapore was the *Guan-Di* Temple.

In the colonial context, the worship of *Guan-Di* can be viewed from two perspectives. *Guan-Di* was worshipped for his personal qualities and his ability to "slash through with a sword" the seemingly insurmountable odds that were so real to the migrants. Second, he provided a common bond and identity in the form of sworn brotherhood. Although *Guan-Di* did not formally come to be the anti-colonial hero, his association with the Chinese-speaking migrants as opposed to the English-speaking Chinese made him one in practice, and he came to symbolise Chinese cultural unity and nationalism. At the height of nationalist fervour, like the other members of the Chinese pantheon, he served to deny Chinese identity to the pro-British and Christian Chinese.

(iv) Cult of the Heavenly Mother or Empress, Tian-Mu or Tian-Hou

The earliest temple built in colonial Singapore was the *Tian-Fu-Gong* Temple, dedicated to the Heavenly Mother, *Tian-Mu*. The most popular and revered deity among the migrants, she was also known as *Tian-Hou* or *Ma-Zu* and was worshipped by seafarers and others connected with the sea, who looked to her for protection as she was believed to possess magical powers to protect fishermen and travellers during their journeys.[4] Her role as the guardian of the sea resulted in the formation of the Cult of Heavenly Mother in Singapore. It was very common for junk owners who acquired good profits from the junk trade to build a temple in her honour. Migrants saw her as the protector for their safe journey from their village in China to Singapore. Upon arrival, the first thing they did was to visit the temple and give offerings to her for her efforts.

(v) Cult of the Goddess of Mercy, Guan-Yin

Among the Chinese migrants, all happenings were viewed as preordained. However, they also believed that individual fate (*ming-yun*) could be changed through divine intervention. Thus, gods and deities known to be compassionate and to possess magical powers were revered. As mentioned earlier, *Guan-Yin*, the Goddess of Mercy, continued to be regarded as one with great compassion and willingness to assist those in need of help. The fact that *Guan-Yin* could take on 88 forms meant that she was imbued with various powers to help with all kinds of problems. People from all walks of life – the coolies, the traders, towkay, the destitute and the rich – went to her with every kind of problem.

Guan-Yin became an extremely important deity with the coming of the Chinese women migrants, who went to her especially seeking good health. *Guan-Yin* was also seen as a deity who could help women conceive and the guardian for safe delivery for expectant mothers. This was very important during the colonial days, when medical facilities were not readily available to women. Both men and women also went to her for help with domestic problems, to acquire wealth and to ensure the smooth conduct of business. A small number of men also consulted *Guan-Yin* before going into business ventures although the important deity for businessmen was *Da-Bo-Gong*.

(vi) Cult of Da-Bo-Gong (Great Paternal Uncle): A Merchant's Deity

Although *Guan-Yin* was everyone's deity, those who were interested primarily in business and trading sought the assistance of *Da-Bo-Gong* or Great Paternal Uncle. Within the business community, the Cult of *Da-Bo-Gong* worship became the most widely-observed practice. *Da-Bo-Gong* was especially closely associated with the Fujianese-speaking Chinese.

Da-Bo-Gong was a local invention whose origins remain unclear, present only among the overseas Chinese.[5] One common view is that the deity represented some early migrants who were deified for the part they played in the development of the Chinese communities in Southeast Asia. They were known as "the ancestors who opened up the land" (*kai-shan-lao-ren*). Myth has it that they were prosperous migrants who had accumulated enormous wealth and contributed significantly to the general welfare of the Chinese community. Through deification, it was hoped that their virtues of frugality and success could be preserved for the Chinese community as a whole and be inherited by the worshippers. Gradually, *Da-Bo-Gong* acquired a mythical status and supernatural power.

(vii) Cult of Domestic Gods and Deities

With the coming of women migrants and the formation of domestic hearths, household gods and deities became important permanent fixtures in Chinese households. Numerous household gods were worshipped, the most common being *Hou-Bo-Gong* (literally Deity of the Back Portion of the House, also commonly known as the Kitchen God); *Tu-Di-Gong* (Earth God) and *Chuang-mu* (Consort of the Bed). These deities were usually worshipped within individual households for peace and harmony within the family. The kitchen and earth gods were worshipped to bless the household with sufficient food for the year as migrants were constantly faced with the question of survival. The Consort of the Bed became a popular deity among the Fujianese-speaking households, and was invoked to protect young children against illness and affliction by spirit attack. Needless to say, the high rate of infant mortality during the early years made this an especially important deity. All these domestic gods were worshipped twice a month, mostly on the first and the fifteenth day of the lunar month.

(viii) Guardian Gods of the Dialect Groups

There were also numerous localised and regional gods worshipped by the different clan and dialect groupings. Each group tends to have its own favourite god to worship. For example, the Fujianese worshipped their regional *Qing-Shui-Zu-Shi-Gong* (Clear Water Ancestor), likewise, the Chaozhouese (Teochew) had their special deity, *Xuan-Tian-Shang-Ti* (a heavenly deity), while the Hainanese worshipped *Shui-Wei-Sheng-Niang* (Goddess of Water Margin) (Yen, 1986: 14-15). Despite these varieties, however, the primary goal of supplicants was to find those gods who answered prayers most effectively and who acted as a protective shield against unforeseen social and economic circumstances.

SURFACE AND DEEP STRUCTURES: RITUALS AND RELIGIOUS IDEOLOGIES

The worshipping of these different categories of deities and gods involved ritual performances on an individual and communal basis and the Chinese attached great significance to these ritual practices, irrespective of the ritual complexity.

Performance of rituals is a universal phenomenon. In all societies, varying degrees of rituals are conducted for both religious and social purposes. What used to be a sacred domain has now been extended to include the secular. But till today, the definition and interpretation of rituals remain an area of scholarly debate. Ritual, according to La Fontaine, is a type of social action, and its performance requires the organised co-operation of individuals, directed by a leader or leaders (La Fontaine, 1985: 11). There are rules concerning the participants and their participation. There are also rules concerning those who are excluded. A prescribed set of actions is to be followed in a specific ritual, and it is seen as having a fixed structure. Thus, rituals are sometimes viewed as a microcosm of the functioning of the social structure. Wilson, in her studies on ritual, writes that "rituals reveal values at their deepest level...men express in ritual what moves them most, and since the form of expression is conventionalised and obligatory, it is the values of the group that are revealed" (Wilson cited in Turner, 1969: 6). Rituals are therefore seen to have transformative powers, moving from one stage to another despite its repetitive performance. It is this power to transform that separates it from other social actions (Watson, 1988: 4).

Given that the central focus of Chinese religious syncretism is on rituals, it is not surprising that Watson argues that "if anything is central to the creation and maintenance of a unified Chinese culture, it is the standardisation of ritual. To be Chinese is to understand, and accept the view, that there is a correct way to perform rites associated with the growth-cycle of human existence, the most important being weddings and funerals. By following accepted ritual routines ordinary citizens participated in the process of cultural unification" (Watson, 1988: 3). He further states that "what is clear and explicit about ritual is how to do it – rather than its meaning" (Watson, 1988: 5). Rawski states that in many cases, most participants do not, or only partially, understand the meaning of cultural and religious events – although this does not mean that an underlying system of religious meaning does not exist (Rawski, 1988: 22).

Watson and Rawski have mentioned two complementary elements of the religious structure – ritual and ideology. The ideology – the deep structure – may be embedded within the religious structure without being articulated by its adherents. On the other hand, the rituals – surface structure – are articulated and expressed openly in the religious performance. However, the ideology provides the

Chinese with an identifiable common cosmological worldview, which is shared by Chinese communities scattered throughout the world. The elaboration or simplification of the ritual content by the Chinese reflects changing socio-cultural, economic and political environments of the time.

It is the surface structure that we are confronted with when we study the religion of the Singapore Chinese. It is this structure that has found favour with many scholars, including anthropologists. This is the Shenist ritual system that is viewed as a system of religious magic by Frazer (1960). However, it is also this rich ritual system that is subjected to harsh criticism by the younger generation Chinese who fail to comprehend the cosmological whole of the Chinese religion from the ritual point of view and thus label this ritual system as irrational magical practices. Because of the magical practices, younger generation Chinese argue, in the same vein as the early Christian missionaries, that Chinese religion is superstition as it lacks a religious canon, is irrational and non-scientific. This is where we have to turn now to the deep structure of the Chinese religious orthodoxy.

As the religious orientations and needs of the Chinese in Singapore change, the question to ask here is whether the existing interlocking system of religious ideologies and universes could continue to serve as the deep structure of the Chinese religion or have they outlived their usefulness. At the conceptual level, it seems easy to remove and replace the system with another set of modern and rational ideologies that the majority of the Chinese could and would subscribe to. However, to remove it would leave the Chinese with a religious vacuum, and disrupt cultural stability. Moreover, a new system would need the various elements with which Chinese could identify and they would feel at home. In short, such a system would have to incorporate the major social and cultural elements that distinguish it as the religion of the Chinese. Put another way, the new religious system would have to be able to provide the Chinese community with a sense of cultural familiarity and identity. As such, the adoption of a totally new system is both impractical and impossible. What the Chinese could do is to select and rationalise aspects of this religious orthodoxy.

At this deep structural level, the Singapore Chinese found it easier to adapt, adjust and repackage the various ideological elements within the religious orthodoxy. In repackaging the product, the main concern is to highlight those that are considered as "relevant", "rational" and "modern" and that appeal most to the new generation of Chinese and yet continue to be regarded highly by the older generation. Essentially, by packaging old wine in a new bottle, the Chinese religion continues to have the same ideological and cultural elements as before. Only this time, the three religious universes are treated separately as three independent universes, each with its own values and ethics. They are highlighted according to their ethical values and rationality. The Chinese could either adhere to one or all of the three. By focussing on the scriptural contents and consciously de-emphasising the magical aspects of the ritual, the Singapore Chinese could now re-evaluate Shenism in light of rationalism and modernism. On the basis of individual belief, one can claim to be a Reformist Buddhist practising Reformist Buddhism, a Confucianist or Daoist. On a communal basis, the Shenist communal religious functions and celebrations are now rationalised as part of the Chinese cultural practices. The syncretic label of Shenism is now being consciously eliminated and it is being replaced by first, the rational and modern individualised religious system conforming to the three religious universes and second, the communal religious system viewed as part of Chinese cultural system.

In reinventing the old, the Singapore Chinese have avoided a religious vacuum. This religious orthodoxy continues to provide the Singapore Chinese with religious and cultural familiarity, hence a sense of social stability and continuity within the Chinese community.

CHINESE RELIGIOUS SYNCRETISM AND RATIONALITY

How should one view Chinese religious syncretism? This is the question that scholars of Chinese religion are interested in. Granet, for example, sees Chinese religion divided along class line – the literati, peasant and the state. Each social group focuses on different religious universes and practices and interprets Chinese religious practices differently (Granet, 1975). Weber, on the other hand, explores Chinese religion with reference to its propensity towards the development of rational bourgeois capitalism and argues that Chinese religion obstructs such development (Weber, 1951, 1958). Yang divides Chinese religion into two main types – institutional and diffused. The institutional religion is practised by the elites while the masses practised diffused religion (Yang, 1961). Here, institutional religion is often regarded as the Great Tradition, while diffused religion is seen as the Little Tradition. Other scholars look at the symbolic interpretations and significance of religious rituals and their relevance to the various Chinese societies scattered throughout the world today (Ahern, 1973, 1981; Wolf, 1974; Freedman, 1958; Weller, 1986; Saso, 1972).

In the anthropological study of religion, one important aspect of religion is its claim to rationality. Is Chinese religious syncretism a rational religion? Within a specific culture, there is a cultural logic that anthropologists are interested in. Rationality too involves this cultural logic. As long as the people within a culture understand this logic, see and organise their world according to this logic, events and inter-relationships would fall into place. In all schemes, there is an order of events and actions. Religious rationality too has to be seen within the cultural logic of a particular culture.

Chinese religious syncretism has therefore to be viewed within the wider Chinese culture. Its rationality lies in its ability to explain to the Chinese the causation of the events in their daily lives; the social, economic and political happenings; and their encounters with the living and spirit worlds. It is also able to solve their problems and cushion them from the unforeseen events. It is this cultural logic – coherence, interpretations and meanings – shared by the Chinese, which constitutes the wider Chinese socio-religious structure.

As the Chinese community in Singapore undergoes a rapid process of modernisation and transformation, the Chinese culture too undergoes a phase of re-evaluation, re-adjustment, adaptation and re-alignment. The cultural logic too will shift its central gravity accordingly. In this process of changes, the element of rationality takes the form of socio-scientific explanation. Religious rationality becomes an all pervasive notion within the religious community. Rationality is equated with meanings and truth and is couched within a Western scientific framework. Here, we see the emergence of a misfit between the two interpretations of religious rationalisation within Chinese religious syncretism. On the one hand, religious rationalism within Shenism is being subjected to Western scientific interpretation, and as such Shenism and its related rituals are seen as not rational. On the other hand, Shenism interpreted from within its subjective cultural logic remains rational to its adherents. The challenge for the Singapore Chinese then is to bridge the gap between these two interpretations and to make Chinese religious syncretism rational to both the adherents and the rest of the population. Can modernity be interpreted along two main streams of thoughts: Western modernity and Asian modernity? This is a question that the Reformist Buddhists and the Singapore State continue to grapple with.

In contemporary Singapore, armed with a Western secular and liberal education, the younger generation Chinese are now using the Western scientific paradigm to explore and explain the irrationality of Chinese religious syncretism. The perception and interpretation of these younger generation Chinese is of great concern to us here for it is they who would seek to rationalise Shenism into a modern religion. The younger Chinese perceive Shenism as synonymous with an elaborate meaningless ritual system. Furthermore, the traditional explanation and interpretation of the ritual practices are often rejected as they do not conform to the modern Western paradigm It has resulted in much hostility towards Shenist rituals and practices.

CONCLUSION

To the Chinese, gods, deities and ancestors serve important functions. They are consulted to help with all problems and affairs of daily living, from the spiritual to the mundane. Although the Chinese migrants sought to reproduce the village form of their religion – Shenism – they did so selectively, in response to their specific functional needs in the colonial and post-independence environment of Singapore. In the beginning, when the Chinese were sojourners, temple religious practice was based on individual needs and catered to them. Communal religious fairs were held on specific days to celebrate those occasions, which were of a cultural nature. With the formation of Chinese families, it was the individual and domestic types of worship that became important. Chinese religious syncretism in Singapore can thus be regarded as two components: a set of private beliefs upon which migrants acted and worshipped individually, both at home and in the temples, and as a communal religion catering to the different religious celebrations that dotted the calendar year.

However, this belief system is subjected to challenges from within the Chinese community. The younger Chinese want to rationalise the practice and make it relevant to suit their modern religious needs.

NOTES

1. For a study of the social conditions that plagued one group of migrants, the rickshaw coolies, see Warren, J.F., 1986, *The Rickshaw Coolies: A Peoples' History of Singapore, 1919-1939*, Singapore: Oxford University Press.

2. For a discussion on the death rites and ancestor worship, see DeGroot, J.J.M., 1964, *The Religion of the Chinese*, vol.1, Taipei: Literature House, reprint.

3. For a discussion on the influence of geomancy, see Freedman, 1958, *Lineage Organisation in South-eastern China*, London: Athlone Press; also ibid, 1966, *Chinese Lineage and Society: Fukien and Kwangtung*, London: Athlone Press.

4. The legendary origin of this deity, *Tian-Mu*, has it that she was a native of *Pu-Tian* district in the province of Fujian and was born into a fisherman's family in 960 A.D. She was known to possess supernatural powers that enabled her to rescue those at sea, especially fishermen and sailors. After her death, she was deified and worshipped by many, especially by these two categories of men. See Yen, C. H., 1986, *A Social History of Singapore, 1800-1911*, Singapore: Oxford University Press, p. 59 fn.17 and p. 105 fn. 116. Also, Bosco, J., 1998, *Tin Hou: The Heavenly Empress*, Hong Kong: Oxford University Press.

5. For a discussion of the origin of *Da-Bo-Gong*, see Hsu, Y.T., 1951, "*Da-Bo-Gong, Er-Bo-Gong yu Ben-Tu-Gong*" in *Journal of the South Seas Society*, 7(2): 6-10; also ibid, 1952, "*zai tan Da-Bo-Gong yan-jiu*", in *Journal of the South Seas Society*, vol. 8(2): 19-24.

2

Communicating with Gods, Deities and Spirits

INTRODUCTION

Chinese Shenism consists of a system of elaborate rituals and practices that are conducted by the individuals, groups of individuals and religious specialists within the domestic households and in the temple. These rituals serve as a system of communication and negotiation with the gods and deities where the inter-personal communication between individuals and deities take place on both a routine basis and on special occasions. Religious specialists such as the Buddhist monks, Daoist priests and spirit-mediums are sometimes asked to intervene in the negotiation process. This chapter explores these various aspects of ritualism and the extent to which this system of communication and negotiation takes place between the individuals, religious specialists and the gods and deities.

COMMUNICATING WITH GODS AND DEITIES

(a) Domestic Worship

Among the older generation Chinese, the worship of deities is considered an important manifestation of religiosity. Images of the deities can be made from wood, metal or marble, or printed on paper (as posters) and encased in photo frames, or represented by written Chinese characters on paper or cloth and framed or pasted on the wall for worshipping. While wealthy worshippers have specially-made altar tables to house the elaborate forms, often sculptured out of marble, the majority have simple forms of representation. To them, it is the piety of the individual worshipper that is the most significant. It is therefore not surprising to find that today, in most Chinese homes, there continues to be a family shrine, in the form of an altar table devoted to one or more deities and to the family's ancestors.

The most common form of communication with the deities is to talk to them in the form of silent prayer, known as "praying to god" (*bai-shen*), either at home or in the temple. At home, communication with these deities and ancestors takes place through a simple offering of incense – usually twice a day, once in the morning and once in the evening. This is also a reflection of an individual religiosity to the deities and ancestors. Other forms of expressing one's religiosity include chanting a Buddhist mantra, the common one being the Amitabha mantra, *Namo-O-Mi-To-Fo*. This form of communication and offering lasts only a few minutes. Sometimes, a person might recite the name of Amitabha Buddha during his or her leisure time with the help of a prayer beads. The string has one hundred and eight rosary beads, which help the pious keep track of the number of recitations. It is believed that the chance of reaching the Western Paradise is positively correlated to the number of times the name of Amitabha Buddha is invoked. For devout individuals, this involves concentration and repetitive recitation of the mantra *Namo-O-Mi-To-Fo* for a specified number of times. The Amitabha Sutra is the most popular sutra. It is mostly elderly women and men who devote their time to this pursuit. Because of this, Buddhism is often regarded as a "religion for the elderly people".

A slightly more elaborate form of offering is given during the first and fifteenth days of each lunar month, coinciding with the new and full moons (the Singapore Chinese, like Chinese elsewhere, observe the lunar calendar for their religious activities). On these two days, offerings of fresh flowers, fruits, wine or water and cooked food (vegetarian for the Buddhist deities and non-vegetarian for the ancestors and others), together with incense and oil lamps, are made to the deities. These offerings are placed on the altar shelf. The fruits and food are consumed afterwards.

Theravada Buddhists, however, discard it or feed it to the animals; the Reformist Buddhists also consider food offered to the Buddha unsuitable for human consumption.

The rationale for the offerings varies among individuals. Elderly male Buddhists see it as part of the required religious practice and do not seek explanation for the custom. When asked for an answer, most simply respond, "Gods are like us, they need to eat too". To most elderly female Buddhists, the offerings have other meanings. It is a way of communicating with the gods and displaying religiosity. It is also to accumulate merits and to propitiate the deities. It is for this reason that they differentiate categories of gods and deities with different kinds of food offerings. It would be disrespectful to serve the Buddhist deities non-vegetarian food while treating the other deities with vegetarian food. It is through this form of categorisation and representation that Chinese women see their religious world.

(b) Temple Worship *(Gong-yang)*

There are many Buddhist and non-Buddhist deities found in the temples. The common Buddhist deities are *Shi-Jia-Mo-Ni-Fo* (Sakyamuni Buddha), *O-Mi-To-Fo* (Amitabha Buddha), *Guan-Yin-Pu-Sa* (Avalokitesvara), *Di-Zhang-Wang-Pu-Sa* (Kistargarbha Mahabodhisattva) and *Yao-Shi-Fo* (Medicine Buddha Bhaisajyaguru Vaiduryaprabha). Non-Buddhist deities include *Tian Hou, Guan-Di,* and other regional gods.

In most temples, these Buddhist deities are either housed within different shrine halls or together in the main shrine hall where monks, nuns and laity perform acts of veneration. Usually, a main Buddhist deity, Sakyamuni Buddha or Amitabha Buddha, is housed in the temple. In the nunneries *(an-tang)*, the most common deity is *Guan-Yin-Pu-Sa*. Some individual households also worship, apart from various Chinese gods and supernatural beings, *Guan-Yin*, Sakyamuni Buddha or Amitabha Buddha.

Sakyamuni Buddha is commonly worshipped because he is the founder of Buddhism. He is worshipped most by the literate laity and the scholar monks who are interested in Buddhist scriptural knowledge. For the elderly Chinese, Sakyamuni Buddha is not a central figure. Many pray to him because "he is there and must not be ignored". As one lay person said, "It is best to pray to all so as not to offend any". Sakyamuni Buddha has no specific function, but because he shares in the general sacredness, most Chinese believe that he also has supernatural power to assist supplicants. However, in South and Southeast Asia, Sakyamuni Buddha is the central figure worshipped by Theravada Buddhists.

Amitabha Buddha and *Guan-Yin* are the two most popular Buddhist deities among the Mahayana Buddhists, who constitute 90% of all Chinese Buddhists in Singapore. Amitabha Buddha (*O-Mi-To-Fo*) is one of the most popular deities found in Mahayana temples. This veneration is carried out individually and communally. Veneration takes the form of chanting the Amitabha Sutra (*O-Mi-To-Jing*), and ritual acts are performed on a communal basis in the temple during the religious days every month.

Amitabha Buddha is venerated by the laity for various reasons. The common purpose, especially for the aged, is to seek salvation. It is widely held that Amitabha Buddha resides in the Western Heavenly Paradise (*Ji-Le-Shi-Jie*). Individual Buddhists aspire to reach this heavenly paradise and the ability to do so represents the enlightenment triumph of an individual. Buddhists in Singapore believe in the progression from earthly sufferings to the plane of eternal bliss. They believed that through constant recitation of Amitabha Buddha's name, one is able to establish a "supernatural link", and upon death, one will be given preferential treatment and granted a place in the Western Heavenly Paradise. This method is known as *ta-li*, "relying on the other power", in contrast with Theravada Buddhist's self-effort, *zi-li*.

In the temples, the monks organise the Cult of Amitabha Buddha, centring around the Amitabha Religious Service (*O-Mi-To-Fo-fa-hui*), that involves the chanting of the Amitabha Sutra. This religious service includes two important rites namely "the rites of purification", *xiao-zai-fa-shi*, and "the rites of compassion", *da-bei-fa-shi*.

Likewise, *Guan-Yin* caters to this-worldly needs. *Guan-Yin* is the most popular deity among women. She is known to be compassionate and merciful to those who seek assistance from her. Hence, those with problems, serious or otherwise, go to her for solutions. Within the Mahayana canon, *Guan-Yin* is also known as Avalokitesvara (a male bodhisattva) who assumes different life forms in order to help those who are in need. She/he is capable of transforming herself/himself into any of the 88 different forms and images and she may play female roles on certain occasions and male ones on others. Canonically, the sexual status of *Guan-Yin* is a subject of controversy. However, among the Singapore Chinese, *Guan-Yin* is taken to be a female figure and most people are unaware of the ambisexual status stated in the canon.

Guan-Yin commonly appears in several popular forms. Depending on individual needs and the perceived complexity of the problems, *Guan-Yin* will be approached in different postures for assistance. In one form she is in the standing posture carrying a vase in one hand and a flower stalk in another, representing her readiness to help all those in need of her. In the standing form, *Guan-Yin* is also known as *Guan-shi-yin-pu-sa*, "awareness of the cries in this world". She is also known as *Guan-yin-niang-niang* meaning simply "Mother *Guan-Yin*". In yet another form, *Guan-Yin* has a thousand hands and a thousand eyes, hence her name *Qian-shou-qian-yan Guan-shi-yin-pu-sa*, symbolising her ability to see and help all in distress. Her popularity is so great that there are many temples devoted solely to her, known as *Guan-Yin-Tang*.

Kistagarbha Mahabodhisattva (*Di-Zhang-Wang-Pu-Sa*) is associated with the dead. He is invoked to assist the rite of passage of the dead from the underworld to the heavenly realm and is also invoked during a funeral service and during the annual Hungry Ghost Festival. The main function of this deity is to assist the dead to move with haste to the Western Paradise and suffer as little punishment as possible in the underworld. The Chinese believe that the dead will be punished in the underworld according to the deeds they performed during their lives on earth. Irrespective of the good secular deeds performed in this world, the expressed piety in religious participation in temples and the individual effort through the recitation of Amitabha Buddha's name, there remains a store of bad karma which invite punishment in the netherworld. However, the degree of punishment is negotiable. Hence, kinsmen of the dead enlist *Di-Zhang-Wang-Pu-Sa* to help lighten the punishment. Monks and nuns are engaged to perform prayers and funeral rites to invoke the bodhisattva to assist in this rite of passage. Only through the intervention of Kistagarbha Mahabodhisattva can one expect negotiation to take place.

Prayers and the chanting of *Di-Zhang-Wang-Jing* are done communally by monks and groups of lay people at the Hungry Ghost Festival during the seventh lunar month. It is hoped that through collective prayers *Di-Zhang-Wang-Pu-Sa* will help the hungry ghosts to be reborn again as human beings. Because of his association with the dead, *Di-Zhang-Wang-Pu-Sa* is rarely found in homes. In temples, he is usually placed within the crematorium, memorial hall (*gong-de-tang*) and collabarium where ancestral tablets and urns of ashes are stored respectively.

While Kistagarbha Mahabodhisattva looks after the dead, Medicine Buddha (*Yao-Shi-Fo*) looks after the health of the living. He is another Buddhist deity found commonly in the temples and is worshipped by both the healthy and the physically impaired and mentally ill. An individual may worship him any time of the month or year, but he is worshipped most continuously for forty-nine days starting from his birthday, which falls on the ninth lunar month. Most temples perform services for *Yao-Shi-Fo* that involve lighting medicine lamps. Families request the temple to light a lamp for a fee. During this period, the temples commonly light hundreds of these lamps, which are usually glasses containing part water and part vegetable oil, with a short burning wick placed in the middle. Hundreds of these glasses, with lights glittering from the burning wick, make a very pretty sight. Sometimes when there are so many participants and there is a shortage of space, the names of some participants are entered on printed sheets of paper specially designed for this purpose which are then pasted on the wall. In most temples, to avoid being seen as partial to some participants, the lamps are no longer assigned a name but instead become communal lamps, with the names of all participants entered on the printed sheets placed on the altar table. This informs *Yao-Shi-Fo* of those who have requested his blessings and assistance.

Worship of *Yao-Shi-Fo* involves intensive prayer and chanting sessions for forty-nine days and nights by the monks, nuns, and the laity, who together chant the *Yao-Shi-Jing* (Medicine Sutra). It is believed that through these prayer and chanting sessions, merit accumulated by these monks, nuns and laity will be transferred to those who have requested for help, and the sick and infirmed in general. All will then be protected.

Within the Mahayana temples, offerings of food (*gong-yang*) to the various Buddhist deities are made before the monks and nuns consume each meal. The Mahayana monks have three meals a day. After a meal is cooked by the temple assistants, a small portion of it, usually rice, is put into a miniature rice bowl and offered to the deities in the temple. Only a single bowl of rice is offered at the altar of the main deity of the temple. A monk or a temple assistant then sounds the gong and recites a short prayer, inviting the deities to partake of the meal. Food is also offered to the wandering souls and spirits. In most temples, there is a memorial tablet outside the shrine hall, but within the premises dedicated to the orphan souls (*gu-hun*) that have not been cared for by their kinsmen. The rice is scattered around the temple premises, along with prayers, to be picked up by these wandering souls. It is given out of pity, not respect. Their memorial tablet is placed outside so that they may not pollute the pure and holy shrine hall. They are also regarded as unwholesome evil beings capable of harming human beings. The shrine hall, housing the Buddhist deities, is considered to be a sanctuary, capable of protecting human beings from harm by evil spirits. Because of the superiority of Buddhist deities over the spirits, the spirits hover around the temple but are never able to venture into the shrine hall. As they are well fed, they do not pose a threat to the devotees. The spirits are also offered incense everyday, but usually only one stick of joss incense is placed in the ash urn where the memorial spirit tablet is located.

(i) Mahayana Buddhist Religious Service, Fa-hui

Within the Mahayana temples, there is a regular monthly religious service called *fa-hui*. Each temple can choose a specific *fa-hui* according to the religious preference of the monk and the devotees. The two most common types are the Great Repentance Service, *Da-Bei-Fa-Hui*, that invokes *Guan-Yin* to assist in this-worldly needs and the *O-Mi-To-Fu-Fa-Hui* that invokes Amitabha Buddha to assist in other-worldly needs. In addition, most temples have a series of religious services devoted to different Buddhist deities throughout the year.

The day chosen for the service is one of great significance. Days like the sixth, fifteenth, eighteenth and the twenty-seventh of the lunar month have commemorative significance and are therefore chosen. They all coincide with the birthdays of the various Buddhist deities. For example, *Guan-Yin's* birthday falls on the twenty-seventh day of the lunar month and is a favourite day for religious service in many temples, and is also the day when all *Guan-Yin* temples have an elaborate religious service.

On the chosen day, devotees arrive at the temple with fresh flowers and joss incense, preferring to bring their own rather than use those provided by the temple as this represents their personal piety. On arrival, they light the joss incense, place the flowers in the vases and pay obeisance to the deities. They then greet the monk. The devotees usually arrive prior to the stated time in order to have a private moment with the deities before the start of the service. Those who arrive late perform these acts at the end of the service.

Devotees and worshippers also arrive early to socialise. Many have known one another for many years. Especially for the elderly, this is an opportunity to engage in gossip. Their conversation revolves round topics of the family, health and their religiosity. They do not generally engage in malicious talk in the temple. However, they do show much concern for the welfare of their fellow believers. It is often in the temple that one finds sympathetic hearings and advice, often of a religious nature.

Preparation for the weekly and monthly religious service, *fa-hui*, begins a few days before the day of the service. The temple and the altar are cleaned by the temple assistants. If the service is held in the morning, a decision is made by the monk and the temple assistants on the type of food to be served for lunch. At night, only light refreshment is served. In most Mahayana temples with long-serving temple assistants, the decision and preparation are left to them.

One of the main highlights of the *fa-hui* is a purifying ritual service aimed at eradicating an individual's misfortune and averting approaching ill-fated events. This is the *xiao-zai-fa-hui*. In Buddhism, all human beings are subjected to karmic influence. Those who have done good will be rewarded with good karma and those who have done evil will be punished with bad karma, where they will suffer not only in this life but also in the afterlife through the cycle of rebirths (Obeyeskere, G., 1968). In Singapore Chinese Buddhism, the adherents believe that good karma could be gained by the manipulation of supernatural forces during the religious services.

The monk records the names of the individuals or the families who want to participate in the *xiao-zai* service in a record book. The devotees usually notify the monk or temple assistants of their desire to participate in this service before the actual day. The regular devotees often book the monthly service en bloc once a year and make yearly payments instead of monthly ones; those who are less regular might ask for a *xiao-zai* service when the need arises. They would then go to the temple, request the service and make payment. A few days before the service, the names of the adherents are also entered on a petition called *xiao-zai zhang-cheng*. The printed papers act as proxy for the individuals during the service. The coming misfortune, through the ritual acts, will be symbolically transferred to these sheets, which will then be burned. This process will enable the individuals to avert the impending misfortunes. The monk makes sure that no one is left out of this service as any misfortune arising from this omission will result in an increased bad karma for the monks.

The devotees need not come personally to the temple. They can either entrust someone else to do the job or telephone the temple to request a service. Although it is not stated, the service caters primarily to the regular devotees of the temple. When one member requests a service for the family, the other family members may or may not know of their involvement. It is commonly the elderly women who request the services for their family members to maintain peace and good fortune.

The *xiao-zai* service acts as a shield against misfortune. Most people I talked to at such services said that they would rather have more when it comes to protection. In some families, educated men, husbands, sons and brothers become critical of the women's attitudes regarding this service. The women's response is often crisp and sharp: "Look at yourself, you have a smooth time. Don't you? If I had not done the *xiao-zai* services for you, do you think you would have escaped this or that misfortune?" Sometimes, women consult the fortune-tellers on behalf of their family members. If it is predicted that a family member will experience ill fortune, the women will request a *xiao-zai* to overcome it. People often point to *xiao-zai* for their good fortune. Some people, otherwise indifferent to religion, will resort to *xiao-zai* if they are under stress or experience a series of misfortunes.

On the day of the *fa-hui*, the main altar is adorned with fresh flowers and stacks of *xiao-zai* petitions are placed on the altar table. At the stipulated time, a gong sounds. Members who have taken the Buddhist vow (*san-gui-yi*) adorn themselves in black robes (*hai-qing*) and assemble behind the monks, who stand nearest to the deities. Other worshippers stand last as the position reflects the depth of religiosity. The monks are the closest because they are the most devout. Those with black robes have entered the lay Buddhist community after formally taking the vow of *san-gui-yi*. Others are only casual worshippers. In the temple, those who have taken the vow are also regular worshippers with a close relationship with the monk or nun and the temple. They are the main supporters of the temple and its monastic residents.

With a *mu-yu*, (wooden fish – actually a wooden gong) and a small bell in hand, the monks lead the service. They first prostrate themselves three times to the main Buddhist deity. Next they begin the chanting of the *Da-Bei-Zhou* (Great Repentance Sutra). The main aim of chanting this sutra is to get rid of one's bad karma through repentance. A woman said to me, "This sutra is so powerful that the first time I chanted it, tears of remorse flowed out automatically and I felt as if all my evil deeds and shame had been washed away. I was so touched by it and spiritually awakened that I undertook *san-gui-yi* there and then and have participated regularly in this service since." Most devotees told me that they feel great relief after the sutra chanting.

In the course of chanting *Da-Bei-Zhou*, the devotees prostrate themselves 88 times, once after each verse. Elderly worshippers do this without any complaint and take pride in the act. They see it as a measure of their own commitment to the religion. Near the end of the chanting, the monks lead the laity round the temple while chanting "*Namo Guan-Shi-Yin-Pu-Sa*" and bow to *Guan-Yin* 108 times. The movement is a symbolic act of invocation of the Goddess of Mercy from all corners of the world for her assistance for the suffering sentient beings.

After this, the laity assemble in the main shrine hall and conclude the chanting session by prostrating to the deity three times. This is followed by the *xiao-zai* act. The laity remain standing in the shrine hall. In front, nearer the altar, the head monk with the assistance of fellow monks and temple assistants, perform the *xiao-zai* ritual and chant a purifying sutra, after which they read out the names that have been entered on the *xiao-zai* sheets. This act informs the deities of the worshippers' request for their assistance in purifying themselves. The *xiao-zai* sheets are subsequently burnt after all the names have been recited. The devotees see the burning of the *xiao-zai* sheets as a symbolic act, extinguishing one's periodic bad karma and misfortune that surface at certain points in their lives. The service ends with the participants partaking of a communal vegetarian lunch. The regular worshippers remain behind to socialise and assist in the clearing up. The monks retire into their own chamber, but may join in conversation if they are not too tired.

(c) Public and Communal Worship: The Hungry Ghost Festival

One of the most public and ubiquitously celebrated communal worship is the Hungry Ghost Festival (*Zhong-yuan-jie*). The

Hungry Ghost Festival is a large-scale communal religious celebration among the Singapore Chinese and lasts the whole of the seventh lunar month. This festival is celebrated at two levels. At the individual level, most households give offerings to the hungry ghosts during this period. At the communal level, business corporations and members of almost all occupation and social groupings give huge offerings. Such is the importance of this festival that it involves almost every Chinese family and socio-economic group in Singapore.

The origin of the Hungry Ghost Festival is very unclear. One of the most common Mahayana Buddhist interpretations is that monk *Mu-Lien*, who was highly trained and had reached a very high level in his spiritual pursuit, possessed supernatural powers. These supernatural powers enabled him to see the sufferings of all, including his own mother in the netherworld. His mother, because of her bad karma, suffered severe punishment. She was prevented from consuming any food as she had a small and narrow neck that made the entry of food difficult. Also, each time food reached her mouth, it turned into burning charcoal. She also had a bloated stomach. *Mu-Lien*, on seeing his mother's suffering, attempted to free her in many ways but without avail. Eventually, out of pity for his filial piety, the Buddha instructed him to assemble a group of monks and perform chanting for forty-nine days, imparting merits to her. She, who had been a hungry ghost, was saved.

According to another belief, the Chinese see the seventh month of the lunar calendar as the time when the hell gate is opened to let all the hungry ghosts roam in the earthly realm. They then prey on human beings in revenge for their deprivation. The wandering souls who have not yet been captured and encapsulated in the ancestral tablets are particularly dangerous because they are neglected souls. Those who have died a violent death and have not been given proper rites also have no place to go and are forced to wander around.

The Chinese believe that those who end up in the hungry ghost realm are those who have done many evil deeds during their lifetime – those who have engaged in family quarrels or other kinds of quarrels, or have cursed others. Hungry ghosts are also those who have died prematurely and experienced violent deaths such as suicides, car accidents and in fights. Because such persons are resentful of their deaths, they avenge themselves by haunting and attacking other human beings.

Among the Buddhists, the hungry ghosts are interpreted as beings devoid of merit. They should be given merits to enable them to advance to the human realm, their only hope of liberation from suffering. This is the common explanation for participating in the Hungry Ghost Festival. Here, it is the transference of merit that is the central ideology. Mass transference of merit to all ancestors and wandering souls is conducted in all temples. When I asked the laity why they participated in this activity, they told me that "one can never be sure if the ancestors are still suffering in hell or are reborn into the human world. It is better to transfer more rather than less merit to them. Even if an ancestor is reborn, the additional merit will add on to his present life and he will experience a more blissful life".

Chinese look on the hungry ghosts with fear. They fear being inflicted with bodily and spiritual harm, being polluted by the "dirty things and beings" and being dragged into the realm of hell by the hungry ghosts to become one of them. Therefore the ghosts must be dealt with by acts of appeasement and propitiation through sacrificial offerings. In Singapore, this offering is done at three levels: within the household; on a communal basis based on occupational and social groupings; and at the Buddhist, Daoist and Shenist temples.

Offerings by Individual Households

The festival stretches for the whole of the seventh lunar month and individual households are free to choose any day of the month to perform the act of propitiation. The common practice among the Singapore Chinese is to give a small offering on the first day of the seventh lunar month to "usher" the hungry ghosts into the human world. A more elaborate offering is staged at a later date. A send-off offering is also given on the last day of the month when the hell gate closes and the hungry ghosts return to their rightful place in the netherworld.

However, in many households, propitiation begins on the first day with offerings of incense sticks, candles, joss paper and paper money to the hungry ghosts. The stems of incense sticks are painted green and the candles white, whereas the gods are given red-stemmed incense sticks and red candles. There are three types of joss money. Of the highest value, offered to the deities and ancestors, is the "golden paper" (*jin-zhi*) – that is, joss paper with a piece of gold-coloured foil stuck into the centre. Less valuable is the "silver paper" (*yin-zhi*) with silver foil, and the ordinary joss paper with a stamp in red ink in the middle. Usually, the latter two types are offered to the hungry ghosts because of the low status of the ghosts. The ghosts are lesser beings and should thus be treated accordingly in order to maintain harmony in the heavenly, human and spirit worlds. A relatively recent innovation, hell money, resembling currency notes printed in high values such as ten thousand or a hundred thousand, is also offered to the ghosts. According to the Singapore Chinese, it is because the hungry ghosts are so poor that they scrounge around, and so the high value notes will appease them. As the ghosts are stupid, they will be fooled by hell money.

It is assumed that when the hell-gate opens, all the hungry ghosts float to this earthly world. They are everywhere but cannot be seen by the naked eye. Offering must be made outside the homes – the ghosts are not invited into the house because of their polluted status. Should they attack a house, exorcism will be needed. Offering is usually made in the immediate vicinity of the house, along the sidewalk. Sometimes, the ghosts are offered their due next to a tree or on a vacant plot – places which are considered to be hideouts of the ghosts. Regular pathways and parks where children play are usually avoided.

One day during the month is chosen for an elaborate offering. Many households favour the fifteenth day, mid-way through the month, to hold the ceremony. Most offerings are modest and can be carried out at any hour. On the selected day, womenfolk in the household prepare propitiatory offerings. Food and ritual items are bought in the neighbourhood, either in the market or in specialised shops. Chicken, duck, pork, fruits, vegetables, tinned food of a few varieties, joss-sticks, candles, joss and hell papers and small triangular-shaped, colourful flags with designs denoting deities or Chinese symbols such as dragons, are purchased. The food is cooked but one or two meat items are left in raw form in order to distinguish between the gods who are given only cooked food and the ghosts.

The food is brought outside of the house and left on a table. Lighted incense sticks are placed in every dish and the triangular flags are placed in an upright position in between the food to inform the ghosts of the offerings. The joss and hell money are stacked and left on the road to be burned after the offering. The usual way of offering joss-paper to the deities and ancestors is by lighting a few sheets of joss-paper at a time. In the offering to the hungry ghosts, they are burned as a stack without any human being doing the offering. The reason is that the hungry ghosts who hover around might accidentally inflict burns on people standing close to the burning joss-papers.

After the offerings, most households eat the food, but the wealthy households throw the food away. People say that the food offered to the hungry ghosts tastes "flat" and funny, unlike that offered to the deities. Some say that the food given to the hungry ghosts turns stale within a short period of time and so must be eaten immediately or thrown away. The offering usually lasts about an hour. Women are more concerned with domestic offering while men are more involved in the communal public offerings, effectively reinforcing the gender divide of the private and public domains between the two genders in a patriarchal Chinese society.

Offerings by Neighbourhood and Business Groups

At communal observances, business companies and other economic groups provide the offerings in a neighbourhood district. The wholesalers and market vendors too have their own communal worship. Every year, a *lu-zhu* or "stove master" is chosen to head the worshipping. He is responsible for the collection of funds from the members, who pay monthly instalments throughout the year. Wholesalers pay a single amount voluntarily. A committee decides on the amount to be contributed. Usually those in larger commercial firms or other organisations pay about two hundred to three hundred dollars a month. The market vendors and petty traders contribute twenty dollars each month. The contributions go into a central pool and are used specifically for the hungry ghost festival. When approached by the *lu-zhu*, everyone contributes his share. Many perceive the celebration to be of great significance – hence their readiness in contributing to it. No one would dream of not participating in the worship. To them, it is religiously and socially a very significant event.

The scale of worship is dependent on the amount of money collected for the occasion, but there are essential items that have to be bought to benefit the hungry ghosts and protect human beings from harm. There is an important balance between ostentation and strict adherence to known ritual practices that must be observed. There are also slight variations in the style of worshipping (the positioning of the various altars, the sequences of events) among the various groups. Below is an example of how a communal worship of the Hungry Ghost Festival takes place in a market place.

The Beach Road Market Hungry Ghost Communal Worship Service

The vendors of a wet market along Beach Road organised this Hungry Ghost communal worship service. In this district, besides shops, there are close to sixty stalls selling vegetables, fruits, fish, meat and cooked food. This celebration has been carried out yearly since the start of the wet market some thirty years ago.

The stove master (*lu-zhu*) played a prominent role in the celebration. He was expected not only to contribute in the administration and the management of the whole function, but also financially, should the funds collected prove insufficient. The *lu-zhu* was chosen not by the members but by the "will of the God" which was determined via the following process. First, those who are interested in competing for the position of *lu-zhu* for the following year make their intention known to the members. Second, before the

71

end of the celebration, the interested members are invited to participate in the selection process.

The selection process is as follows: the participants are required to throw the wooden blocks, *mu-bei*, in front of their guardian god and seek his approval, which is given if when thrown, one *mu-bei* lands with the flat face down and the other with the face upwards. The person with the highest number of positive throws becomes the *lu-zhu* for the following year's ceremony, and one or two of the others become the assistant stove-masters (*fu-lu-zhu*), again chosen in the same way. The god is called to witness and judge the selection process and to ensure impartiality. Once chosen, the *lu-zhu's* authority is sacred and indisputable.

According to one of the organisers, if the *lu-zhu* does not perform his job well or if he is an unsuitable candidate, the deity will give telltale signs. Members would then gather to discuss a solution. The organiser told me that there was a case of a dishonest stove master who pocketed some of the money contributed by the members. The deity brought this dishonesty to light in this way: "The opera stage collapsed in the midst of a performance and yet the troupe was unharmed. Incidents like this just happened and things did not go right. Members and outsiders were then aware of the existence of dishonesty within the committee". The committee subsequently met, forcing the culprit to own up to his "mistake". In most cases, according to my informants, people do own up to their dishonesty and return the money. In another instance, a contestant for *lu-zhu* was not moving along the "right path", as he was connected with some undesirable groups. To prevent him from vying for the position, "the deity made him ill at the selection time".

Preparations for the ceremony involved gaining permission from several government departments and booking various facilities at an early date. The committee rented open space between the market and the housing units. They first applied to the Police Department for a clearance permit for a permit that would entitle them to hold this religio-cultural function involving public participation and gathering. The permits required a deposit of one hundred dollars and a nominal daily rent of twenty dollars. The police monitored the noise level and traffic congestion. The rent paid to the Ministry of Culture was for the use of the space: should any damage need to be repaired, the deposit would be forfeited. Applying for the permit and booking the facilities had to be done at least two to three months in advance.

The committee also booked an opera troupe. There is usually some competition among the worshipping groups for good opera or musical groups. Traditionally, the Hungry Ghost Festival is celebrated with an opera performance (*da-xi*), but in recent years, pop music groups had been hired to play for both the gods and the general public. *Da-xi*, performed in Chinese dialects and traditional singing style, has become less popular with the younger population.

The *lu-zhu* and the committee decided on an invitation list, and a month prior to the celebration, they sent out invitation cards to the participants and contributors to attend the religious function and the dinner on the main night. Other preparations involved the renting of chairs and tables and the erecting of the temporary shelter and the opera stage. Because of heavy demand during this season, everything had to be booked well in advance.

Religious paraphernalia and food for sacrificial and propitiatory offerings were bought later. Giant-sized, cylindrical-shaped joss sticks about three feet in height, with pictures of dragon and phoenix affixed to them; candles of similar size; and large quantities of joss papers and hell notes were purchased. Various figures, of human size, of Buddhist deities such as *Guan-Yin*, *Yan-Luo-Wang* (King of Hades) and other deities associated with the netherworld, shaped out of colourful papers, were ordered for the occasion.

The actual worship lasted three days. During the main religious day, all the market vendors stopped trading. For most of them, this was one of the few occasions to take a break from working, as most open shop seven days a week. A few days before the actual celebration, temporary shelters and the stage were erected to house the deities and the hungry ghosts. Tables and chairs were arranged for the dinner feast and for the food offering. The general mood was one of festivity. The working committee supervised the work, busying itself with last minute preparations. Everything was carefully laid out according to plan. There was not to be any mistake, because any mishap would be interpreted as divine punishment for the wrong leadership. This was a particularly tense period for the *lu-zhu* and his assistants, given the expectation the participants had of them. Men did virtually all the work. Women only participated in the worshipping.

During the celebration, all the items were arranged in order and offered to the ghosts. During the day, passers-by made obeisance by clasping both hands together to show respect to the deities and the hungry ghosts. At night, the place became lively with bright lights and men hanging around. The women were less conspicuous. However, for the final dinner feast thrown by the committee, men, women and children turned out in numbers.

One of the highlights was the auctioning of the various items that were considered to be auspicious. Auctioning took place at the dinner amidst the noises from the opera show. It was a very noisy event. Various items were auctioned, ranging from food to toys to images of deities. However, the most treasured item was the "black gold", a piece of charcoal, the possession of which would bring prosperity and wealth to the possessor. Because of its alleged property, it was much sought by businessmen. As a result, the bidding price for it was unusually high. In a big celebration, when wealthy businessmen gather for the night, the price of the black gold can reach over ten thousand dollars. For this particular celebration, the market vendors bid two thousand dollars for the black gold. Other items of low value fetched several hundred dollars each. From the auction, several tens of thousands were netted, which would to be used to fund the following year's celebration.

The opera performance captivated the attention of some passers-by and the residents from the nearby housing units. However, for this particular celebration, the organiser had also staged, a religious performance. Youths from a religious organisation were invited to chant Buddhist sutras, including the *Di-Zang-Wang-Jing*, to transfer merits to the ghosts. This was a new move, an addition to the efforts to propitiate and appease the ghosts through the offerings of food and entertainment. It was seen as an important act by the Reformist Buddhists to rationalise a traditional Chinese religious celebration into a partly Buddhist one. The chanting emphasised the importance of the merits to the ghosts as compared to the giving of paper money and other material goods. However, all informants generally stressed the importance of the food offerings and said that the hungry ghosts were the result of their this-worldly craving. The offerings of food served to satisfy their cravings and hence calm them down. With a calm mind, these ghosts would be able to concentrate on their spiritual salvation and be reborn into the human realm again. Thus, the food offering was again given a Buddhist (karmic cycle) reinterpretation.

Significance of Propitiating the Hungry Ghosts

Hungry ghosts are the result of the failure to install the dead in proper burial grounds and worship them as ancestors. They therefore become wandering souls without a permanent abode, known as floating souls (*you-hun*) or lonely souls (*gu-hun*). They are thus frustrated spirits capable of inflicting harm on humans and the rituals involved in the hungry ghost worship are ways to negotiate, bribe and solicit sympathy from the spirits to prevent them from harming humans.

As a result of their state of misery and deprivation, the spirits inflict harm to gain attention. Individual spirits can attack and make the victims sick or possess the victims to alert the humans to their plight. One way out is through appeasement and propitiation through offerings of food, paper money and rites as in the Hungry Ghost Festival. Another way is to negotiate and encourage the spirit to leave the victims through a religious rite of exorcism and the provision of material benefits to the spirit in order to rest its soul in the netherworld.

The seventh lunar month, known as the month of the hungry ghosts (*gui-jie*), is an important month where the humans and the spirits interact in a mutually- acceptable manner. It is a time of giving and a time of receiving: the humans give while the spirits receive. But beneath this simple transaction, there is a subtle negotiation going on. The generous gifts of food, money, material goods and religious merits are given with the understanding that the spirits will leave the humans alone, so that, when the hell gate closes after the designated month, no hungry ghost will choose to hover around the human world. The seventh lunar month can thus be seen as a month of "betwixt and between", where liminality is at its zenith. The criss-crossing of the human and spirit paths is potentially dangerous, polluting and harmful. Precaution has to be taken concerning the behaviour and actions of the humans, so that they do not offend the spirits, lest they retaliate. It is a time where each group re-establishes its own boundary and establishes its standing with the other. In short, humans and spirits are two separate types of being occupying two different worlds. At times, the spirits might cross over to the human world where they are welcomed as guests by their hosts. But there is a limit to which their presence is appreciated. Beyond that, it is a different story.

The dead ancestors are normally regarded as the "good spirits or ghosts" and are worshipped separately as ancestors and are not seen as part of the Hungry Ghost celebration. They are seen as inherently kind and continue to be part of the family and lineage structure. They are willing and capable of helping the living members of the family and lineage if treated in a proper manner. The veneration of ancestors and the creation of the cult of ancestor worship serve to place the dead and the living in a reciprocal relationship. The Confucian ideal dictates that the living respect the dead, to express "gratitude toward the originators and (recall) the beginning" (Yang, 1961: 44). It is also important "for the purpose of stabilising and perpetuating the kinship system as the basic unit of social organisation" (Yang, 1961: 51). The most common situation is that the dead ancestors are worshipped because of filial obligation. A secondary motive is for peace, prosperity and general protection. They are pure and wholesome beings, generally benign and rather passive.

On the whole, there is very little tension between the living and their ancestors. The Chinese do not expect their ancestors to harm them at all if they have performed their duties in a filial manner. If the ancestors were uncomfortable or suffering in the underworld, there would be signs given to the living, often in the form of dreams in which the ancestors bemoan their suffering. The descendants would, without hesitation, give food and monetary offerings to the ancestors as well as the guardian spirits of the underworld. Some might request the services of priests or monks to make merits and pacify the unsettled souls of the ancestors. Others consult a spirit-medium to perform a séance and communicate with their dead ancestors.

To ensure that the ancestors are not reduced to the state of pauperism in the underworld, it is common for descendants to perform the rite of meritorious deeds, *gong-de*. This is usually performed either 49 days, or three years, after the death. Sometimes, because of unforeseen circumstances, this rite is performed only many years after the death of an ancestor.

As the name suggests, *gong-de* is a merit-making ceremony. It can involve either Buddhist or Daoist rites. Monks, nuns or Daoist priests are engaged in this ceremony. It usually lasts for three to seven days. It is performed either in a temple or at home. Each day, several sessions of Buddhist or Daoist prayers are offered. Elaborate religious paraphernalia accompany the ceremony, including a mansion (beautifully decorated, at times of several storeys); all kinds of modern equipment (car, television, video recorder, air conditioner, etc); and items for daily needs. All of these items are made of colourful paper. The central idea behind this ceremony is to provide for the spiritual and material needs of the ancestors. Buddhist prayers serve to impart merits to the dead so that they can be reborn as human beings in their next cycle of rebirth. The religious paraphernalia are for their use in the netherworld. In short, the ceremony enables the living to look after the welfare of the dead. It also allows some people to compensate for their unfilial treatment of the ancestor before their death and thus serves as an avenue for the absolution of their guilty feelings.

INTER-PERSONAL COMMUNICATION
AND TRANSACTION

Another reason for approaching the gods, deities and spirits and performing rituals for them is to communicate and negotiate with them. The Chinese approach their gods and deities to help them solve their problems, both this-worldly and other-worldly ones, believing that the fate and life of humans are intertwined closely with that of the godly and spiritual beings. Each needs the other to survive. Because human beings have form and are capable of actions and words, it is therefore left to the humans to initiate the dialogue with the godly and spiritual beings, in which the gods respond. Negotiation is possible because the Chinese view the spirit world as resembling that of a human world (Ahern, 1981). The gods and spirits therefore share the same kinds of ideals and needs as humans. They are intelligent, reasonable, understanding and rational. Because they are rational, it is possible to reason with them. But the success of the negotiation is highly dependent on the skills of the person.

Scholars of Chinese religion (Ahern 1981, Saso 1972, Wolf 1974, and Weller 1986) have written about the different methods used by the Chinese to communicate with their gods, deities and spirits. There are four ways in which a worshipper could establish a dialogue with the gods and deities: through interpersonal communication, through written bureaucratic communication, through divination, and through magic.

One of the simplest methods is simply to communicate with the deities on an interpersonal level. At this level, all that is needed is for the person who has a problem to confront the god or deity directly. He or she can go to the family altar or to a temple, pick out a specific deity, confide his or her problems to the deity and ask for assistance. Affirmation of the willingness of the deity to assist is through a simple ritual procedure of the throwing of the *mu-bei*. Two flat or two concave sides mean a negative reply and unwillingness to help. This is construed as the fault of the supplicant, who has unintentionally offended the deity or has not performed correctly the desired rituals when soliciting assistance. Usually, the supplicant will implore and coax the deity for further consideration, giving various reasons why its assistance is needed. At the same time, the supplicant engages in negotiation with the deity, promising certain rituals and rewards to the deity when the supplicant's problem is solved. This is the most common method used by the Singapore Chinese. It is not uncommon for older women to consult the gods and deities on the smallest move that they intend to make or on small obstacles that they encounter in their daily discourse. To a large degree, it is psychological comfort that they are seeking and they find solace in the gods and deities.

When a supplicant has a specific and slightly more complex problem, he or she is even more likely to consult the gods and deities in the temple. The choice of the god is dependent on the supplicant. Among the Singapore Chinese, *Guan-Yin* is the favourite. People go to her with a wide range of problems including domestic quarrels, emotional problems, problems of health, study or money.

The person with a problem who wishes to seek advice or remedy from *Guan-Yin* will take off her footwear and enter the shrine hall. She first lights three joss sticks, clasping them in both hands and waving them three times before depositing them in the incense holder. Again, depending on her wish, the supplicant might bring some fresh flowers and offer them to the Buddhist deity. The flowers are put in vases in front of the altar. The supplicant then prostrates fully or partly by kneeling on both knees and bending the body forward till the forehead touches the ground. In part-prostration, the person kneels, clasping both hands together in front of the chest and then waving them from the chest outward three times. Having done this, the devotee articulates her problem silently or in a murmur to *Guan-Yin* and begs for help. The advice from *Guan-Yin* comes in the form of *qian-si*, slips of paper with printed remedies and advice.

The process of seeking an answer is as follows: first, the person asks a question and petitions for help, then she picks a container containing 99 bamboo sticks called *qian* and shakes out one of them. Each *qian* has a number written on it. Next she ascertains the status of the particular *qian* by throwing a pair of *mu-bei*. If the *mu-bei* gives a positive indication, she carries the numbered *qian* to the counter to exchange for a slip of paper of the same number as the *qian*. The slip of paper, which bears a message, is known as *qian-si*. The wording is non-specific and must be interpreted according to the question posed by the devotee. If literate, the supplicant might decipher the meaning by herself. Otherwise, for a small fee, she might engage a professional *qian-si* interpreter to do the job. The interpreter is usually a man who works at the temple. The person then follows the advice or the remedy given. Subsequently, if her problem is solved, the outcome is attributed to the effectiveness of *Guan-Yin*. The devotee will then return to the temple and give offering to the deity. If not, she can either come back to seek further assistance from *Guan-Yin* or go to other places to try there.

In another type of communication, *Guan-Yin* speaks through a spirit-medium. Often in the *Guan-Yin* temple a spirit-medium, usually an elderly woman, goes into a trance and in this state, is taken as a manifestation of mother *Guan-Yin*. She acts as a mediator between the supplicant and the transcendental *Guan-Yin*, her body serving as a conduit for *Guan-Yin* to manifest herself.

Consulting a spirit medium is carried out as follows: a person wishing to consult the spirit medium visits the temple and makes her request known to the temple assistant, who then informs the spirit medium. The medium will then take her position on a chair with a table next to her in front of the *Guan-Yin* altar. The believer sits on the chair next to the medium. *Guan-Yin* is invoked and possesses the body of the spirit medium through the ritual acts of incantation and the burning of incense. When in trance, the medium is ready to answer questions posed by the believer. The believer begins by outlining the problems she has encountered and then asks for assistance. A temple helper acts as a translator for the believer, helping to translate the words of *Guan-Yin* which are spoken through the spirit medium. Asked if this really happens, most people told me that it does because the voice of the spirit medium changes. The session lasts from 10 to 20 minutes depending on the complexity of the problems and the solutions needed.

At the end of the session, *Guan-Yin* returns to the altar, the spirit medium is sprinkled with holy water and awakes from her trance. The medium is often exhausted after each consultation.

People approach the medium for emotional troubles, marital disharmony, problems with children or health, and for safe voyages, and also when they suspect spirit possession or being affected by an evil eye. The believers are also given protective amulets, *fu* for extra protection. Usually two kinds of *fu* are given, one to be burned into ashes and consumed with drink and the other to be kept next to the body for physical protection. The consumption of *fu* serves as a ritual act of cleansing.

The medium also acts as a protector of sickly children. This is the fostering of children to Mother *Guan-Yin*. When a child is frequently or chronically ill and when medical treatment brings no improvement to the child's health, he or she is considered to be "a difficult child to rear". A difficult child will have characteristics such as an ill-defined horoscope, a deficiency in *yang* elements and an excessive amount of *yin* elements. Such a child is prone to attack by evil spirits and so falls sick easily and thus must be placed under the guardianship and protection of mother *Guan-Yin*.

To do this, the child is brought to the temple, usually by the mother, who informs the temple assistant, who in turn informs the spirit medium of the believer's request. The medium then initiates the child into the Buddhist family by chanting prayers and making known the intention of spiritually fostering the child to *Guan-Yin*. The child is then given a special name. In most temples, a shirt of the child is stamped with a seal in red ink to denote his or her entry into the relationship. The child will wear the stamped shirt during the day of initiation; it will then be kept at home to protect him/her. He/She is also given an amulet to be worn at all times, for additional protection. After the initiation, the mother of the child contributes a small sum to the temple for the service. Most parents whose children have been fostered to Mother *Guan-Yin* told me that they have witnessed an improvement in the health of their children: they cried less, had better appetites and were more active.

Children can be fostered to Mother *Guan-Yin* from as young as a few months to a maximum age of sixteen years. In one temple where Mother *Guan-Yin* is seen as efficacious, over 200 children have been placed under her foster care. The foster children are expected to attend and participate in temple celebrations. Once a year, on the birthday of *Guan-Yin*, a procession is organised in which the foster female children act as flower girls and the boys act as "the red children" (disciples) and march in the streets along with the sedan chair carrying *Guan-Yin*. This fostering system binds the children – and indirectly the parents – to the temple, so that it is guaranteed of a constant flow of reliable social and economic support.

The consultation of the deity for assistance is usually a simple procedure. The devotees usually place their faith in the deity and are confident that with proper ritual procedures, help will come their way. In the constant process of negotiation between humans and deities, reaching an agreement must be mutually beneficial – otherwise, either one or both parties might suffer bad consequences. The Chinese usually negotiate for protection from both fellow humans and from other spiritual beings. At the individual level, they ask for protection for safe passage, childbirth, health, fertility, passing examinations and wealth. At the communal level, the welfare of the family and the community may need protection. At the national level, the welfare of the Chinese community and the nation state comes under protection too. Various gods and deities are invoked at different levels of negotiation. For those that prove efficacious, the human rewards are very substantial.

NEGOTIATING WITH THE SPIRITS

When dealing with the spirits from the underworld, the situation is much more complicated. It involves a lengthy process of negotiation, bribery and blackmail. These spirits are seen as malignant, unreasonable, vicious, and irrational, and often cannot be reasoned with. So, when a person crosses the path of these spirits, they will be inflicted with bodily and psychological harm, with physical illness or mental disorder. It is the latter that is most frightful. Ahern distinguishes between illness from "within the body" and illness from "being hit" (*zhuang-dao*). While illness from "within the body" is the result of the yin and yang imbalance, "being hit" is the result of crossing the path of the ghosts and spirits (Ahern, 1981: 9). At times, the ghosts and spirits take hold of the body and reside in it. Like the Taiwanese counterparts whom Ahern discusses, the Singapore Chinese resort to the aid of the gods and deities to assist in curing those who have been hit by the spirits and to rid the unwholesome being from the body.

The ritual procedure for exorcism may be a long and complex one, depending on the spirit involved in the collision, or who has possessed the body. It frequently involves some form of reasoning, negotiation and bribery. I give an example of how this negotiation is carried out:

> An informant whose daughter, aged seventeen, was noticed behaving in an abnormal manner, complained to her mother that she was often visited by a male spirit. She had not been concentrating on her studies or on any other thing. She complained of excessive fatigue. She lacked interest in joining her friends in their activities and kept to herself most of the time. She was also very nervous.
>
> She claimed to be continuously troubled by the unknown spirit, at first only occasionally during the night, later during the day as well. The number of visits made by the spirit had increased and at one stage, occurred on a daily basis. When the spirit became familiar with her, he began a love affair with her and they started making love.
>
> She began to talk to "him" constantly, including during school hours. The teachers in her schools noticed her strange behaviour and reported it to her parents. At first, both the teachers and her parents thought that she was unwell and consulted a trained medical doctor, then a psychiatrist. But her symptoms continued. She lacked concentration and was, at times, nervous. Her parents, on medical advice, decided to suspend her studies temporarily and continued counselling and psychiatric treatment. The treatment went on for half a year but without much improvement. During this period, they thought that she was suffering from puberty blues, nervous tension and schizophrenia.

The parents, on the advice of some kinswomen, sought the assistance of the Daoist priest for they now became convinced that she had met a polluting, unwholesome spirit. By then she could describe very vividly what "he" looked like (in human form), the conversation between them and their love relationship.

A Daoist priest was consulted to exorcise the spirit. The priest, on behalf of the teenage girl and her parents, entered into a lengthy negotiation process with the spirit to implore "him" to leave her. Various rituals were performed, and the male spirit was asked the reason for his invasion and what he required. If he agreed to leave the captive host peacefully, his needs would be catered for. He was offered paper money and food. The spirit was also told that he could not have a relationship with a human and that a female substitute (*nu-ti-shen*) would be arranged for him as a companion. This ritual was performed several times before a noticeable improvement was realised.

After several ritual performances, the teenage girl felt that "he" did not communicate with her as often, although there was still some contact. He would still visit her "once in a while" and they would be on intimate terms. She was happy when "he" came to see her and was glad that he continued to "love" her.

Having realised that the spirit continued to visit her, the priest felt that the spirit had refused to honour their negotiation. At the same time, the priest felt that it was the girl who had intentionally or unconsciously invited him back. The priest proclaimed that she was by then in a fairly clear stage of mind. The priest suggested that the girl learn Buddhism. The priest felt that the negotiation had to be left to the girl and the spirit. The learning of Buddhist prayers, under a monk or nun, would enlighten the thoughts and consciousness of the girl, enabling her to differentiate between human and spirit forms. The priest also believed that the mystical power of Buddhism would slowly dispel the unwholesome spirit from her as she gradually purified her thoughts and body.

On the advice of the priest, the parents brought the girl to the temple on a very regular basis, two or three times a week, where she socialised with other laity and learned Buddhist dharma and prayers. Her condition, according to some of the laity and her parents, improved tremendously and they were hopeful that she would return to her normal self and resume her studies. When I spoke to her, she seemed happy with her Buddhist teaching and expressed her desire to go back to school.

Anthropologically, this case study highlights several points. The human and the spirit beings can communicate with each other. The spirit being is able to cross the boundary to the human world. The human, who is in contact with the spirit, is regarded as being in a dangerous phase. At this phase, she is a danger to herself, and at times to others. In this case study, the male spirit was obviously a forlorn and forsaken being and was, to a large degree, harmless, having inflicted little harm on the girl (she sustained no physical injury, although she was mentally troubled). The ritual act of cleansing was an important process of negotiation, where the spirit was asked not to trouble the girl if he were to be given a substitute. However, spirits, like humans, have feelings and attachments. The male spirit, having formed a union with the girl, did not "leave" her, probably on her request, as she was "happy to see him" again. His not leaving also reflected on the negotiating power of the rituals performed by the Daoist priest, who invited the spirit to leave the girl alone. But alas, love is such a powerful idiom that the two did not want to separate. The only recourse was then to force the girl to work on cleansing herself through religious self-cultivation (*zi-xiu*) and she was taught Buddhist dharma and prayers by a monk in order that her ties with the spirit could be severed through the mystical religious power she would gain. It would have to be the girl who would negotiate and invite the male spirit not to visit her again.

At the time of the fieldwork, she was in this process of self-cleansing and self-healing and she was gradually losing her affinity for the spirit, to the relief of the priest, monk, her parents and friends.

CONTEMPORARY RELEVANCE

The essence of Shenism is ritualism, both on the communal and individual level. The ritual action, irrespective of whether it is conducted by the individual at home or through a monk or priest at a temple, is essentially the same and its meaning is largely propitiatory and supplicative. Although underlying the ritual action there are cosmological and eschatological tenets, the purpose of ritual action is manipulative and this-worldly. The priest or the individual is "the trickster". The beliefs, as such, are diffused and do not contain soteriological elements. This is so even when the action is addressed to a Buddhist deity such as Sakyamuni Buddha, in the temple. There is, for example, little direct hint of the goal of reaching the Western Paradise or nirvana, among the laity. Since the late 1970s, with Buddhicisation of Shenism, there is a gradual move towards the Buddhist understanding of karma, merit-making and enlightenment in the Western Paradise.

An important aspect of Shenist ritualism involves dealings with the gods and deities. Chinese gods, deities and spirits are represented in national, regional and local polities. Their status is ordered according to their popularity. Their popularity is dependent on the extent to which the Chinese can negotiate and bargain with them to achieve their desired ends. In their relationship with the spirits, the Chinese adopt various strategies – they propitiate, offer, negotiate, bargain and blackmail – according to the types of spirits they are dealing with. With the godly beings, they are more likely to show a high level of respect, with which propitiation and offerings are more appropriate. They also negotiate and bargain with lesser gods. With the underworld spirit beings, they propitiate out of fear and whenever possible, bargain or blackmail them to achieve their ends.

The current ritual action expresses individual and familial concerns. Religion, in a sense, is now privatised. This is so even during the Hungry Ghost Festival where, along with the communal celebration, each family nowadays propitiates ghosts on its own. In the past, the celebrations were exclusively communal and temple-based. In this sense, the shift also reflects the changed structure of Singapore society.

While this ritualism continues to form an important aspect of the religious landscape for the Chinese, this is only so for the elderly. Among the younger generation Chinese, such ritualism is increasingly being seen as "superstitious practices" and is devoid of meaning, as it fails to answer other religious needs, for which they turn to Reformist Buddhism in their quest for individual salvation.

PART 2

State, Society and Religious Engineering

CHAPTER 3

Bureaucratising the Temple and the Sangha

INTRODUCTION

Apart from reproducing the religious ideologies and ritual practices, the Chinese during the early years also reproduced the familiar institution of the village temple in colonial Singapore. Among the common terms for a temple are *miao*, *gong*, *she* and *tang*. These various terms are used interchangeably to denote Buddhist, Daoist and Shenist temples. The village temple emerged to cater to the functional needs of the peasants and later, in Singapore, of the migrants. Most Chinese were intimately involved in the religious life of the temple, for it fulfilled their individual religious needs. It was important for the Chinese, especially the women, to visit the temple and pray to their gods and deities for help and favour. Members of the Sangha, i.e., monks and nuns, lived in the temples. They were often seen as the embodiment of the institution of the temple because of their status and the roles they played within it. Traditionally, the temple and the Sangha functioned as a single entity.

However, in present-day Singapore, the temple and the Sangha are subjected to the process of bureaucratisation to make them "modern", "rational" and accountable to the general public. As a result of this process of bureaucratisation, both the temple and the Sangha have different roles. The temple as a religious institution is engaged in both religious and secular activities while the Sangha as a monastic institution is engaged in the pursuit of religious activities. Only certain types of secular activities that are closely linked to religion such as those related to welfare and education can be pursued by individual Sangha members.

This chapter discusses how the process of bureaucratisation results in the separation of the Sangha and the temple. It also discusses the modernising roles played by the monks and nuns, the lay community and the Singapore State in restructuring Chinese religion and Buddhism to suit the modern needs.

EARLY TEMPLE STRUCTURE

In traditional China, there were two main types of temples, the large monasteries and the village temples. They emerged to cater to two separate groups of people. The monasteries were built for those who had chosen a monastic way of life, whose primary preoccupation was the pursuit of enlightenment. They were also seats of power, learning and much scholarship as well as significant economic institutions that controlled large stretches of rural land (Welch, 1967; Chen, 1973). These monasteries were idealised images that were seen as both impractical and at times, incomprehensible to the majority. Their institutional set-up and their inmates' renunciation of ordinary life were a far cry from the Chinese understanding of the dictates of daily routine. They remained the abode for only the selected few who experienced a spiritual calling.[1]

On the other hand, the village temple structure was a simple one. It can be best understood functionally. Temples came to absorb continuously the surplus rural population that an agrarian economy failed to accommodate. In an agrarian society where the socio-economic institutions were geared towards agricultural production, an increase in population, changes within one or more parts of the social system or a natural or socio-political disorder, created pressure on the existing resources and resulted in economic hardship for the people. At various stages in Chinese history, one can see a recurring pattern in which displaced and unemployed workers and redundant familial child labourers entered the Sangha. Under extreme economic hardship, even in ordinary times, adult males might enter the order. Among the poorer families, one son was normally given to the order, arguably to gain merit for the parents.

Other Buddhist societies have developed different ways of placing their surplus population into the monastic order. In Thailand, it is customary for young male adults to enter the order for the lent period at least once in their life.[2] In Burma and Sri Lanka, it became customary for a family to send one of the sons to the monastery.[3] Among Tibetans and many other Himalayan peoples, large numbers of young men regularly entered the monastic order to keep the societies viable. In rural South China, the peasants were confronted with a rigid socio-economic structure that was incapable of expanding with increases in population. Their impoverishment was accentuated by the constant occurrence of natural disasters. The Confucian norm of having large families ran counter to the resources of many peasant families. Poverty usually landed young boys from the poorest families in the temples. This was the situation right up to the eve of World War II.

The majority of monks who lived in small village temples had neither land nor wealth of other kinds. Most were no better off than the poor peasant families whence they came. Their monastic vocation was neither highly regarded nor deemed desirable by them or the village community. Sending a son to a monastery was an admission of failure for most families, as they had made such a son contradict the Confucian principles of filial piety and obligation to the living and dead forebears. The entry into monkhood, *chu-jia* (leaving the family), effectively destroyed this cherished familial ideal. Yet the harsh socio-economic conditions in China led some families to give up one or more of their children to the temple for adoption. Once in the temple, a child could legitimately beg for food and was entitled to it at the monasteries. He (or she) could also hope to learn and acquire the skill of ritual performance and other skills and become self-supporting through the exercise of these skills for laymen.

The early temple structure was patterned after the family system. It consisted of a head monk, his disciples and the temple assistants, also called vegetarian aunts, *cai-gu*. These vegetarian aunts were not part of the Sangha. Within an individual temple, the head monk ran the temple in a patriarchal and authoritarian manner as he would if he were the head of a household. He controlled both the religious and administrative activities and assigned various tasks to his disciples and temple assistants. These temple assistants were usually homeless women, taken in by the monks. In exchange for board and lodging, they assisted the monks in the maintenance of the temple. As they lived in the temple, they consumed only a vegetarian diet and are thus called vegetarian aunt, *cai-gu* by the devotees. The monk was assisted by his disciples in ritual services. He instructed his disciples and preached to the *cai-gu* occasionally, and chose his successor when he felt old or was infirmed, or when he knew that he was dying.

The head monk communicated directly with the lay worshippers and responded to their needs, which were largely of a ritual variety. Occasionally, he would be approached to perform exorcisms and dispense charms. His relationship with them was of a patron-client character, where the lay people demanded religious services and in return they provided financial and material support for the monk and his temple. He also acted as spiritual guardian and provided advice to devotees who came with their personal problems, ranging from domestic to business and spiritual problems. He occasionally preached dharma to individuals who requested it. Finally, he might have knowledge of Chinese herbal medicine and practised as a herbalist.

The head monk functioned as a sole proprietor and did not have formal rules governing the functioning and activities of the temple. There was no written instruction, nor was there any written code of conduct, but the head monk observe monastic rules concerning morality and personal behaviour. His knowledge of the religious services and the dharma was learnt through apprenticeship, and in turn he imparted it to his disciples.

The temple and the monk derived income from the provision of religious services and donations from the worshippers. Infrequent but substantial financial contributions were also given by wealthy merchants out of piety, but more often because they have derived huge benefits from the services rendered by the monk. Assistance was also given for repairs of the temple building. In most cases, the monk eked out subsistence living in an increasingly competitive secular environment that granted few priorities for its religious activities. Often, the temple had a humble beginning, made out of mud and thatch. However, over time, it might be given a concrete floor or a brick structure when the monk accumulated enough money through his religious services to pay for them, or managed to convince wealthy laymen to sponsor renovation of the temple. Despite public contributions, the ownership laid with the monk and no one disputed this, as a religious gift could not bring merit if its alienation was only partial.

THE TEMPLE AS A MODERN DAY BUREAUCRACY

One common feature of temples is that devotees are free to walk in and perform worship on their own. A worshipper or devotee may visit any temple or shrine freely, at any time. There is no congregational membership, and worshippers are not required to have allegiance to any one temple; and in fact, many have no allegiance to any temple at all, but visit different temples for different needs. The lay worshippers practise a similar form of worshipping and offerings at all the temples. It is a common sight to see a temple filled with worshippers, mostly women, offering joss sticks, candles and joss-papers, and reciting prayers to the gods. A worshipper may choose to worship at a particular temple more than others, or may have preferences among the gods who serve the same utilitarian functions – mainly, that of solving the mundane, albeit varied, problems of the worshippers.

The village temple that served the early Chinese community well is no longer considered an appropriate institution in contemporary Singapore society. In a modern society, all institutional activities are being rationalised and made accountable under an auditing system put in place by the government. This is the bureaucratisation process and the temple is not an exception to this. This new arrangement means that there is a clear distinction between the temple as a religious institution and the monks and nuns who are part of the Sangha order. In the village temple structure, the sole-proprietor nature of the temple meant that the monk was in fact accountable only to himself for success or failure, and for the resources (monetary and non-monetary assets) that he might accrue in his professional course. Today, the temple is regarded as a public institution and its activities are accountable to the public (practitioners who have supported it). They are required to register as religious organisations and are governed by the guidelines laid down by the Registrar of Societies, and their activities are governed by the policies of the Ministry of Culture and Home Affairs. Likewise, the conduct of the monks and nuns are subjected to rules and regulations spelt out in the constitution of the Sangha Council.

As a bureaucratic organisation, a temple needs to have a constitution outlining its aims and objectives. It also needs a management committee to manage temple affairs. The temple is now divided into two main functional parts: one that deals with the religious activities and the other deals with the secular affairs including routine administration. The incorporation of lay members into temple administration has led to the creation of a lay religious community. While some monks and nuns may be involved in the administration of the temple, many are confined to the religious sphere. This formalisation is what Durkheim called the division between the sacred and profane and is seen by the Singapore state as essential for avoiding a conflict of interest between the lay and religious communities. The separation of the sacred from the profane has several repercussions on the familial-styled temple structure and the relationship between the Sangha and practitioners.

To start with, bureaucratisation has resulted in a high degree of differentiation in administrative practice. The temple is run by an executive committee which is the highest authoritative and the main decision-making body. At the apex is the chairperson who holds the seal of the temple. He wields the greatest actual power. He is formally empowered to make decisions and initiate activities on his own. Yet he rarely does this without consulting his committee. In most temples, the chairperson is a successful businessman given to taking important decisions on his own. In few cases, the chairperson can be the monk himself. A vice-chairperson assists him.

Both of them oversee the routine running of the temple, which includes administering the temple properties and carrying out the various functions, such as communicating with members and devotees and relating to special government departments.

The secretary-general and his assistant assist the chairperson and vice-chairperson. This involves keeping records of all meetings, formally communicating to all the members the legal responsibilities arising out of membership, informing members of on-going activities of interest and generating and organising new social activities. The office of the secretary also handles all forms of internal and external correspondence. The secretary has routine contact with other temples, charitable organisations, government bodies and private individuals.

The treasurer, under the law, is entitled to serve for only one term. He is responsible for the collection of subscriptions from members, for donations, for profits from temple earnings, for interest from the temple's bank accounts and so forth. He holds the petty cash account and defrays small expenditures incurred by the temple. Large expenditures need the approval of the main committee. Together with either the chairperson or secretary, he authorises financial transactions on behalf of the temple. He reports the financial affairs to the main committee at their monthly meetings and the annual account to the members in an annual report. Two qualified auditors, usually a member and an outsider, audit the account. A formal account is also submitted to the Taxation Department. As religious organisations, most temples apply for tax exemption and do not pay tax. (The personal income of the monk, however, is taxable). Ordinary committee members can participate in the decision-making process and supervision over the administration and the activities of the temple. They attend all committee meetings and have voting rights.

Numerous sub-committees, headed by a leader, help with numerous tasks, including publication of the temple's newsletter and other publications, fundraising, the Sunday school, library, sports and recreation, charity works and temple building. Together they initiate, plan and implement projects and activities. However, their plans need the formal approval of the executive committee. In many temples, endorsement of the chief monk is sought before they are implemented. The leaders of the sub-committees sit on the executive committee and are accountable to the executive committee for all their activities.

Under this bureaucratic reorganisation, the status and roles of the resident monk have been specifically defined in the constitution. He is confined to the role of religious specialist and adviser. He has little or no administrative responsibilities. Even as the temple moves towards bureaucratisation, the monk continues to wield much power. In some temples, the monk continues to assume the status of chairperson although his actions are now governed by a management committee and he has to abide by the rule of the majority instead of making decisions by himself. In other temples when the chairperson is a lay person, almost all decisions (including economic ones) made by the committee are informally endorsed by the head monk before they are implemented. Although the executive committee holds power *de jure*, in many cases it is the monk who is the *de facto* head of the temple, ruling it with an invisible hand. The committee members permit the monk to exercise this power because the monk is seen as the "grandfather" of the temple. The kinship (Confucian) norm that governs the members, and also most Buddhists, is that one does not quarrel with the *pater familias*. The metaphor of the temple as a family exists because most of the devotees have paid allegiance to the temple for a long period of time. The extended family or the kinship ethos therefore exists outside the formal temple structure and severely modifies the bureaucratically-defined role of the monk. In many cases, practitioners and members of the committee have known the monk prior to the bureaucratic reorganisation. The paternal affection and regard they have for the monk is thus borne out of socialisation among interacting individuals. Fundamentally however, there is still the belief that the temple belongs to the monk and the laity are there only to facilitate and assist the monk in meeting the bureaucratic requirements, at which they are adept. This conceptualisation ultimately rests on the classical concept of alms-giving, *dana* or *bu-shi*, which in this case means performing works for the temple and in assisting the Sangha fully without asking for rewards. It is only through alms-giving that one can accumulate merits for oneself.

In some temples, however, where the bureaucratic functioning has deepened, the lay committee does not wish the monks and nuns to interfere with the administration of the temples. This reorganisation has allowed for a high level of efficiency and for the productive use of the limited collective resources. It also provides accountability to the public for its resources, movements, activities and behaviour of the religious personnel who function within it. It has also resulted in a high level of tension between the two groups. Sometimes the tension is overtly expressed, to the dissatisfaction of many adherents, who continue to feel that the monks and nuns should be given power to administer.

Another area where the Singapore State has influenced the running of the temple is in the control of the temple's publications. Many temples produce their own newsletter, which is distributed free to all members and interested laity. Often, the newsletter contains temple news and announcements of new developments, celebrations, the admittance of new members, activities of the temple and their charity works. As with all publications, the temple needs to apply for a publication licence from the Ministry of Home Affairs before its newsletter can be produced for circulation to its members. To apply for a licence, a temple needs to submit to the Ministry of Home Affairs the objectives of the publication, as well as, sample copies, for inspection, and obtains approval before circulation is permitted. Deviation from the stated goals may lead to interrogation of the editorial board by the Ministry and may result in the withdrawal of the permit for publication.

Because of the strict control over publication by the Singapore state, temples producing newsletters must have within its constitution a section that states the objectives of its publications. Temple publications have to abide by the Newspaper and Printing Presses Act of 1974,[4] and their objectives have to relate to the publication of materials on Buddhism and members' activities. It is strictly barred from publishing information relating to or with political overtones. For example, a temple publication cannot publish articles that concern trade union activities. As a result of this restriction, the executive committee of many temples interprets the Newspaper and Printing Presses Act of 1974 in the narrowest possible manner and exercises neutrality. In this area, the Singapore state is thus instrumental in setting a bureaucratic framework in which the temple conducts its activities and thereby restructures its organisation.

In addition to the influence of the state in restructuring the temple and its activities, the temple is also restructuring its activities in response to the needs of its lay members. As mentioned earlier, the needs of the younger generation Singapore Chinese have resulted in a reorientation of the temple activities. Unlike the Shenist temples where practitioners visit the temple when the need arises, many Buddhist temples have regular religious and social activities including the study of Buddhist scriptures, sports and recreation.

Some Buddhist temples have weekend school or classes on Buddhism for both adults and children. The Sunday schools are patterned after the Christian Sunday schools and cater to different age groups. Many Reformist Buddhist parents send their children to attend Buddhist dharma classes. Dharma classes are also conducted at night for working adults. Since the late 1980s, there has been a large increase in demand for dharma classes as more Singapore Chinese, Buddhists and non-Buddhists alike, have expressed interest in studying the dharma. Buddhist libraries, either found in the temple or in public places, have been set up to cope with the demand as the result of the expansion of Buddhism.

The young Buddhists are not only interested in the acquisition of Buddhist knowledge, they are also interested in social activities. Many temples today also have activities to cater to their young adherents. They include various kinds of sports and recreational activities in addition to cooking and flower arrangement classes for the women. The temples hope that through the introduction of these activities, they will be able to be seen as "modern" and hence attract more members.

Temples also want to be seen to be socially relevant and have responded and collaborated with other social organisations to promote various social activities and policies. For example, many temples respond to the Red Cross Society's blood donation campaign by lending their premises to the blood bank, and by encouraging their members and the public to donate blood. Likewise, they respond to the government-organised campaigns such as "Respect the Elders" campaign by organising outings and banquets for their senior members.

What is noticeable in the bureaucratisation of the temples is the high degree of formalisation. The temple structure has taken the form of a total bureaucracy, relinquishing the informal village familial organisational structure altogether, with clear division of labour between the religious personnel and the lay people. Here, the monks and nuns have been relegated to the label of ritual and dharma experts. This formalisation has changed the relationship between the state, the Sangha and the laity. The fact that the state is able to impose legal-bureaucratic constraints upon the temple and the Sangha in the name of a good and democratic management marks the state as being the ultimate guide of the religious order. The state has thus become the overarching authority, where individual sub-structures obey as secular, mechanical parts within the wider civil bureaucracy.

In Singapore, the relationship between the laity and the Sangha has changed. The laity, who previously regarded the temple as a place of worship and the monks as the embodiment of the temple, have now taken on administrative tasks as ordered by the bureaucratic state. They have done this partly because they themselves are products of the same bureaucratic system, which has persisted since the time of the British. Yet they still regard the monk as the main *de facto* administrator. This ambivalence reflects the mutual exclusivity of the Sangha and the laity.

Prior to religious modernisation, Shenist temples existed largely for the mundane needs of the lay population and did not possess a single religious ideological order. The gods, deified heroes, deified animals and inanimate objects are the mythological and legendary elements of the folk culture of the Chinese. However, with religious modernisation, the move now is towards religious purity based on religious scriptures. Temples are now classified more specifically as

Buddhist, Daoist or Shenist temples, reflecting the growing trend towards religious purity. Likewise, within the Buddhist sphere, the adherents call themselves Mahayana, Theravada or "Buddhayana" (non-denominational) Buddhists. Today, there is a growing demarcation between Buddhist and Shenist temples with clear membership boundaries and role differentiation among them.

THE SANGHA

Like the temple, the Sangha is also subjected to bureaucratic reorganisation. Monks and nuns no longer function as the embodiment of temple organisation but are governed by the Sangha Council, which laid down strict guidelines governing the activities, functions and behaviour of its members. Those who fail to abide by the guidelines may be censured by the Council, and those who commit serious offences may be expelled. The primary aim of the Sangha Council is to ensure that its members are involved in activities confined to the sacred sphere. Within the religious sphere, monks and nuns continue to function freely. They can choose freely to perform various religious tasks: as ritual experts, dharma teachers or monastic recluses. At the same time, they can also perform social and welfare tasks.

In Singapore, the total number of Buddhist monks and nuns is around 200 members. In a survey conducted in 1985, I interviewed a total of 62 fully ordained monks and 64 nuns. In terms of age distribution, about 40% were above 60 years old, 23% were between 41 and 60 years old, 37% were between the 21 and 40 years old and less than 1% was below 20 years old. These monks and nuns came from different countries: 41% were local Singaporeans, 29% from China, 13% from Malaysia, 7% were from Thailand, 4% from Sri Lanka, 2% from Taiwan and Cambodia and less than 1% from Tibet, the Philippines and Indonesia. The composition of the monks and nuns reflect the different Buddhist traditions that are being practised in Singapore today. Today, about 80% of the monks and nuns are Singapore citizens or permanent residents. There are also a substantial number of visiting monks and nuns who come for a short period of time. About 80% speak Mandarin and/or Chinese dialects. About 20% also speak the English language. In terms of education, about 25% were not formally educated; 22% had primary education, 29% had secondary secular education, 10% had post-secondary secular education, while 14% had some form of monastic education.[5]

PURSUIT OF MONASTIC IDEALS VERSUS VOCATION

Ideally, individuals who aspire to enter the Sangha gain entry on a voluntary basis and are in pursuit of enlightenment. In reality, the pursuit of the monastic ideal, of achieving nirvana, although desired, is not a priority for the majority of monks and nuns, for most of whom the reality of monasticism lies with the immediate environment. The early monks to Singapore sought to establish a religious structure similar to the one found in the rural village where Shenism was mixed with Mahayana Buddhism. The Mahayana Buddhist notion of mass salvation as found in the bodhisattva ideal, was interpreted to mean that the monastic order was there to serve the functional needs of the practitioners. Monks and nuns were involved in fortune-telling, divination, geomancy reading, *feng-shui*, faith-healing and funeral rites for the dead.

Within the Buddhist canon, when a person moved out of the family, *chu-jia*, to become a monk and nun, they also left behind this-worldly life in pursuit of a religious life. Here a monk or nun follows the Four Noble Truths and Eightfold Path where emotions, feelings, and material desires are consciously denied, the ideal being to reach enlightenment through the pursuit of dharma and the practice of meditation. They are expected to observe the monastic rules laid down in the Vinaya texts, which require monks to observe a minimum of 227 rules and nuns to observe 400 rules governing their moral and ethical conduct. In an ideal situation, these people who renounce worldly pleasures live in monasteries or forest dwellings, away from the population. In Singapore, monks remain within the society because of the demands placed upon them to perform the various religious tasks.

Among Chinese Sangha members, the acquisition of deep Buddhist knowledge, dharma, is desirable but most times, impossible. This is because many are semi-literate or illiterate and therefore find the reading of the Buddhist texts an extremely difficult task. Over half of the monks and nuns interviewed do not read scriptural texts at all, relying on the teachings and interpretations taught to them by their master through oral transmission.

Although monks and nuns are required to observe 200 and 400 monastic rules respectively, among the Singapore Chinese, there are five important precepts that the Sangha members are expected to follow. The first is the precept on celibacy. Moving out of the family also means that "one has seen through the world and jumped the red wall" (the wall of sensual pleasures). It is therefore inconceivable for monks and nuns to be in any kind of relationship. For those who have been married, renunciation means a break from matrimony; others expect to remain unmarried. This is unlike in Thailand and Sri Lanka, where young men who have come of age are expected to spend a "Buddhist lent", a rainy season, carrying out their religious responsibilities, be ordained as novices and perform the desired merit-making for their parents and relatives. After which, they will resume their normal lives. In Singapore the monastic vocation is for life and very few get out of it. It is also unlike Japanese Buddhism with a married Sangha. Celibacy is highly prized as it separates the sacred from the mundane domain, and Buddhist monks and nuns who strictly observe this precept are seen as pure and are regarded highly among the Singapore Chinese. Those who violate this precept are considered to be polluted, with no possibility of reaching enlightenment. There have been cases where a monk established a sexual relationship with a lay woman in secret. When such a relationship is known, it often creates tension between the monk and the members of the temple. Topley also writes about nuns having lesbian affairs (Topley, 1958). But in most cases, the close relationship between these nuns does not mean that they are having lesbian relationships. In the Singapore culture, it is not uncommon to see women holding hands in the public, which reflects the culture rather than sexual orientation.

Another important precept is not to kill. This is taken to mean abstaining from eating animal products and observing a vegetarian diet. This interpretation is especially strong among Chinese Mahayana Buddhist monks and nuns. For the elderly monks, whose early childhood life in China was one of poverty and whose diet consisted primarily of rice, vegetables and beans, consuming a vegetarian diet is regarded as an extension of their pre-ordained dietary habit. Under such circumstances, filling one's stomach was the priority, the types of food eaten being dependent on availability. Most elderly monks have found that their diet has undergone a vast improvement since the 1970s.[6] But to many young monks and nuns, consuming a vegetarian diet requires conscious effort.

This is made easier as the monks and nuns in Singapore have their own kitchen in the temple, which allows them to exercise a greater choice in their diet. This again differs from Southeast Asian and South Asian monks who go on morning alms collections and consume what has been prepared for them by the laity (Bunnag, 1973). Few monks and nuns prepare their own meals but rely on temple assistants to perform the task. Their diet consists mainly of rice, vegetables, fruits, bean and nut products.

The existence of a kitchen within the temple frees the monks and nuns from the chores of alms-collection and allows them to spend greater time catering to the religious needs of the laity. It also means that the Sangha need not adhere to a strict mealtime. In the Theravada tradition, monks have to finish collecting food and consume it before mid-day. Traditionally, they are restricted to one meal a day. However, Singapore monks and nuns, like the rest of the population, have three meals a day. The kitchen also allows for the provision of special vegetarian feasts for participants of special religious events. Instead of a one-way alms-giving process, the Chinese Sangha thus participates in a reciprocal relationship of communal sharing. As M. Douglas (1975:249-275) has argued, food can be seen as a code of inclusion and exclusion, carving out the insiders from the outsiders. Instead of alms-giving as a means of accruing merits, the Singapore Chinese provide monetary donations to purchase food as a means to accrue merits.

FACTORS INFLUENCING ENTRY
INTO THE MONASTIC ORDER

There are several factors that influence a person's entry into the monastic order. One of the most important reasons is poverty. 58% of the monks and nuns entered the monastic order because of strained economic circumstances. 13% entered the monastic order because of family problems, 5% joined because of poor health, 13% joined because of their deep interest in Buddhism and their desire for spiritual enlightenment, 2% joined because of opportunity for better education and 9% joined because of influences from family members.

(a) Orthodox Monks

In Singapore, there are four categories of monks. The first are those who have been monks in their childhood in China prior to their migration to Singapore. These are the elderly monks and they joined the monastic order because of family poverty and poor health. Below is the story of an elderly monk who joined the monastic order as a result of poverty and influences from a family member:

> When I was seven years old, I started to help my father on the farm. We did not own any land, but my father rented land from the village headman. I usually followed my father to the field, at the first light. I did what my father ordered me to. Often, I would go to the nearby hills to gather firewood for boiling bath water and for cooking. My mother stayed at home and looked after my three younger brothers. She also worked as a seamstress.
>
> We were always strained and had very little food to eat. Mostly, I had porridge, with a few vegetables in it. We rarely had meat – maybe once or twice a year, and then only on special occasions.
>
> I visited the temple often with my mother who prayed a lot to the gods. The temple belonged to my uncle, my mother's brother. One day, my uncle suggested to my mother that he needed a disciple and that I would be a good choice. He told my mother that if I were to be his disciple, he would feed me and my family would

have one mouth less to worry about. He would also teach me how to read and write. Because we were related, my uncle felt that he should help us by taking me instead of a total stranger.

My mother discussed the matter with my father and they agreed to send me to the temple. Initially, my father was not very pleased with the idea as I was the eldest son and would be responsible for carrying the incense urn (*xiang-lu*) at his funeral. Besides, I was already seven years old and a good farm hand for my father. My relationship with my father had been very close and he was reluctant to lose me to the temple. But my mother reasoned with him saying that it was better for them to send me to a temple than to work as a coolie, where my fate would be in the hands of a total stranger. At least, they would be assured of the fact that my uncle would not ill-treat me. Besides, they just could not afford to feed four mouths with their meagre income. My father earned about fifteen to eighteen yuan and my mother earned about ten yuan a month. As my three brothers were growing and demanding more food, I became the one who had to starve if there was not enough to go round.

Another factor that persuaded my father was the fact that my uncle was literate and had promised my mother that he would teach me reading and writing. My mother felt that if I were to become literate, then I could teach my younger brothers reading and writing and they could then take on some other jobs that paid better than farming. They would then not be poor forever.

This was how I became a monk.

A second factor that influenced the choice of monkhood was the health of the child. The Chinese understanding of poor health is attributed to several reasons: poor dietary intake and the imbalance of *yin* and *yang* as a result of spirit disturbances and/or attack. Children with a *yin* horoscope are prone to spirit attack and therefore likely to have poor health. Under such conditions, these children will be either fostered to a deity for protection or in extreme cases, join the monastic order in order to purify and absorb the *yang* elements. One monk told me the following story.

> I was a sickly child. I always had this or that illness. I often refused
> to eat or play with other boys. I always stayed at home and helped
> my mother. Every time I fell ill, my mother would bring me to
> the village temple to pray. Because I went there so often, I got on
> well with the temple monk. He told my mother that the reason
> for my frequent illness was that I did not have enough *yang*
> element. That was why I was prone to spirit attack. I was given to
> the temple at the suggestion of the monk.

The second category consists of monks recruited from local boys
in Singapore. From the 1950s to 1970s, individual monks and nuns
attempted to recruit or adopt orphan boys and girls into the monastic
order. Adopting infants instead of boys and girls into the order is a
novelty within the monastic order. This type of recruitment by
adoption largely transformed the character of the monastic order,
which can be seen as a surrogate family. Infant adoption weaves the
monastic family into the social structure. The adoption of infants
into the temple poses the problem of childcare for the monks, whose
official status is that of persons outside of the ordinary social realm
and who are in pursuit of enlightenment. Such persons cannot be
seen to be involved in the mundane chores of child rearing. Often
temple assistants helped to look after the infants. In Singapore, a monk
would normally recruit or adopt only one or two children to succeed
him because of the lack of resources.

From the 1970s, adoption of children into the monastic order
became difficult as they were few in number because of the
expanding economy and the successful family planning policy
launched by the government. Those who could not afford to look
after a large family gave the surplus children to childless couples.
The monks and nuns had to compete with childless couples for
the unwanted babies. From the 1970s to 1980s, a total of 17 boys
and 47 girls were adopted into the various temples. More girls
were given away for two reasons. First, Chinese families continued
to prefer sons to daughters, and the latter continued to be regarded
as a profit-losing commodity (*shi-ben-huo*). However, the temple
continued to be the last resort, when all other avenues to place the

daughters for adoption had failed. Second, the temple serves as a ready avenue for unwed mothers who needed to dispose of an infant swiftly. The monks and nuns rarely enquired about the parentage of the babies brought to them.

When a monk took on a young boy and girl as a disciple, the master shaved the head of the disciple and he or she becomes a shaven-head disciple (*ti-tou-di-zi*). Like in the traditional village temple, the head-shaven disciple who would eventually succeed the monk and maintain the monastic lineage genealogy.

The third category of monks are those that joined the monastic order in their adult life in Singapore. Five adults entered the monastic order in 1980s for a variety of reasons. One did so to avoid compulsory conscription into the army, as religious personnel are exempted from military training. The other four entered because they were dissatisfied with their existing lifestyles and were disenchanted with this-worldly existence. Four have a tertiary education and one had completed secondary education. All five were from devout Shenist-Buddhist families and had some knowledge of Buddhism prior to their entry into monkhood. One of them recounted his involvement in Buddhism that eventually led to his entry into the monkhood:

> I was first introduced to scriptural Buddhism by a fellow Buddhist at the university. After joining the university's Buddhist Society, I participated actively in promoting its activities. These were about Buddhist dharma and we practised meditation. All of us regarded Buddhism as a superior religion capable of explaining our theodical problems, our existence and our sufferings. None of us at that time contemplated a drastic move such as renunciation.
>
> After graduation, I worked in a bank for seven years. During these seven years, I was very unhappy with many things that were happening around me. I felt life was meaningless and I began to search for an answer. I went back to Buddhism. I began to read more deeply into the scriptural texts and found myself thoroughly encaptured by the Buddhist outlook to life. This was the beginning of my path towards monkhood. But it was very difficult to move out of secular life. It took me another one and a half years of

searching before I finally decided that this was the life I wanted to lead.

I had to inform my parents about my decision and it was the hardest act of my life. I was the only son in my family and my parents were extremely upset when I told them of my decision. They implored me not to do it. My feelings towards renunciation were so strong that I somehow pressed on.

Finally, they agreed, and I was ordained in 1981 at the age of thirty-one.

(b) Reformist Monks

The fourth category consists of the Reformist monks. From the 1980s onwards, the rise of Reformist Buddhism has led to new needs and a demand for monks and nuns with a reformist outlook, and who are able to teach in the areas of Buddhist scholarship and meditation. Today, the population of the local and foreign Reformist monks stands around 30. They are well-versed in Buddhist dharma, meditation and the rituals. The local Reformist monks were ordained in adult life. Prior to becoming monks, they had held professional occupations and were middle class in social status. They entered the monastic order because of disenchantment with this-worldy life and they believe in this-worldly asceticism for their goal towards enlightenment. One of them recounted his entry to me:

(i)   Reformist Monk A

I was brought up in a fairly middle class household. My childhood was rather peaceful. I was able to continue my studies and I did a degree in science overseas. When I returned I worked in the private sector for almost ten years. I had a steady income and I was relatively happy.

While studying overseas, I was exposed to fundamental Buddhism. I had the opportunity to read up on Buddhism. I found that it was so very different from the type of Buddhism practised locally in Singapore. The local brand of Buddhism is really not Buddhism at all. It is a syncretic mix of various elements of

Daoism, Confucianism and Buddhism. But above all, a large dosage of folk practices. This was all new to me.

I then realised that Buddhism in fact is very much of a philosophy. It teaches moral philosophy and how one could attain inner peace and harmony.

When I started working, I was not actively involved in Buddhist activities, although it was in the back of my mind all the time. But working life is very different from student life. There are more responsibilities and also more social interaction. There is also quite a bit of office politics. Although it was bearable, I was increasingly becoming very dissatisfied with my working life. I found that the pursuit of this type of career is rather meaningless.

By the time I reached thirty years old, I began an earnest search for the type of life I wanted to lead. Also, a few years back, I started to read widely on Buddhism. I began to feel an attraction to the philosophical exposition behind Buddhism. I found everyday life meaningless unless one has an objective. The routine lifestyle where work becomes a dominant partner and where materialism starts to take precedence over the simplicity of living distorted one's priority. It was as if I was lost in a deep ocean and I needed to find myself again – especially my soul – in order to be a whole being again.

I found my answer in Buddhism. It suited my temperament better. I found myself unable to accept the Christian notion of a God-created world. Neither could I accept the notion that we are all sinners. On the other hand, the Buddhist notion of karma is very appealing. It offers an explanation of why the world is full of suffering, and a way out of it. Its reasoning is grounded in human attitudes and human actions. Our karma is dependent on our actions and thoughts. So we must consciously be aware of our own actions and thoughts in order to bring out our good karma. One way to bring it out is to renounce the world. Renunciation is more than just moving out of this world and leading an other-worldly existence. It is only the first step, for we must try to get rid of the cause of suffering which is our desire to crave for all things, especially material and sensual pleasures.

To me, Buddhism offers an alternative form of thinking and an alternative lifestyle, which I found suited my character, and I began to consider it seriously.

However, it was never an easy path. For I happened to be an only son, and it is always hard on the parents if you are the only son. One has to be responsible to one's parents as well. So I had to request my parent's permission before I could renounce. This is clearly specified in Buddhism. It took me quite some time to persuade my parents that I was serious about this move and that I had thought it through very carefully; that I did not do it in a spur of the moment. Of course, they too have the responsibility even though I am an adult. They found it hard that I, a university graduate with a good job, good friends and good lifestyle, would want to be a pauper monk. I had to start by explaining to them what Buddhism is all about and in fact, teach them the basic Buddhist philosophy. Only when they understood its philosophy did they agree to my ordination.

I was eventually ordained. But I did not do it locally. I went to Sri Lanka for my ordination. Part of the reason is that they have a monastery there and I could learn to adapt to the monastic life, whereas in Singapore there are no such facilities. Upon training, I came back and assumed the task of educating the public in Buddhist philosophy, which is important for the public to know, instead of mistaking the Chinese beliefs as Buddhism. I feel that it is my responsibility to spread the true Buddhism, because I stumbled on it only by chance, and I believe that there are people out there who want to know more about Buddhism but did not know where to search for it. So I should bring it to them.

(ii)   Reformist Monk B

I am now twenty-nine years old. I first got to know about Buddhism when I was a second year undergraduate. At that time, I was not involved in any Buddhist society. At university, I knew a fellow student who was also very keen on Buddhism. One day, I went to his hostel and found that his bookshelf was filled with books on Buddhism. I borrowed one titled, *Jin-Gang-Jing*, read it, returned the book to him and never went back to it.

Later, the Buddhist Society in the university conducted some activities for freshmen and I went along to the meeting. From then on, I became very intimate with Buddhism.

Most of my time was spent in searching for the truth of what Buddhism really means, for I still was very confused about its philosophy. As I started reading more deeply into Buddhism, I found that the views expounded by Sakyamuni Buddha are very similar to my own. This intensified my search. At the same time, I also explored other religions, mainly Christianity and Islam. In Buddhism, I continued to find flaws in the teachings. At university, where both the Buddhist and the Christian societies were trying to proselytise and recruit new members, I would often engage them in discussion. As I began to explore and understand the various religious doctrines, I began to reject Christianity and Islam. This was mainly because Christianity did not provide a logical answer to the question of existentialism. It failed to answer my quest for the issue on life and death. Both Christianity and Islam believed in a God. This is in contrast to Buddhism. Buddha is not the founder of life and death, but he found the answer to it. He only advised. Even if I did not choose to be a Buddhist, I would also not be able to accept a God-created religion.

Prior to my knowing Buddhism, my own philosophy of life was that all knowledge is passed down and accumulated. Nothing belongs to oneself. This is also what Buddhism teaches. I also did not believe in a beginning and an end. Most people believe that there is a beginning and an end and that is why they search for such a beginning and place their belief in a God. I also cannot accept the fact that God is omnipotent and omnipresent. I felt this was unreasonable. I was then a free thinker.

I decided to stop my search in Christianity as I had by then come to reject it as a possible answer to my spiritual quest. I began to concentrate on Buddhism.

At the university, Christian groups usually invited many famous priests to give talks. They were usually well trained and knowledgeable. But they would also attempt to destroy the Buddhist faith. Because of their attacks on Buddhism, I would seek further clarification of their viewpoints to further understand Buddhism from the Christian angle. Often I would argue with them. After several times, I was provided with a stock answer that "Buddhism is very good. But how come it is not as popular as Christianity?" I found myself defending Buddhism during these sessions.

I also began to have a little inkling of renunciation. This was largely influenced by my discussions with the Christian ministers. They argued that Christianity is superior by virtue of the well-trained clergy and that most professionals turned to Christianity, whereas Buddhism was confined mainly to the lower working class. I wanted to challenge their view on this.

During my time, searching for Buddhism was a very difficult task. One has to do intensive reading by oneself. There were very few people erudite in Buddhist theology that could provide guidance. And I had very little dealing with the monks, nuns and temples. I rarely went to them. I did not even consider myself a Buddhist then.

My family *bai-shen* (is Shenist). But through the years, my mother came into contact with Buddhism, except that this had no influence on me at all.

Fortunately for me, I continued to read as much on Buddhism as I could, and gradually, I joined the fellow student (whom I had visited in his hostel room once and borrowed a book on Buddhism) and his dharma discussion group. By the end of my second year, I was ready for more action. The dharma group had decided that one needed to practise what one knew about the religion. One of the Buddhist precepts was against killing, and hence we decided to do our bit by not consuming meat. We formed a vegetarian unit to provide a common objective and encouragement in our religious pursuit.

By the end of second year, I felt that it was no longer very meaningful to study and research chemistry and mathematics. Gradually, my energy was directed towards Buddhism. The more I read into Buddhism, the more I felt that I had close affinity with the religion and that at times, when reading the scriptures, I felt that they provided me with clues to my past lives and I began to get a sketchy picture of my previous lives. Also at times, my dreams produced a pattern and had Buddhism as the underlying theme. I felt that this was fate (*yin-yuan*).

I only told my parents of my desire to enter the monkhood shortly before my graduation. But I promised that I would work for two years to repay them for bringing me up. However, after graduation, I decided to embark on the religious career immediately. My parents disagreed. They wanted me to work first, for they were afraid that I might be under influences from different quarters and that I might have made the wrong decision. My brothers and sisters suggested that I should try it out for one year initially. But I insisted on a full commitment rather than a half-hearted commitment. Eventually, my brothers and sisters were supportive of my decision although my parents found it hard to accept. But I was ordained anyway.

These reformist monks' entrance into the monkhood in their adult life often entailed giving up a successful career, so that they have a different outlook from that of the traditionalist monks. As a result of their personal religious experience, they are highly motivated to reform traditional Chinese religious syncretism into Buddhism.

Foreign monks are also invited on short- and medium- term bases to teach Buddhist dharma and to perform rituals. They come primarily from Southeast Asia, Tibet, Sri Lanka, Taiwan, America and England. They constitute about 20% of the monastic population in Singapore. These monks could either speak Chinese or English. Visiting missionary monks were also invited periodically to give public lectures and expound on dharma and meditation.

(b) The Nuns

50% of the monastic population in Singapore are nuns. Nuns can be divided into two main groups. The first group consists of the elderly nuns who worked as domestic servants throughout their life prior to retirement. These were formerly Cantonese-speaking *mui-tsai*, who came to work in the Nanyang region. These women had formally renounced the idea of marriage in China and when they arrived in Singapore, they worked as domestic servants within Chinese households. They usually devoted their lives to one household and were considered as trustworthy, dedicated and loyal servants. [7]

After their retirement, a few banded together and lived a pious life, devoting their time to spiritual cultivation (*zi-xiu*). Through time, this form of communal living evolved into a semi-religious style of communal living and the home became a home-based nunnery (*an-tang*). The nunnery as a religious institution became formalised only when the inhabitants in the house ordained themselves formerly as nuns and called their home a religious institution. Even so, many *an-tang* continued to function as private residences and are not open for public worshipping.

The formation of the *an-tang* at the initial stage can thus be seen as a culturally-viable solution in response to the needs of these women without a family or sons to look after them. As these women only renounced lay life in their later years, they did not undergo monastic training, nor did they feel the need to acquire it. Their primary aim is to engage in spiritual self-cultivation, *zi-xiu*, to reduce their bad karma. All of them know and recite the various Buddhist sutras and mantras on a daily basis. They believe that through continuous and pious chanting and recitation they will be able to achieve an acceptable level of enlightenment. Enlightenment to them is to be reborn in the Heavenly Western Paradise (*ji-le-shi-jie*).

Like the monks, these elderly nuns too consider the question of succession. They too resort to adopting infant girls and raising them as their daughters in order to provide for themselves a security blanket in their old age and to ensure that there will be somebody who will perform ancestral rites upon their death. From the 1970s to mid-1980s, a total of 47 girls were adopted into the nunnery. They were "given to *an-tang* as babies"; "raised in the *an-tang*" and stayed there "out of a sense of obligation to the mistress who brought them up". This second group of nuns are local born, adopted and brought up in the nunnery.

During their early years, the girls were raised as daughters rather than novices until after they complete their primary education. At a young age the girls generally are not bound by monastic rules, and they are given very little training. While most of them start learning the sutras when they are able to talk, there is no serious attempt to teach them until they are in their early teens. This is also the case for their dietary intake. Although the older nuns themselves are strict vegetarians, the young girls are raised on non-vegetarian diets until they are old enough to subsist on vegetarian food. One of the teenage girls told me that she was given a choice. She had tried non-vegetarian food, did not like the taste and rejected it outright. Her friends remarked that she has Buddha's body (*fo-shen*) (i.e., a born Buddhist) and therefore should not force anything unwholesome on herself.

In Singapore, there are no monastic schools and monks and nuns have to leave the country if they want to receive monastic education and training. As such, they were sent to a secular school for education. Of the local-born nuns, in the 21-40 year age group, 35% received six years of primary education, 62% received 10 or more years of education and 3% were not sent to a school at all. Education is considered as an important asset by elderly nuns who themselves are illiterate or semi-literate.

The amount of education these local-born nuns received is highly dependent on the resources of the nunnery and the attitude of the mother-nun. In some cases, the girls were taken out of schools after primary education so that they could start monastic training as a novice. In other cases, the girls were encouraged to continue their education, either secular or monastic. Currently, those who want to pursue tertiary education are encouraged to pursue monastic tertiary education, either in Taiwan, Japan or Sri Lanka, where they would be taught, amongst other subjects, Buddhist education, theology, philosophy and psychology. Sending them abroad to a Buddhist university has several advantages to the monastic order. First, it provides them with better education. Second, the girls will mix with like-minded members where each will hopefully reinforce the others in their commitment to the order. And third, they will be exposed to the functioning of the Buddhist institutions in the host country and, hopefully, when they return they will be able to initiate modern changes in face of the new demands placed upon the Buddhist Sangha.

These are the stories of how the nuns viewed themselves and their monastic status:

(i) Nun A

I am now in my fifties. I was brought up in the temple by my mother-nun. When I was growing up, I was sent to a girls' school. My mother-nun just let me go on with my studies when I finished my primary education. So, I continued and finished twelve years of schooling.

After my studies, I was allowed to choose between working in the temple or working outside. I chose to work in a trading firm. All these years I continued to live in the temple and I contributed part of my income to the temple. I worked in several trading firms until the last few years when my mother-nun, who was very ill then, told me to take charge of the temple.

My personal life was very tied up with the temple life. Although I worked outside and was a lay person until a few years ago, I still helped in the activities of the temple during weekends and on special occasions. So I am basically a religious person.

At the same time, I also went out and socialised with friends. I went shopping and to the movies. I did what normal women would do. But when it came to meal times, I would always ask for vegetarian food. Perhaps this is where the dividing line between myself and the rest is.

But I was never involved with any man. Somehow it is probably because of my close association with the temple and with the nuns and that I was usually busy that I never got round to associating with men. I had also very little interest in courtship. It was probably because deep in me I always knew that I would be a nun so I did not consciously pursue romance like other girls of my age.

Finally, when I was in my late forties, my mother-nun asked me to take over the temple, as she was too old and sickly to do her job properly. It was only natural that I took over from my mother-nun as I was her only adopted child. And I also knew that the time had come for me to be ordained and to assume the role of a nun. So I was ordained and assumed the position of the head nun. I have no regrets over my late ordination. Nor do I have regrets over the fact that I did not get married and have a family. I think it was never my life to begin with.

The years when I was holding a secular occupation made me see much of the world and I am now in a better position to render my assistance to those who are in need of religious counselling. Besides, I have years of administrative experience, which I can now put to good use in reshaping the operation of the temple.

I suppose my experience has shaped my way of dealing with the temple girls. We have another girl who was very good in her studies. She finished her pre-university studies shortly after I took over the leadership. She had decided to pursue a course in nursing as she felt that she could contribute more than if she were to remain in the temple. She asked for my opinion and I agreed that if this was what she wanted, she would have my moral and financial support. She went on with her nursing career and later went to Britain to further her nursing studies. I tried my best to provide her with some financial assistance.

After her studies, she returned to Singapore and worked as a nurse. She was staying with us until she got married recently. I am happy for her. She still continues to visit us very regularly. The good thing about her is that she did not attempt to hide her background and remained supportive of the temple and the nuns.

I think it is never easy for any temple girl, brought up in the temple to move away from the temple. In her case, she has decided to lead a secular life and has made the best use of it. She now has a daughter to whom I am the grandmother-nun.

There is also nothing to regret or moan over the loss of her. If you are a Buddhist, you will believe in the theory of causation (*yin-guo*). If it is your life, it is your life, you cannot escape from it and you cannot force it if it is not to be.

The most important thing is to achieve an inner peace within oneself.

(ii) *Nun B*

I was always dressed up to look like a boy. My hair was also cut in the boy's style and I was made to look ugly. When I was young, my mistress would tell me that I was given to the temple because I was ugly, that my parents were afraid that I would not be able to find a husband when I grew up.

I was not sent to school and had no education at all. I know only a few basic characters and can speak some Mandarin. Mostly, we converse in the Cantonese dialect.

When I was seven years old, my mistress shaved my head and I was ordained as a novice nun. I could not go out of the *an-tang* without her permission. I was forced to learn chanting and the various rituals and rites. When I was thirteen, she took me with her on her religious services. She never left me alone.

What can I do? I can't get out of it. I don't read, write or have any skill to earn a living. I also do not have friends outside the monastic order. Everyone I know is close to the monastic order. If I leave the temple life, they will never ever talk to me. To whom could I turn to? No one. I don't even know who my biological parents are. Even if I did, I would not turn to them. I am doomed to be a nun.

This nun was very articulate. She felt deeply that she was brought up harshly. She was not given a chance to go to school like most of the other temple girls. She felt inadequate compared to the others, as she was not literate. Although she was reconciled to her status, she insisted that she had been forced into ordination without her consent and above all, felt trapped in a life without a future. But she was afraid to leave the *an-tang*, as it would bring shame upon her and the *an-tang* and she feared social ostracism from her fellow nuns in other *an-tang*. Moreover, having being brought up and lived in the *an-tang* all her life, she was uncertain of her ability to lead a normal secular life. So she had become resigned to a fate that she considered a cruel one.

Another nun told me that although she did not really want to be a nun, she felt that her circumstances had placed her in a position where she was obligated to become a nun. She told me she was treated fairly but there was an enormous amount of moral persuasion placed on her to accept her position.

(iii)   Nun C

My mistress was very honest with me. She told me of how I was given to the *an-tang* at birth. I was the sixth girl of a family. Because my family was poor and could not afford to feed me, I was given away. It was also because my biological father was hoping for a boy and when he saw me, he was so disappointed that he did not want me.

When I was seven years old, I was sent to a school to study. I studied till I finished my G.C.E. O level examination. I would have continued my studies had it not been that my biological parents came to the *an-tang* with the intention of reclaiming me.

My mistress was very upset. She told me how hard it was for her as a nun to bring me up and provide me with an education. She had to take on extra religious work in order to bring in extra money to finance my education. And that it would be ungrateful for me to leave her now as she was getting old and needed someone to help in the temple. She also warned me of the likelihood of losing all my friends in the order if I left the *an-tang*. Besides, what kind of life would it be if I were to go and live with my parents, especially since they had given me away? It would be like living with some strangers. They might even force me to get married if I didn't get along in the family.

Although I don't like a nun's life because it is so restrictive, I dare not tell my mistress. She would be very upset and maybe angry.

Shortly after my parents' visit, she asked me whether I want to be a nun and live in the *an-tang* or not. If I do, then I should have an ordination. And I was ordained as a nun.

THE ROLES OF MONKS AND NUNS

Monks and nuns can be divided into three main types according to their religious skills although some have multiple skills. They can be seen as ritual experts dealing with magic, exorcism, death rituals and a variety of religious rituals and rites; as dharma teachers specialising in teaching Buddhist dharma and expounding on Buddhist sutras; and as welfare specialists. It is not uncommon for the monks and nuns to be involved in two or all of the above. At a general level, elderly monks and nuns tend to be ritual specialists catering to the needs of the primarily elderly devotees while the younger Reformist monks and nuns are actively involved in the dissemination of Buddhist dharma and welfare works.

There are no stereotypes of the monks and nuns of Singapore. One of the best ways to understand the richness and diversity of their skills is through looking into the life histories of some of the monks. A number of accounts are given below.

(i) The Late Venerable Shong Kai – A Multi-Skilled Monk

The late Venerable Shong Kai was a Mahayana monk. He was sixty-seven years old during the time of interview and had been in the order for more than fifty years. He was born in the Fujian province in South China. At the age of thirteen years, he was ordained to become a monk in China. Buddhism came naturally to him as he put it. He was born into a Buddhist family where his family members were all "full-time vegetarians". Being a full-time vegetarian is symbolic of devoutness. His late father and uncles were both monks. It was through them that he was eventually drawn into the order. Two major considerations governed his entry. He wanted to learn the dharma, which implied that he would have an opportunity to be educated.

This was an important factor because Venerable Shong Kai did not come from a rich family. A second consideration for him was the opportunity to learn the martial art of gong-fu. He was not a very healthy child. The master of the temple to which he went was a martial arts specialist. Venerable Shong Kai was able to build up his physique after joining the order.

In China, he lived in three different temples, first out of economic necessity and then, to take up the art of Chinese medicine and healing. He moved away from his second temple to avoid Communist persecution. In his first temple, he was given several years of monastic education that included Chinese literature and poetry. In his second temple, he learnt the art of Chinese healing and acquired knowledge of herbal medicine. This learning he took along with him on moving to Singapore where he helped establish the Buddhist Free Clinic in the later years. Prior to Singapore, he went to Hong Kong for four years when the Red Guards took over China in 1949.

His move to Singapore was more than a coincidence. He was advised by his fellow monks to migrate to Singapore where they said there were great opportunities for a monastic career. In the year he arrived, he and some fellow monks formed the Singapore Buddhist Federation. Since then, he had never been out of the limelight, ever increasing his participation in the activities within the Buddhist community and moving from religious to social services. It was the nature of his work, which was aimed at the general public that has won him respect among his fellow monks and the lay community.

His involvement in the activities of the Singapore Buddhist Federation and his appointment as the secretary-general from 1963 till the late 1980s showed the amount of trust his fellow monks and lay colleagues have in him. They had come to recognise Venerable Shong Kai as a competent and resourceful administrator and someone who was willing to shoulder responsibilities. They also respected his literary skill, which he used for proper administration, and communicating with the outside world. His learning got him acceptance outside the Buddhist circle. In Singapore where the majority of the monks were poorly educated and semi-literate, learning commanded great respect.

From the vantage point of the Singapore Buddhist Federation, Shong Kai assisted in the early fire and flood relief projects, initiating Buddhist involvement in the social services. As a trained Chinese physician, he worked at the Chung Hwa Free Clinic. He was the only monk at that time to work outside the religious sphere on a full-time basis. He felt that he was offering an important service to the public because there was a shortage of medical facilities and he was doing it for free.

Soon after he started practising medicine in the 1950s, he initiated the establishment of a Buddhist Free Clinic. However, his plan of formally incorporating free medical services within the religious organisation was not realised because of lack of funding. In the mid-1960s, he solicited the support of the abbot of Phor Khar See Temple to fund the clinics. The surplus money from the fairs and his share of it was to be used to set up a free clinic. The surplus proceeds of $67,000 was used to fund the project. This amount, together with some donations from supporters, established the first Buddhist Free Clinic. Venerable Shong Kai undertook to organise the project, ranging from the selection of the premise to the planning and running of the clinic. In 1969, the Buddhist Free Clinic was officially declared opened.

By involving himself in the Federation, he was able to gain wider contacts within the monastic order and the lay community. This separated him from other monks who were involved only in the provision of ritual services to a small number of persons. By not going into the traditional sphere of providing religious services, and instead, into a new field, he carved out a niche for himself and gained prestige because of it. His ability to articulate plans and put them into practice and thus be of service to the people enabled him to push Buddhism along a new path.

His ability to align Buddhism with the government policy of using religious education in schools to create a new morality and consciousness earned him a reputation among the non-Buddhists. As the secretary-general of the Singapore Buddhist Federation, he involved the Federation in the Religious Knowledge programme by providing advisory services to the Ministry of Education. He also involved other prominent scholar monks to participate in the programme. Furthermore, he was instrumental in establishing a Buddhist Secondary school in 1984. (There are also two primary schools run by the Buddhist Federation). His ability to mount these projects and bring them to fruition was an important indicator of the willingness of the monastic community to be involved in the secular activities, actions that won him credits for his pioneering efforts.

Venerable Shong Kai was a highly-respected monk in Singapore. His intelligence, skills and his ability to use them to achieve concrete results placed him in a league ahead of many of his contemporaries.

(ii) The Late Venerable Yuan Pei – A Scholar Monk

The late Venerable Yuan Pei was also a Mahayana monk. During the time of the interview he was sixty-six years old and was also a migrant monk from China. He too moved out of China after the Communist victory. He first went to Taiwan, then Hong Kong and finally to Singapore. It was in Taiwan that he became a student of a very well-known scholar monk and learnt dharma and the art of propagating dharma. These skills had brought him to the forefront as a scholar monk in Singapore. His belief in education as the only way of "building up Buddhism and the Buddhists" was matched by his uncompromising attitude against ritualism of the monastic order and the laity. This educational approach and his proselytising zeal have won him approval from both monks and the people. Monks believed (some enviously do so) that Venerable Yuan Pei had charisma. But most of his fellow monks also admired his learning and approved of his proselytising. Many of his members were proud of having such a scholar monk in Singapore.

He arrived in Singapore in 1963 and lived in a temple temporarily. There he started preaching Buddhism to the public. He was among the first few monks to conduct public lectures, *jiang-jing*, where he spoke on public morality according to the sutras. Master Yuan Pei institutionalised the public lecture system, carving out a specific role for himself within the order and the community. Upon the death of a monk whom he knew in the 1960s, he was invited to

125

take charge of the school for nuns as he was then the most qualified to teach the monastic code.

Master Yuan Pei planned the curriculum of the school for Buddhist teachings and secular literacy. He was the only teacher. He continued to conduct the discourses for the public and so gathered a number of lay supporters around him. Most of them recognised the sincerity of his purpose and argued that he had no this-worldly goals for himself. He was highly sought by the lay Buddhists to administer the Buddhist vow, *san-gui-yi*. He told me that he had administered *san-gui-yi* to about four thousand Buddhists from all over Singapore. They were technically his disciples. This figure was unusually high compared with the other monks, few of whom have even fifty followers.

With the declining number of young children entering the monastic order, the school was forced to close. In its place, he started a welfare service for the aged. Though not the first to provide it, he was the first to interact with the government in this field. He and his ordained female disciple, a nun of Filipino origin, did the co-ordinating work for the placing of the aged in various institutions. His own temple was until recently too small to take in inmates. He also organised visits to the Home for the Aged and encouraged his own followers to participate in this. In the 1980s, Master Yuan Pei built a new temple together with a well-equipped Home for the Aged on the temple premise so that he and his disciple became even more involved in welfare works.

Although the home is independent of the Ministry, Master Yuan Pei and his disciple had chosen to work closely with the government. One reason might be that by associating with a government body made the project credible in the public eye. Another reason is that he and the nun, at the initial stage, lacked the expertise needed in caring for the old and the infirmed. So they relied on paid social workers.

His project was privately funded. The construction cost of the new temple was approximately $3,000,000. The Home received a subsidy from the government to help defray the costs of keeping one hundred inmates. Master Yuan Pei had some difficulty in getting large contributions from businesses. Lay people were the main donors and he enjoyed a high prestige with both the monks and the people.

One event in 1984 that brought him into the limelight was when he was invited by the Ministry of Education as an instructor to help train the teachers in Buddhism. This firmly established him as one of the main scholar monks in Buddhism in the Singapore society.

The late Master Yuan Pei was seen by many as a monk who refused to compromise Buddhism by rejecting syncretic practices, thereby seeking to redefine the role of Buddhism in modern Singapore society. He was succeeded by his disciple, a nun Venerable Guan-Yen, who continued his welfare work.

(iii) The Late Venerable Yin Shih – A Ritual Specialist

The late Venerable Yin Shih was considered to be "an old veteran Mahayana monk" and was reasonably well-known. Yet he did not have as high a status as the above two monks but people went to him for ritual services, especially funeral rites. Many saw him as a competent professional ritualist.

He was seventy-three years old at the time of the interview. He was born in the Fujian province and was not very well-educated. Venerable Yin Shih could only speak the Fujianese dialect and read some Chinese. He was ordained as a novice monk at the age of ten because his family was too poor to afford him. Following the migrants after the communist victory, he came to Singapore in the early 1950s. Yin Shih had no one to turn to when he first arrived but was fortunate to lodge at a temple for a brief period and set up his own temple soon after. He was able to survive and accumulate some capital from the ritual services he rendered.

In the early 1960s, he built his own temple in what was then a remote rural area. Being new, he had yet to acquire supporters who would help him. So he built the temple using his own labour and that of a few helpers. According to those who have been with him for the past two to three decades, Yin-Shih was much respected for his hard work and perseverance. They recalled those earlier years when he worked practically on his own. He would work on the religious services during the day and build the temple continuing into the middle of the night when everyone was asleep.

He was an entrepreneurial monk. After the temple was completed, he aligned himself closely with a clan association, ensuring support from them by becoming the caretaker of the clan temple, which was situated next door to his. At the same time, he catered to the ritual needs of the clan members. In this way, he attracted members and money. He eventually got one rich clan member to help construct a memorial hall for housing ancestral tablets, thereby providing the temple with a steady source of income. He also performed the rite of merit-making, *gong-de*, to the general public. It was this service that attracted many Chinese lay members to him and popularised him as one of the few monks who provided such services. Because demand was great, he was able to charge a high fee, as high as five thousand dollars, for the *gong-de* service.

His entrepreneurial acumen showed up again when he detected a shift in the interest of the laity from ritualism to dharma and meditation. Being uneducated himself, he invited a young scholar monk from Taiwan and organised dharma lectures and seminars for the public. Public lectures were held in the main shrine hall on a weekly basis. Through this, he was able to publicise his temple to the younger Singaporean Chinese. However, things did not go as smoothly as he anticipated, resulting in tension between him and the Taiwanese monk. Venerable Yin Shih was fundamentally more interested in increasing the number of devotees, hence generating a larger income so he could expand his temple but the young Taiwanese monk favoured learning and scholarship.

In assessing Venerable Yin Shih's monastic career and the status accorded to him, one can say that he was well-known for his ritual skills, and such were the *raison d'être* of most monks in the Chinese community even up till today.

(iv) Venerable Shi Fa Zhao – A Reformist, Ritual and Welfare-Oriented Specialist

Venerable Shi Fa Zhao is a modern breed of young Reformist monk. He became a monk in his late adolescent years and is now in his early forties and has accomplished much by monastic standards. He is the abbot of the Golden Pagoda Temple with a large group of adherents and members. His members range in age from the teens through to elderly men and women. He is highly respected by the adherents and members.

During the early years of his monastic career, he was trained in rituals and therefore provided ritual services to the general Chinese population. Today, he continues to provide monthly religious services to his members and conduct funeral services on request. Furthermore, he also visits the sick and infirmed members in the hospitals and goes round the business premises of his members to perform ritual cleansing and blessing when required.

However, since the 1980s, in addition to ritual services, he has been very active in catering to the welfare needs of the Singapore population. In 1992, he founded the Metta Welfare Association that now operates nine centres providing care and welfare services that are described in greater detail in the next chapter. Apart from this, Venerable Shi Fa Zhao also popularised pilgrimage tours for the members. Each year he and his committee organised tours to Buddhist countries in Southeast Asia and South Asia and enabled the members and adherents to understand the different Buddhist traditions and interact with other Buddhists.

Furthermore, he did not neglect his spiritual cultivation. Periodically, he goes on a full-year spiritual retreat where he engages in spiritualism. During this period of time, he lives in confinement in a small room in the temple and does not step out of his room. Food is placed in his room through a small door opening. No one is allowed into the room. He does not see anyone, communicate with anyone nor does he perform any religious service or concern himself with the welfare work and secular life. To many adherents, this is a great act of the venerable as he not only cares for the people but also does not neglect his monastic calling.

CONCLUSION

The reorganisation of the traditional village temple structure into two separate entities has effectively established a clear division of labour and roles between the temple and the Sangha. The bureaucratised temple structure is now being governed by a committee of lay people who are accountable to the members and the Singapore state for their functions and activities. Thus the temple is free to conduct all types of religious and secular activities for its members. Today, many temples continue to have an array of religious activities for their members. In addition, they also run welfare homes and business enterprises, and organise sport and recreation activities. Members of the Sangha, on the other hand, increasingly confine their duties to the religious sphere. For those who continue to be involved in the non-religious activities, the administrative duties are increasingly being taken over by the lay management committee. In a way, the executive powers that the monks once enjoyed are no longer in their domain.

NOTES

1. For a discussion of the large monasteries, see Welch, 1967.

2. For a discussion on the monastic life in Thailand, see Bunnag, J., 1973, *Buddhist monk, Buddhist layman*, London: Cambridge University Press, p. 36-85.

3. For a discussion on the monastic recruitment pattern in Burma, see Spiro, M., 1970, *Buddhism and Society*, New York: Harper and Row, p. 321-350.

4. The Newspaper and Printing Press Bill passed in 1974 was designed to ensure that newspapers (and other mass publications) are not used as instruments of subversion. It is also used to prevent local newspapers and so forth from being influenced and manipulated by "black operations". "Black operation" is a term used by the Singapore government to refer to illicit activities by foreign powers in Singapore, designed to manipulate the politics of the island and destabilise the political order. See Chan, H.C., 1985, "Legislature and Legislators" in Quah, J. S. T., Chan, H. C. and Seah, C.M. (eds.), *Government and Politics of Singapore*, Singapore: Oxford University Press. In 1986 a new Press Act was passed under which foreign publications can have their circulation in Singapore progressively cut if

they are deemed to engage in "domestic politics". See Far Eastern Economic Review, 4 Sept 1986, p.12.

5.   There are presently no formal monastic schools in Singapore to train Buddhist monks and nuns. An aspiring monk or nun would have to travel to Taiwan, Thailand or Sri Lanka to receive a monastic education. A novice could, however, learn some dharma, rituals and prayers locally as an apprentice to older monks and nuns.

6.   When the Chinese community was first established, as well as after the war, poverty was widespread. Most of the monks and nuns suffered alongside their fellow Chinese. The monks and nuns, by the nature of their status, are dependent on the Chinese community for support. From the 1970s onwards, however, general economic prosperity has meant that more money and resources flowed into the temples and individual monks and nuns are better provided for financially and materially. The livelihood of the monks and nuns has improved greatly.

7.   For a discussion on the *mui-tsai*, see Jashok, M, 1988, *Concubines and Bondservants*, Hong Kong: Oxford University Press. Also, Gaw, K, 1991, *Superior Servants*, Singapore: Oxford University Press.

CHAPTER 4

Establishing an Ethno-Religious Framework and the Religious Law[1]

INTRODUCTION

As Singapore is firmly established as a multi-religious society, the state has proceeded to protect the link between multi-ethnicity and multi-religiosity. This is done through the establishment of an ethno-religious framework that the state believes is the key to stable ethnic relations. To ensure that this link remains a permanent feature within Singapore society, it has established the "Maintenance of the Religious Harmony Act" which serves to police the functions and activities of the religious institutions, religious personnel and the lay community.

STATE AND ETHNICITY

To understand the significance of the ethno-religious framework in Singapore, it is important for us to understand the background to the relationship between state and ethnicity. The relationship between the Singapore state and the construction of ethnicity is a close one. In post-independent Singapore, the state has consciously created a multiracial framework for its diverse ethnic population, an issue that has been studied by various scholars. Multiracialism is seen as a founding myth of the Singapore state (Benjamin, 1976) on the one hand and as an issue of orientalism by others (Purushotam, 1995). To Benjamin, it is this strict division of ethnic groups as the central tenet of multiracialism that inhibits the growth of a truly Singaporean national culture and identity, resulting in a process of "cultural involution" (Benjamin, 1976:128). Purushotam argues that the management of ethnicity by the Singapore state somehow has not managed to get out of the colonial experience. In fact, the state further reinforces the stereotype grouping of ethnicity by using the existing colonial categories. Thus, she argues, what we see today is a localised form of "orientalism" by the national elite.

In Singapore, ethnicity is taken to be synonymous with race, and it is to the concept of "race" that the political elite subscribe to. Thus, in all official discourses, the state alludes to multi-racialism rather than multi-ethnicity. All citizens are required by law to specify their racial backgrounds. Since independence, the government has consciously maintained this ethnic distribution. This issue has been discussed variously by scholars such as Benjamin (1976), Clammer (1982, 1985) and Purushotam (1995).

There are four main official race categories: Chinese, Malay, Indians and Others. Offspring of inter-ethnic marriages are required to slot themselves into one of these four official categories, which then define them. This form of legally-prescribed race status, while allowing the state to define clearly the various groups and to formulate social policies for them, does not fully represent the diversities found within the four official categories.

The categorisation into four official races is based on phenotype – that is, the differences among these four groups of people are spelt out clearly by their skin colour and their general physical appearance. The differences are reinforced through a definition of the cultural contents of these ethnic groups: linguistic skills, religion, cuisine and art. Hence, the state draws close links between race and language, race and religion, race and value. The attempt to standardise the ethnic categories is significant in the formulation of social policies in the areas of multi-culturalism, multi-lingualism and multi-religiosity (Siddique, 1989: 563-578).

Under the official banner, the link between language and ethnicity is spelled out thus: the mother tongue of the Chinese is Mandarin; for the Malay, it is Bahasa Melayu; for the Indians, it is Tamil; and for the Others, it is English. This correlation between race and language means that other variations cannot exist in the legal sense, although, informally, everyone is aware that they do. Likewise, the correlation between race and religion creates the general impression that the Chinese are Buddhist (including Daoists and practitioners of Chinese religion); Malays are Muslim; Indians are Hindus; and Others are Christians. At the official level, their status continues to be prescribed within this "CMIO" (Chinese, Malay, Indian and Others) framework. The race status is also patriarchally oriented, recognising only the patrilineal descent pattern. Thus, those groups with matrilineal descent are forced to identify their racial origin according to their male ancestors.

Today, this multiracial framework is widely referred to as the CMIO model (Siddique, 1989). To ensure the operational success of this framework, the state steadfastly adheres to the pre-independence ratio distribution of its ethnic population and the present-day ethnic profile conforms closely to it: Chinese (consisting of the various dialect groups – mainly Fujianese, Chaozhouese, Cantonese and Hakka) – constitute 76.8% of the total population, the Malays (which include Javanese and Boyanese) constitute 14% and Indians (mainly Tamils, Malayalees and Punjabis) constitute 7.9% of the total population. The remaining 1.4% belong to "Others", mainly of Eurasian and Western background (Department of Statistics, 2001 (2): viii).

This effort to create a multicultural framework is seen as an attempt by the Singapore state to establish an acceptable set of criteria for ethnic relations in order to ensure social stability within the new nation-state. In a post-colonial environment, independent new nation states are not unlike what Anderson termed imagined communities (Anderson, 1980). In Singapore, this sense of imagined community includes two sets of identities: an imagined national (Singapore) political identity on the one hand and an imagined sense of multiracialism among the ethnic groups. These two identities have had to be invented for post-colonial Singapore. Hobsbawn and Ranger (1983) argue that an invented tradition would become part of a dominant tradition through time. In Singapore, after 30 years of nation-building, multiracialism has become an accepted part of the social rubric of the society.

The construction of the close links between ethnicity, language and religion can create deep divisions among the ethnic groups. When the People's Action Party first took office, one of their main tasks was to break down ethnic allegiance and to forge a Singapore national identity. The contest of loyalty between ethnic identity and national identity has continued right up till today.

The question of loyalty to the new nation state and the fear of ethnic rivalries resulting in open conflicts such as the 1964 Riot,[2] are two main reasons for the adoption of the CMIO model. Its policies are aimed at containing ethnic sentiments and tensions within a manageable framework that is backed by Singapore law. The policies include an integrated educational programme and an integrated school system, where students from different ethnic backgrounds are placed in a common school environment;[3] a civic education programme that focuses on Singapore as a nation with the creation of a national identity as its main goal; and an integrated public housing programme, which provides an ethnic quota for the new towns that have been built by the Housing and Development Board authorities. The policy of the Housing and Development Board authorities, from the 1960s through to the 1970s, was to encourage ethnically-mixed residential estates through the housing allocation system according to a proportionate ethnic population formula. This differed greatly from the early years, when Chinese lived in shophouses within the city precinct and the Malays lived in kampongs in the outlying districts. From the 1980s, preferential allocation of HDB flats in ethnic districts was given to the existing ethnic population.[4] The Housing and Development Board spelt out ethnic quotas for public housing (Lai, 1995: 121-132).

In 1990, the state announced a system of "Shared Values" for its citizens to expedite the formation of a national identity (White Paper, 1991; Quah, 1990).[5]

ETHNICITY AND RELIGION

As part of the policy of multi-ethnicity, the Singapore State is also committed to a policy of multi-religiosity. This is the "Buddhism, Daoism/Chinese religious beliefs, Islam, Hinduism and Christianity" model; which is in accordance with the prescribed CMIO ethnic model. Referred to as the BDIHC model, this has become the blueprint for the religious landscape in modern Singapore society. The link between ethnicity and religion is spelt out as the CMIO-BDIHC formula for the majority of the population.

In the official census, this link has been clearly spelt out. There continues to be a correlation between the ethnic population and the established religions. In 2000, the census shows that about 54% of the Chinese population continues to adhere to "Buddhism" while 11% adhere to Daoism and traditional Chinese religion, 99.6% of the Malay population are Muslims; however, only a little over 55.4% of the Indians are Hindus and 53% of the Others are Christians (Department of Statistics, 2001 (2): 112). Among the Chinese ethnic group, 16.5% are Christians and 18.6% claim to have no religion. Among Indians, 23% are Muslims, 12% are Christians, 0.2% follow other religions and 0.5% have no religion. For the Others, 14% are Buddhists, 22% are Muslims, 1% follow other religions and 8% have no religion. The Malays are much less varied in religious commitment. Only 0.03% has declared themselves to have other religions and another 0.05% claim to have no religion (Department of Statistics, 2001: 3).

This official categorisation of the various types of religion that are practised in Singapore stands in contrast with the great variations that are found within each of these official categories. However, the population is expected to adhere to this categorisation when stating their religious affiliation on official documents. The division between the Buddhists and Daoists/Shenists reflects the growing trend of Buddhicisation among the Singapore Chinese. However, there continues to be no official recognition of other forms of religion practised by the Chinese such as Confucianism, although it is viewed by the state as a Chinese moral ethical system. Likewise, all Malays are Muslims, which ignores the Malays' own categorisation of themselves as Sunni or Sufi or Islamic fundamentalist. For the Indians, this homogenisation of the Hindu faith totally ignores not only the many variations found within the religion but also the entirely different religious systems of some

Indians such as Sikhism, Zoroastrianism and Jainism which are also practised by small groups of Indians in Singapore. Likewise, Judaism, which is practised by a very small Jewish community, is not seen as a separate religious category.

This official categorisation has led to the perpetuation of the stereotypical images of Chinese as "Buddhists/Daoists/Shenists", the Malays as "Muslims" and Indians as "Hindus", unless they state otherwise.

Only the Christians do not fit this ethnic mould. There are two reasons that explain why the Christians are outside this ethno-religious framework. First, Christianity was associated with the colonial regime, hence its status as a colonial religion. Second, its present status is associated with claims of modernity. Christianity is seen as having the ability to transcend the ethnic boundary, since it draws its adherents from the various ethnic groups in Singapore. Although the majority of the Christian believers come from the Chinese population, a sizeable number of Indians and a very small group of Malays are also Christians. Of the three ethnic groups, the religious boundary of the Malays can be seen as the least elastic, with the smallest number of converts, while the Chinese and the Indians register a much higher percentage of conversion to Christianity.

Traditionally, Buddhism, Hinduism and Islam in Singapore have abstained from engaging in proselytising with the view of gaining more converts. They each spread in their own time and gradually encompass like-minded communities. Identity between religious belief and community membership has thus remained unbroken among them. This has helped to create a stable relationship among the major ethnic communities in Singapore, where religion continues to be a focus of ethnic culture and ethnic identity.

There is also a tacit understanding between the Singapore state and the various religious leaders that a policy of non-conversion is the key to maintaining ethnic relations not only in Singapore but also within the geopolitics of the Malay Archipelago. Such a policy has allowed the main ethnic groups to enjoy their own religions and engage in religious activities. It has also allowed individuals to either participate actively or passively in their own religions with no worry about losing members, as religious affiliation comes with membership within the community.

However, recent developments in the religious sphere in the local and global context have upset this balance. For the first time, apart from Christianity, Islamic fundamentalist groups are engaged in aggressive proselytisation with the view to converting the general population to the faith. As elsewhere in the world today, there is a strong resurgence of numerous religious movements. In Latin America and parts of Asia, especially in the Philippines, there is the emergence of the Christian Liberation Theology Movement. In the Middle East and other Asian countries like Malaysia and Indonesia, a strong Islamic Dakwah movement has taken place.

This rise of pan-religious movements across Asia and the Middle Eastern countries has set a trend for a renewed awareness and sensitivity towards the need to participate in such movements. The pan-Islamic Dakwah Movement has galvanised forces among the Islamic states, including Malaysia and Indonesia. Likewise, the Hindu Revivalist Movement has set the Indian communities throughout the Asian region in motion, and Buddhist Revivalism, brought about by the formation of the World Buddhist Council, has penetrated these countries as well, affecting those that are suffering a decline in religious membership and facing competition from Christian evangelists.

There are two main types of religious revivalism. The first is fundamentalist revivalism which is: (1) a counter-movement to rationalisation – that is, against the "demystification of the world"; (2) an attempt to overcome the pressures of modernisation; (3) a type of anti-imperialist, anti-hegemonic movement; and (4) an expression of renewal generated from within a given religion (Evers and Siddique, 1993: 2). Fundamentalist revivalism is seen as "an attempt to restructure the past in a form relevant to contemporary concerns" (ibid: 2). The other type is "innovation in scriptural interpretation, a less stringent application of religious codes, secularism, liberalism and rationality: in short, the adaptation of religious ideas and practices to modern culture" (Caplan, 1987: 9). This trend attempts to cope with the impact of modernity on the society by assimilating it as the Reformist Buddhists attempt to do with Shenism.

In line with global trends, in recent years, there has been a general revival of the main non-proselytising religions in Singapore. the Islamic Dakwah, the Hindu Revival and the Buddhist Revivalist movements have gathered momentum since the late 1970s, in part, in response to the actively proselytising Christian evangelical movements. In all these movements, the crux of the action is a self-renewal process – of renewing one's position and identity in a world that is increasingly compressed in time and space. Rapid modernisation has brought about communication and technologies that allow each nation to have instant contact with the others. Diffusion of cultural values, popular cultures, attitudes (predominantly American and European), technological transfer and economic welfare have resulted in a level of cultural homogenisation among nations. In Asia, this has been so. In Singapore, it is especially acute, especially with its information open door policy and its secular liberal education. The process of homogenisation has denied individuals or groups the unique identity that was once available at their disposal. Thus, those who seek to proselytise and those who have converted are most concerned to locate the identity within a recognisable framework. Religion has once again become an important idiom for the transmission of identity in contemporary Singapore.

THE POLICY OF MULTI-RELIGIOSITY

When the PAP government inherited a multi-ethnic population, the dice had already been cast. For the sake of social and political stability, the PAP government adopted a policy of multi-racialism and multi-religiosity. At the first session of the first Parliament of independent Singapore in December 1965, the newly-appointed government spelt out the multiracial policy and appointed the Constitutional Commission to enact this policy. The following was expressed by the then Minister of Law and Development:

> ..one of the cornerstones of the policy of the Government is a
> multi-racial Singapore. We are a nation comprising people of
> various races who constitute her citizens, and our citizens are equal
> regardless of differences of race, language, culture and religion.
>
> To ensure this bias in favour of multi-racialism and the
> equality of our citizens, whether they belong to majority or
> minority groups, a Constitutional Commission is being
> appointed to help formulate these constitutional safeguards
> (Vasil, 1984: 99).

Literally, a multi-racial Singapore society expects its citizenry
to "intermingle and interact with each other in a spirit of tolerance,
understanding and mutual appreciation" (Ling: 1989: 693). The state
would facilitate and, if need be, intervene to ensure that such an
attitude becomes the prevailing norm of the nation. The Singapore
state is a secular and religiously-neutral state and therefore does not
take the side of either majority or minority religions. It deals with
problems of a religious nature in a bureaucratic manner.

As early as 1949, the Inter-Religious Organisation was formed
in Singapore. This was

> ...an association of individuals in Singapore professing the
> different faiths prevailing in the island. Since 1949 it has worked
> assiduously yet unobtrusively in Singapore to create a climate of
> religious understanding and co-operation in order that religion
> should be a source of national unity rather than disunity (Ling,
> 1989: 695).

To ensure that each religious group functioned within its own
boundary, the government has never failed to use appropriate
occasions to remind the religious leaders and adherents of their
responsibility to the wider community at large. On one occasion,
addressing the conference organised by the Tamil Muslim Union in
1966, Prime Minister Lee Kuan Yew expressed his hope that:

"the leaders of the Muslim community would always interpret Islamic doctrine in a way that would be to the benefit of its followers and the general good of the community" (Ling, 1989: 694).

Implicit in Lee's statement was the hope that the interpretation of the Islamic doctrine would also express the values espoused by the state, i.e., multiracialism, multi-religious tolerance, forbearance and togetherness (Ling, 1989: 694). Likewise, Encik Rahim Ishak, the then Minister of State for Education, a Muslim himself, urged the Islamic leaders to shoulder wider responsibility and reminded them of the "abundant opportunities that existed in the Republic for Muslims to improve themselves educationally and economically" (Ling: 694). The state has, since independence, acknowledged that the Malays as a minority group have to be treated sensitively. The Administration of Muslim Law was enacted and came into effect in 1966. Around the same time, the Council of Muslim Religion (Majlis Ugama Islam, or MUIS) was established officially in 1968 to "assist Muslim organisations in Singapore to regulate their affairs and to administer the Muslim Law" (Ling, 1989: 694).

The Buddhists were also reminded of their social responsibility when Lee addressed a Buddhist convention in 1967. He told the congregation:

> Let us face up to this problem of multi-culture, multi-religions and multi-languages. Alone in Southeast Asia, we are a state without an established church (Ling, 1989: 695).

In the 1970s, the fervour of nationalism and national identity was at the forefront of many of the Southeast Asian states. In Singapore, nation building was one of the top priorities during this period. However, the state continued its policy of religious neutrality. The former Prime Minister Lee continued to reaffirm this state policy and reminded the general population that "religion in a secular state like Singapore must never become a source of friction and animosity between the different religious groups" (Ling, 1989: 695). He urged the Buddhists, when addressing the Thirty-fifth Anniversary of the (Singapore) Buddhist Union to "grow in strength, and help make Singapore a more tolerant and a harmonious nation despite our many different religions" (Ling, 1989: 695).

The PAP government has adopted a very consistent policy since 1965 in regards to its multi-religion policy. Two racial riots have made the newly-independent regime extremely cautious and sensitive of the ethno-religious balance in the new nation state, for it believed that any slackening in vigilance in religious affairs among the ethnic groups could result in sectarian violence. The two riots were the Maria Hertogh incident that occurred in 1951 and the 1964 Racial Riot. These two incidents have convinced the government that the only way to prevent sectarian strife from destroying the fragile ethno-religious fabric of the nation is to spell out clearly the roles and responsibilities of each religion and their organisations in Singapore.

a) The Maria Hertogh Incident

One of the most tumultuous events related to the ethnic relations of the newly-independent Singapore State was the Maria Hertogh Incident. This was a case that involved a Dutch Eurasian girl. She was baptised as a Christian after her birth in 1937. However, she was given away to a Malay family in 1943 when the Japanese arrested her parents. She was adopted and raised as a Muslim. In 1948, her parents discovered her whereabouts and brought out a lawsuit for custody of her. In May 1950, the Dutch Consul, acting on behalf of the Dutch parents, obtained a court order for her custody. This order was reversed as a result of a legal technicality in July 1950. Upon returning to her foster parents' home, Maria Hertogh was rushed into marriage with a Malay, which was allowed under Islamic law. This act aroused much dissatisfaction within the Eurasian and Christian community and they called for legal action. Maria was removed from her husband's family and placed in a convent. This led to a lawsuit by the groom's family.

During this period, both the Eurasian and the Malay communities expressed dissatisfaction with the other party. This heightened the ethnic tension within the community at large and between these two communities in particular. The demonstration during the hearing of the court case turned into riot, first at the court and later spreading to various parts of Singapore, with a total of 18 people killed and 173 injured, with 72 vehicles burnt and another 119 damaged (Clutterbuck, 1973: 72 –73).

Although the riot was quashed, the ethnic tension never went away. It continued to simmer at the latent level and awaited an opportunity to erupt, as it did in the racial riot of 1964. In the immediate post-independence years, the ethnic tension shifted to that between the ethnic Chinese and the Malays as a result of economic success of the ethnic Chinese, thereby creating a great disparity of wealth between the two ethnic groups.

b)   The 1964 Racial Riot[6]

The ethnic relations between the Chinese and the Malays were simmering behind what seemed a peaceful environment. However, the political contests between the People's Action Party (PAP) and the United Malay National Organisation (UMNO) brought this tension to the surface (Bass, 1973: 267-269). The catalyst for the 1964 racial riot was the outbreak of violence during a procession in commemoration of the Prophet Mohammed's birthday. There are two versions of this outbreak, one by the People's Action Party (PAP) and the other by the United Malay National Organisation (UMNO). According to the PAP version, a group of Malay stragglers attacked members of the Federal Reserve Unit who were lagging behind their main troop. According to the UMNO version, it was a Chinese bystander who threw a bottle at the Malay marchers. The result was that clashes between the Malays and Chinese spread to various parts of Singapore, from the Malay enclave to Chinatown. At the end of the riot, a total of 22 dead and 78 injured were recorded (Bass: 269-270).

These two events highlighted the ethnic tension in Singapore and how religion was and could still be used as a catalyst for ethnic violence. Given this fact, the Singapore government has been very conscious and sensitive in its treatment of ethnicity and religion.

STATE AND RELIGIOUS LEGITIMACY

In the early 1980s, the recognition by the state of the legitimacy of the various religious systems and their contribution to moral values in Singapore (through the moral education programme in school) encouraged the main religions to adopt a higher public profile than before. This, together with the global trend in religious revivalism, has led to aggressive proselytisation by some Christian evangelical groups and the Islamic Fundamentalist Dakwah members. The aggressive proselytisation has led to conflicts of interest and dissatisfaction at both the inter-religious and intra-religious levels. The established Buddhist/Daoist/Shenist, Islamic and Hindu communities were dissatisfied with the proselytisation carried out by Christian evangelists. Likewise, some Muslims saw the Dakwah members and movement as a threat to their Islamic practice. The Buddhists and Hindus were also forced to respond to this intense religious competition by modernising and rationalising their religion and religious practices to suit modern needs – yet they adopted a passive approach to retain old members while attracting new ones.

At the geopolitical level, the present trend towards Islamic fundamentalism has been further reinforced by the great economic divide between ethnic Chinese and Malays. This is especially so in Indonesia and Malaysia where Islamic fundamentalism has become an attractive alternative moral system for those who are worried by rapid modernisation and the acquisition of wealth by the new Malay middle class. Islamic fundamentalism has established a stronghold in various parts of Malaysia and Indonesia and is an emerging force within the Singapore society too. It has attracted an increasing number of Muslims.

Amidst all these rivalries and competitions for membership, the state responded with the introduction of the Maintenance of Religious Harmony Act, henceforth known as the Act, to prevent such tensions from becoming overt violence. This swift and decisive action was to prevent a repeat of the 1964 Racial Riot between the Malays and Chinese which carried strong religious overtones.

WHITE PAPER ON MAINTENANCE OF RELIGIOUS HARMONY (MRH)

When addressing the Parliament in January 1989, the President stressed the importance of maintaining religious harmony in multi-religious Singapore.

> **Religious Tolerance and Moderation**. Religious harmony is as important to us as racial harmony. Singapore is a secular state, and the supreme source of political authority is the Constitution. The Constitution guarantees freedom of religion. However, in Singapore racial distinctions accentuate religious ones. Religious polarisation will cause sectarian strife. We can only enjoy harmonious and easy racial relationships if we practise religious tolerance and moderation (MRH: 1).

The Religious Harmony Act that came into effect in March 1992, has allowed the government to take action against the various religious groups that violate the Act. It allows the authority to serve restraining orders on leaders and members of a religion who threaten Singapore's religious harmony by their words or actions, and those who conduct political and subversive activities under the guise of religion (MRH: 9-10).

To maintain this harmony, it is the government's policy to prevent aggressive proselytisation and conversion. In the White Paper on Maintenance of Religious Harmony, the goal is:

> to preserve harmony, Singaporeans, whether or not they belong to any organised religious group, must not cause disharmony, ill will or hostility between different religious or non-religious groups. In particular, religious groups, in exercising their freedom of religion, should:
>
> a.   acknowledge the multi-racial and multi-religious character of our society, and the sensitivities of other religious groups;
> b.   emphasise the moral values common to all faiths;

c.   respect the right of each individual to hold his beliefs and
     to accept or not to accept any religion;
d.   not allow their members, followers, officials or clergy from
     acting disrespectfully towards other religions or religious
     groups; and
e.   not influence or incite their members to hostility or violence
     towards other groups, whether religious or non-religious
     (MRH: 5).

The state keeps a close watch on the religious activities of the
various groups. So long as the groups adhere to the guidelines laid
down in the Act, the state has, till recently, refrained from intervening
in religious affairs, and religious groups have been allowed autonomy
in running their activities. Here again, the emphasis is on religious
sensitivity. The government argues that respect for and sensitivty to
other religions are important for the social stability of the nation-
state. The Maria Hertogh Incident and the 1964 Racial Riot continue
to have an impact on the government's treatment of religions,
reflecting on their fear of another eruption of ethnic violence if
religious issues are not handled carefully. Added to this is the global
trend towards ethno-religious revivalism and the outburst of violence
among religious sectarian groups in Sri Lanka and ethnic cleansing
in some East European countries, which have served as reminders of
the potentially volatile situation at home.

(i)   Religion and Politics

The Singapore government views the ethno-religious conflicts in
Sri Lanka and the former Yugoslavia as examples of the failure of
the state to separate religion and politics in a clear fashion. They
also exemplify the weakness of states which cave in to the pressures
and ethnic chauvinism of one ethnic group, as the Sri Lankan case
has illustrated, where the majority urban Buddhist Singhalese were
determined to re-establish Sri Lanka as a Buddhist state and the
Tamil minority retaliated with militancy to protect their own
religious interests. The bitter war fought between the Christian

Orthodox Serbs and the Catholic Croats emerged as a result of the disintegration of Yugoslavia where, without a strong central government, the original ethnic proclivities reasserted their territorial claims.

The government is determined to prevent any overt conflict by monitoring closely influences from overseas. The Christian Liberation Theology Movement which found its followers among the underclass in Latin America and the Philippines was closely monitored by the state when it started appearing in Singapore. Likewise, prominent foreign Muslim leaders and scholars expounding the Dakwah ideology were also subjected to close observation.

Several events in Singapore in the mid-1980s illustrate the volatile nature of, and the need for careful treatment of, religious activities. One widely publicised incident was the arrest of several Catholic priests and lay workers by the government.[7] This action was criticised by some Singaporeans and given wide foreign media coverage.

The incident began in the early 1980s when a number of Catholic priests became interested in the discussion of various social issues surrounding the nation. Most of the priests were already involved in some kind of welfare work – for example, visiting prisons and preaching to the prisoners. Several of the Catholic priests, namely Fathers Patrick Goh, Edgar D'Souza, Joseph Ho and Arotcarena, formed the Church and Society Group with the objective of discussing social issues, and made known their views to the congregation.[8] Through various in-house publications, including the *Catholic News*, the team sought to discuss various social topics. These included the roles of the trade unions, National Wage Council and rights of workers; the roles of multinational corporations in Singapore; the amendments to citizenship laws; the Newspaper and Printing Presses Act; government policies on TV3; and foreign workers.

The tone of the publications, according to the state, was an attempt to appeal to the masses on grounds that they were "victims of injustice, lies and untruths" (ISD in Act: 16). It upset a government that prided itself on fair treatment and justice for the people. To the government, the tone was irresponsible. If Liberation Theology were of this nature, then it had no place in Singapore society, for the government perceived its motive was to rock the very basic stability of the nation which the PAP government had so painstakingly created over the past three decades.[9]

According to a report, the Catholic priests and lay workers, in line with the teachings of Liberation Theology, felt that it was their responsibility to be involved in social issues and to create social consciousness among their congregation. The general view was that the citizens were apathetic, apolitical and, at times, too afraid to speak their minds. They should be encouraged to do so, as in the socially-liberal societies of the European and American worlds. Such actions were seen as leanings towards Marxism, hence a Marxist conspiracy to subvert the existing socio-political system.[10]

The conflicts of ideology between the government and the Catholic priests reflected deep-seated differences between the pragmatists on the one hand and the social democrats on the other. Being rationalists and pragmatists, the government – having gone through the decolonisation process, the separation from Malaysia and the struggle for survival during the early years of independence, finally reaching the present stage of industrialisation and economic progress and achieving the status of a developed nation – was not prepared to let a few radical voices destroy what it considered a fragile fabric. They felt that the three decades of progress could be destroyed within a matter of months if the radicals managed to incite a mass movement. Also, attempts to bring the various ethnic groups together to mutually co-exist in harmony by implementing all the "multi-ism" policies could also be destroyed overnight. The government has consistently stressed that the interests of the wider state is paramount and all other sentiments should be subsumed under it.

While arrests were made of individual members, the government assured the general population that it was not an attack on the Church itself. The Church continued to function as before, but religion and politics were to be clearly separated.

A second incident revealing the need for the separation of religion and politics was a series of lectures given by foreign Muslim theologians which the government regarded as provocative and aimed at inciting resentment against the government.

In 1973, a lecturer named Imaduddin Abdul Rahim from Indonesia was invited to deliver a religious talk to the Muslims in Singapore. During this period, the government was carrying out massive resettlement schemes for its population. Many villages and rural populations were resettled in new towns. It was an extremely difficult task to persuade villagers and families to relocate, and acceptance was slow in coming from these people. Abdul Rahim's speech argued that such policy would eventually lead to a demolition of mosques and that "in new housing estates such as Queenstown and Toa Payoh one could see church steeples piercing the skyline and large non-Muslim prayer houses around" (MRH: 16). He further branded "local Muslims and Malays as 'stooges' in their own country for failing to fulfil their obligations" (MRH: 16).

In 1982, another Muslim theologian, Ahmed Hoosen Deedat, in a speech, compared Singapore Muslims with South African Malays and commented that Singapore Muslims were passive and soft and that they should be more militant. He accused "the early local Muslim inhabitants of being complacent and failing to convert the Chinese immigrants, so that the Chinese had taken over power from the Muslims" (MRH: 17). He was also heard making disparaging remarks about Christianity.

In 1984, a Malaysian religious teacher, Mat Saman bin Mohamed, at a religious function in Singapore "expressed his disappointment over the demolition of mosques in areas affected by urban redevelopment, saying that this was tantamount to the destruction of Allah's house" (MRH: 17). In 1986, again at the invitation of Muslims, he was reported as making a speech asserting that "Singapore belonged to the Malays as they were natives of the island" (MRH: 17). He further commented that "Malays had become a minority as a result of the influx of foreigners to Singapore, and were now subservient to the non-Malays" (MRH: 17), calling for Malay unity against the majority race and saying that their plight would be supported by the Malaysian Malays (MRH: 17).

With the resurgence of ethnic nationalism and chauvinism throughout the world, it was not surprising that some radical theologians should expound such views, but it was equally predictable that the Singapore government would react by banning the three from entering the country again. It should be clear by now that ethnic sensitivities have been accorded top priority in governmental policies and have been taken very seriously by all concerned. The issues surrounding Malay identity and Islam continue to be very sensitive in this part of the world, where the Singapore nation state, with its Chinese majority, has to co-exist peacefully in a fragile geopolitical balance with its Indonesian and Malaysian neighbours, which have majority Muslim populations.[11] The policy of giving preferential treatment to the bumiputras in Malaysia has also caused discontent in some Muslim quarters in Singapore. While Singapore has adopted a policy of meritocracy, it also has had to calm down latent tension and dissatisfaction in the discontented quarters. The 1964 racial riot was simply too high a cost to be repeated. The government thus does not tolerate incitement of any kind from external forces, neither is it prepared to allow its Muslim population to be influenced by them. To the government, the speeches made by these Muslim theologians justified the ban on their re-entry.

Another incident concerned the Sikh and Hindu communities in Singapore. The assassination of Mrs Indira Gandhi by Sikh extremists in 1984 brought about increased tension between the two groups in Singapore. There were four reported cases of assault on Sikhs, acts of vandalism on Sikh properties and several threatening phone calls to Sikh individuals and institutions. Some Indian stallholders refused to serve Sikh customers while some Sikhs closed their shops when they anticipated trouble.

Some Hindu temples and organisations made plans to hold condolence gatherings for the late Indian prime minister. There was also a Brahmin temple planning to place a condolence message in the *Straits Times*, which held prayers for Mrs Gandhi. The government viewed the activities of the Sikhs and Hindus with alarm. It acted by advising against such a display of emotions both in the temple and in the newspaper as it felt that such actions would only aggravate the already tense situation between the two communities in Singapore. It also argued that the politics of India should not concern the Singapore Hindus and Sikhs, and advised calm in response to the assassination.

In 1984, some Sikh temples commemorated the storming of the Golden Temple, and prayer sessions were held for those Sikhs who were killed. Speeches were also made condemning the Indian Government and urging the Singaporean Sikhs to assist their Indian counterparts in their struggle for an independent Sikh state. In 1989, a few Sikh temples held requiems for the two Sikhs executed by the Indian government for the assassination of Indira Gandhi. They also placed an announcement in the obituary column of the *Sunday Times*, giving the intended prayer time for these two executed Sikhs. Photographs and newspaper cuttings were also displayed at the temple. The government reacted swiftly to this. The police called up the Sikh leaders and temple officials, warning against holding further requiems for the two and against importing foreign politics into Singapore or involving their religious organisations in politics (MRH: 18).

The government advised the Sikh temples and their members against providing funds and logistical support to militant Sikh separatist groups, who were fighting for an independent Khalistan state in Punjab, in India and the United Kingdom. While it is difficult to stop individuals from donating to such causes, the government came down hard on those temples that allowed their leaders or members to make emotional appeals to their congregations for donations to the cause.

(ii) Religion and Subversion

Another area of controversy is how different groups of people view certain actions as being politically subversive. The so-called Vincent Cheng and Marxist Conspiracy incident,[12] which attracted international media coverage and the attention of human rights groups, fully illustrated the fear of the government, and the difficulty in defining what constitutes social consciousness and what constitutes subversion. Cheng and his cohorts were arrested under the Internal Security Act and imprisoned without being given a trial. Subsequently, most have been released after they publicly confessed to their activities and admitted their mistakes.

To officers in the Internal Security Branch (ISB), Vincent Cheng and his cohorts were engaged in activities that were aimed at destabilising the country. He was seen to be using Christianity (specifically, Liberation Theology) and the Church to advance the Communist cause (ISB in MRH: 18)[13]. He was seen to embark "on a systematic plan to infiltrate, subvert and control various Catholic and student organisations, including the Justice and Peace Commission of the Catholic Church, and Catholic student societies in the universities and polytechnics. He planned to build a united front of pressure groups for confrontation with the government" (ibid: 18). The Internal Security Branch further reported that "under the aegis of the Justice and Peace Commission, he organised talks, seminars and workshops to arouse feelings of disaffection with society and the urge for revolutionary change. He was seen to manipulate Church publications like the *Highlights* and *Dossier* to subtly propagate Marxist and leftist ideas, and to politicise his readers who included priests and lay Catholics. Some of the articles were perceived by the government as adopting familiar Communist arguments to denounce the existing system as 'exploitative', 'unjust' and 'repressive'" (MRH: 18). In an extracted confession broadcast to the public via the Singapore Broadcasting Corporation, Cheng was heard to make the following remark:

> I would foresee that the building up of pressure groups would develop to a stage where they would come into open confrontation with the government. This confrontation...would start off with peaceful protests, public mass petitions, which could lead further to more mass events like mass rallies, mass demonstrations, strikes, where more people are mobilised. And leading to public disorder and maybe even rioting, bloodshed (FEER, 27 Oct 1987: 23).

The link between Cheng and the exiled radical student leader of the 1970s, Tan Wah Piow (who was stripped of Singapore citizenship in 1985 under a new law), led the government to conclude that there was some kind of Communist conspiracy plot brewing (MRH: 22-25).

In a highly critical article, Haas (1989) charged that the Singapore government has confused political freedom with subversion and leftist leanings with Communism, that there was no basis to prove that Cheng and his cohorts were Marxists, nor was there any plot to overthrow the government. Haas also argued that the government's theory of "nip in the bud" was a dangerous way of viewing social events. He said "to analogise politics to the biological determinism of a bud opening into a flower or the growth of cancer is to espouse an organismic theory of politics, long discredited ...." (Haas, 1989: 68). He further argued that to arrest without trial under the Internal Security Act goes against the very grain of what the PAP government had fought for in the 1950s against the British colonial rule. In 1955 when the British colonial administrators enacted the Internal Security Act, Lee Kuan Yew spoke against it:

> If it is not totalitarian to arrest a man and detain him when you cannot charge him with any offence against any written law – if that is not what we have always cried out against in fascist states – then what is it?... If we are to survive as a free democracy, then we must be prepared, in principle, to concede to our enemies... as much [sic] constitutional rights as you concede yourself....We say we dislike communism because, under that form of government, they have arbitrary powers of arrest and detention without trial....
>
> ...to curtail a fundamental liberty, and the most fundamental of them all – freedom from arrest and punishment without having violated a specific provision of the law and being convicted for it... But no man should be deprived of his liberty (Haas, 1989: 70).

The case of Vincent Cheng, his involvement with Liberation Theology and his activities, has once again drawn attention to the difficulties inherent in the political structure. It has also touched upon the inherent differences between politics and academic discourses. The hard-line approach taken by the government in invoking the Internal

Security Act and arresting Vincent Cheng and his group was seen by many critics as tantamount to the "storm in a teacup" syndrome. But the government's critique of bystanders is that they are not in the forefront of decision-making and are ultimately not responsible for the actual course of events. Given the course of history, the government, in the final analysis, would prefer to err on the side of caution.

The Ikhwan, or Muslim Brotherhood, was considered to have subversive intentions, hence it is undesirable in Singapore. The Internal Security Branch reported that:

> A few Muslim activists have also attempted to carry out subversive activities under the guise of conducting religious activities. In mid-1978, a university graduate formed a clandestine group of extremists called "Ikhwan" or Muslim Brotherhood, with the long-term aim of establishing an Islamic state, by armed means if necessary. The group comprised 21 members, mostly recruited from religious classes conducted by a Malaysian religious teacher then living in Singapore.
>
> Ikhwan planned to recruit pre-university students and undergraduates by setting up religious discussion groups in their respective schools and institutions. They were to be trained as writers and religious teachers in order to disseminate revolutionary ideas and sow disaffection among the Muslims. Led by the Ikhwan, the Muslims would then demand that the Government implement Islamic laws similar to those in Saudi Arabia or Iran. If the Government refused, the Ikhwan would spearhead an armed uprising.
>
> By September '79, the Ikhwan had managed to penetrate the Malay language societies of the then Ngee Ann Technical College and the Singapore Polytechnic, and to take over a moribund Muslim organisation, the Pertubohan Muslimin Singapura (PERMUSI), as a front for their clandestine activities (ISB in MRH: 19).

In this case, the Singapore government invoked the ISA to arrest five leading Ikhwan members while others were given a warning. The religious adviser from Malaysia was expelled and prohibited from entering Singapore. The government reassured the Muslim population that the arrest targeted individuals whose intention was to subvert the state, but not Islam per se. Islamic militancy has now become the hallmark of many Islamic Jihad groups throughout the world and any seed for the germination of such a movement in Singapore would not be viewed kindly at all.

The separation of politics and religion was henceforth spelt out clearly in the Act. Thus the White Paper states that:

> Religious groups must not get themselves involved in the political process. Conversely, no group can be allowed to exploit religious issues or manipulate religious organisations, whether to excite disaffection or to win political support. It does not matter if the purpose of these actions is to achieve religious ideals or to promote secular objectives. In a multi-religious society, if one group violates this taboo, others will follow suit, and the outcome will be militancy and conflict.
>
> We will spell out these ground rules clearly and unequivocally. All political and religious groups must understand these ground rules, and abide by them scrupulously. If we violate them, even with the best intentions, our political stability will be imperiled (MRH: 1).

(iii) Inter and Intra-Religious Tensions

Part of the reason why this Act was introduced was the perception, hence fear, of the state over the implications of uncontrolled religious activities that would tear the basic social structural fabric of Singapore society. Hence, it viewed the recent heightened religious fervour in this light:

> In recent years, there has been a definite increase in religious fervour, missionary zeal, and assertiveness among the Christians, Muslims, Buddhists and other religious groups in Singapore. Competition for followers and converts is becoming sharper and

155

more intense. More Singaporeans of many religions are inclining towards strongly-held exclusive beliefs, rather than the relaxed, tolerant acceptance of and coexistence with other faiths.

This trend is part of a worldwide religious revival affecting many countries, including the US and the Middle East. Its causes lie beyond Singapore, and are not within our control. But in Singapore this trend increases the possibility of friction and misunderstanding among the different religious groups. Religion is a deeply felt matter, and when religious sensitivities are offended emotions are quickly aroused. It takes only a few incidents to inflame passions, kindle violence, and destroy the good record of religious harmony built up in recent decades. The Maria Hertogh riots were a classic example (ibid: 3).

We therefore cannot assume that religious harmony will persist indefinitely as a matter of course. Conscious efforts are necessary to maintain it, especially by religious leaders and groups. So long as Singaporeans understand that they have to live and let live, and show respect and tolerance for other faiths, harmony should prevail. Religious groups should not exceed these limits, for example by denigrating other faiths, or by insensitively trying to convert those belonging to other religions. If they do, these other groups will feel attacked and threatened, and must respond by mobilising themselves to protect their interests, if necessary militantly. Similarly, if any religious group uses its religious authority to pursue secular political objectives, other religions too must follow suit. Tensions will build up, and there will be trouble for all.

Two vital conditions must therefore be observed to maintain harmony. Firstly, followers of the different religions must exercise moderation and tolerance, and do nothing to cause religious enmity or hatred. Secondly, religion and politics must be kept rigorously separated (ibid: 4).

(iv) Aggressive and Insensitive Proselytisation

Various reports commissioned by the government regarding religious activities in Singapore have concluded that there is an increasing trend towards aggressive proselytisation by different religious groups.[14] This has coincided with numerous complaints received by various government bodies over aggressive evangelism, carried out mostly by some Protestant churches and organisations. The Internal Security Branch reported the following:

> University students have been harassed by over-zealous Christian students. These student-preachers tried to convert fellow students who felt depressed after failing their examinations. In hospitals, some doctors and medical students have tried to convert critically ill patients to Christianity on their death beds, without regards for their vulnerabilities or for the sensitivities of their relatives (ISB in MRH: 13).

It also reported on the inter- and intra-religious tensions among the various religious groups as a result of proselytisation where each group tried to convert others to their faith. The following comments were extracted from their report :

Christians and Hindus

The complaints by other religious groups are more serious. Hindus have been perturbed by aggressive Christian proselytisation. In August 1986, officials and devotees of a Hindu temple found posters announcing a forthcoming Christian seminar pasted at the entrance of their temple. The Hindus also objected when Christian missionaries distributed pamphlets to devotees going into temples in Serangoon Road (ibid: 13).

Christians and Muslims

The Muslims are extremely sensitive to any attempt to convert them to other faiths. They reacted indignantly when some Christian groups stepped up evangelical activities in 1986. A few groups distributed pamphlets in Malay that used the word "Allah" for God. The Muslims accused these groups of harassing and misleading them, since to them the word "Allah" was specific to Islam. Some Muslims also received extracts from an unidentified book containing inflammatory remarks - that Islam was a "cruel" and "devilish" religion which encouraged "the killing of Christians" (ibid: 13).

Burial of Muslim Converts

There have also been disputes over the funerals of non-Muslims who had converted to Islam. Two cases in July 1988 and January 1989 involved Chinese converts. One belonged to a Christian, and the other to a Buddhist family. The families wanted to cremate the bodies according to their respective Christian and Buddhist rites. But a Muslim organisation applied for court orders to claim the bodies and bury them according to Islamic rites. This naturally upset the families, who considered themselves as next of kin entitled under the law to decide on funeral arrangements. Fortunately, these two disputes were settled amicably out of court after government officials mediated (ibid: 14).

Intra-religious Tensions

a)   Muslims and Ahmadis

There is a long-standing dispute between orthodox local Muslim organisations and their (sic) Ahmadiyya Muslim Mission. In the mid-1980s, when the Ahmadis called their new building at Onan Road a mosque, local Muslim organisations protested. In early 1989, the Ahmadiyya mission deposited literature in letterboxes, including boxes belonging to Muslim residents. Some orthodox Muslims were enraged, and expressed grave concern that the pamphlets would mislead and confuse Muslim youths. Meanwhile, the Ahmadis continued to assert that they were true Muslims, and mounted a propaganda campaign to refute allegations that they were a deviant sect (ibid: 14).

b)   Hindu

In October 89, a Hindu sect, the Shiv Mandir, burnt an effigy of Ravana, a Hindu mythological king, during a religious festival. The Shiv Mandir claimed that the ritual was an ancient practice marking Lord Ramachandra's triumph over the demon king

Ravana and symbolised the triumph of good over evil. Tamil Hindus were incensed by the ceremony. Some saw it as an Aryan attempt to humiliate and belittle the Dravidians, for Ramachandra was an Aryan while Ravana a Dravidian. A few asserted that Ravana was not a demon king. They wanted to stage a protest demonstration at the Shiv Mandir function and threatened to burn the effigy of Lord Ramachandra in retaliation (ibid: 14-15).

c)   Christians

Some Protestants have distributed pamphlets and booklets denigrating the Roman Catholic Church and the Pope. Some of these materials described the Pope as a Communist, and even as the anti-Christ. The Catholic Church publication, the *Catholic News*, has responded by condemning these attempts by "fundamental Christian groups to confuse Catholics". Some Protestant groups have also criticised other denominations, including Charismatics and Ecumenists, in their publications (ibid: 15).

These cases involved complaints to the government departments that took action to mediate the tensions among the groups concerned. In all cases, the leaders of these religious groups were summoned to the Internal Security Department and warned against instituting activities that would cause misunderstanding and conflict. In all cases, the groups involved halted their activities.

The recent rising tide of religious fervour among all religious groups has meant that groups and individuals alike have been swept along with the whirlwind, which has created its own momentum. The state is determined that this whirlwind force would not get out of control. The White Paper elaborated on this issue further:

Many religions enjoin their followers to proselytise others who have not embraced the same faith, in order to propagate the religion. Christians refer to this as "bearing witness", while Muslims engage in *Dakwah* activities. This liberty to proselytise is part of the freedom of religion protected by the Constitution.

159

However, in Singapore it must be exercised very sensitively. It is one thing to preach to a person who is interested in converting to a new faith. It is another to try to convert a person of a different religion by denigrating his religion, especially if he has no desire to be converted. In such cases, the potential for giving offence is great. For this reason, the Government has always discouraged Christian groups from aggressively evangelising among the Malay Muslim community in Singapore.

Harm can be done even without the direct contact of proselytisation. Each religion has its own comprehensive doctrines and theology. Some faiths, for example Buddhism, readily accept other religions and practices, but others, including both Christianity and Islam, are by their nature exclusive. Each religious group, in instructing its own followers, will naturally need to point out where its doctrines differ from other religions, and indeed from other branches of the same religion, and why it regards the others as being mistaken. While it is legitimate, it is possible to go too far. An unrestrained preacher pouring forth blood and thunder and denouncing the followers of other faiths as misguided infidels and lost souls may cause great umbrage to entire communities. If they then retaliate with equal virulence, or worse escalate the quarrel by attacking the persons and desecrating the places of worship of the opposing faithful, the tolerance and mutual trust which forms the basis of Singapore society will be permanently destroyed.

The futures of Christianity, Islam, Hinduism and Buddhism as world religions are secure regardless of how many Christians, Muslims, Hindus or Buddhists there may be among Singaporeans. However, if any religious group in Singapore seeks to increase the number of its converts drastically, at the expense of the other faiths, or attempts to establish a dominant or exclusive position for itself, it will be strenuously resisted by the other groups. This is a fact of life in Singapore that has to be faced squarely (MRH: 4-5).

Another area that the Act specifically seeks to prevent is the use of religion for political causes. This was in response to the emerging Liberation Theology Movement found in certain sections of the Christian churches and the Fundamental Islamic Movement which led to the arrest of some Christian clergy and lay Christians and the expulsion of some Muslim theologians in the mid-1980s. The Paper states that:

> ...religious leaders and members of religious groups should refrain from promoting any political party or cause under the cloak of religion. The leaders should not incite their faithful to defy, challenge or actively oppose secular Government policies, much less mobilise their followers or their organisations for subversive purposes...
>
> Members of religious groups may, of course, participate in the democratic political process as individual citizens. They may campaign for or against the Government or any political party. But they must not do so as leaders of their religious constituency.
>
> Religious leaders are in a particularly delicate position. An Archbishop, Pastor, Abbot, or Mufti is a religious personage, whether or not he puts on his robes or mounts his pulpit. It is not to be expected that every religious leader will always agree with every policy of the Government. But whatever their political views, they should express them cautiously. They should not use their religious authority to sway their followers, much less actively incite them to oppose the Government (MRH: 6).

The Paper also stipulated that the views of the sacred and the profane might differ vastly, especially on issues which to the Government are legitimate concerns for public policy, but which to some faiths pose moral and religious questions. But issues such as these should be left to the individuals to decide:

> Many Christians, particularly Catholics, consider abortion to be morally wrong. The Government's policy is to allow women wanting abortions to get one. However, whether or not a pregnant

woman wants to undergo an abortion, and whether or not a doctor or nurse wants to carry out abortions, are clearly issues of conscience, to be decided by each person for himself or herself. On such issues, religious groups may and do properly take positions and preach to their followers.

Jehovah's Witnesses believe that their religion forbids them to do any form of National Service. Under the law this is a criminal conduct, not conscientious objection. Followers of this sect who refuse to obey call up orders are court martialed (sic) and serve jail sentences.

Some Christian groups consider radical social action, as practised in Latin America or the Philippines, to be a vital part of Christian faith. Whether or not this is the practice elsewhere, if para-religious social action groups become an active political force in Singapore, they will cause heightened political and religious tensions (MRH: 7).

In formulating the Maintenance of Religious Harmony Act, the purpose **"is to establish working rules by which many faiths can accept fundamental differences between them, and coexist peacefully in Singapore"** (emphasis-mine) (MRH: 7).

Under this Act, the government is empowered to take actions it deems appropriate to prevent religious disharmony. Individuals engaged in the following types of conduct could be prosecuted in the court and be subjected to fine or imprisonment:

a.   causing feelings of enmity, hatred, ill-will or hostility or prejudicing the maintenance of harmony between different religious groups;

b.   carrying out activities to promote a political cause, or a cause of any political society while, under the guise of, propagating or practising any religious belief;

c.   carrying out subversive activities under the guise of propagating or practising any religious belief; or

d.   inciting disaffection against the President or the Government (MRH: 9-10).

The Order has the power to prohibit the individual from:

a. addressing any congregation, or group of worshippers on any subject specified in the order;
b. printing, publishing, distributing or contributing to any publication produced by that religious group;
c. holding office in any editorial board or committee of any publication produced by that group (MRH: 10).

(v) Establishing a Stable Tension – Presidential Council for Religious Harmony

Shortly after the introduction of the Act, a meditating body, the Presidential Council for Religious Harmony, was set up "to consider and report on matters affecting the maintenance of religious harmony", which are referred to it by the Government or Parliament. It will also consider Prohibition Orders issued by the Minister" (MRH: 11). The Council which was established in August 1992 has representatives from the main religious bodies in Singapore, including one representative each from the Buddhist, Muslim, Roman Catholic, Christian Protestant and Hindu and Sikh communities. Included in this is a former Chief Justice, who is the chairperson, and two government representatives.

The main objective of the Council is to ensure religious harmony among the various communities. The functions of the Council include the following. First, to consider and report to the minister on matters affecting the maintenance of religious harmony which are referred to by the minister or Parliament. Second, to consider and make recommendations on restraining orders referred to it by the minister. Third, the council could advise the President whether he should confirm restraining orders imposed by the minister. Fourth, it could also summon those under restraining orders to hear their views (*Straits Times*, 2 August 1992: 1).

In a way, this Council serves as a bridge between the state on the one hand and the religious organisations and public on the other. In creating this Council, the state has in fact passed the responsibility of the maintenance of religious harmony to the people themselves. The leaders of each religion are to ensure that those under their care fall in line and that tension and violence do not break out. In short, self-imposed restraints become important. While not denying that tensions would always remain in situations of intense competition and rivalry, the idea is to establish a stable tension among the religious groups.

Enshrined in the Constitution of Singapore is the clause pertaining to the freedom of worship. The Religious Harmony Act spells out precisely what this freedom of worship means. Individuals can choose whatever they want to worship. They can also encourage family members, friends and colleagues to participate, but cannot coerce or force them to join. The line dividing the acts of persuasion and coercion is very thin. If there are no complaints, then it is an act of persuasion; but if there is dissatisfaction and complaints, it becomes coercion. Also, when a group engages all its members to go out and persuade others whom they do not know, particularly in public places, it is coercion. Within the law, they can be stopped from such acts of proselytisation.

Religious competition can be seen as a healthy sign. It prevents the various religious groups from becoming complacent. In a way, it forces groups to be vigilant and to cater to the needs of their adherents. The demands of the adherents can set in motion the internal dynamics that can usher in changes and development. Alternatively, they could revert back to orthodoxy. In the case of Singapore, the two forces of change and a return to orthodoxy are in action. The availability of different religions allows lay people to shop for the one that suits their needs best. However, each group is not allowed to dominate through the use of force, or intense and unscrupulous acts of proselytisation. The Act thus intends to define and maintain the religious boundaries of these groups. So long as all the players adhere to the rules of the game, the maintenance of a stable tension would be upheld and beneficial to all. The Singapore State, once again, dominates and sets the agenda for acceptable religious competition in Singapore.

CONCLUSION

To the State, there is a close connection between ethnicity and religion on the one hand and a clear separation between the religious and secular spheres on the other. Any activity that falls outside the realm of religion should be treated as secular. Introducing the Maintenance of Religious Harmony Act sent a message to the citizens to confine religious pursuit within the known religious boundary. Any other non-related and non-religious activities within the religious boundary would not be acceptable to the State. Furthermore, the religious leaders from the various mainstream religious groups were recruited as members of the Presidential Council for Religious Harmony. In doing so the state has, in fact, placed not only the responsibility for religious activities but also the maintenance of religious harmony among the major religious and ethnic groups squarely on the shoulders of these religious leaders. In short, these religious institutions through their leaders are now accountable to the state for their own conduct as well as the religious well being of other groups, ensuring that the ethno-religious framework is maintained.

NOTES

1. A different version of this chapter is published under Kuah, Khun Eng "Maintaining Ethno-Religious Harmony in Singapore", in *Journal of Contemporary Asia*, April 1998, 28(1): 103-121.

2. Inter-ethnic relationship continues to be an extremely sensitive issue in contemporary Singapore and is handled with great caution. The Singapore state is determined to keep it under control. The early examples of ethnic distrust and suspicion had led to conflicts between the Chinese and Malays, resulting in the 1964 Racial Riot. See Bedlington, S., 1978, *Malaysia and Singapore: The Building of New States*, Ithaca: Cornell University.

3. During the early years, the various ethnic groups established their own schools and students were taught in the vernacular. There was no common teaching curriculum, the result being that each group adopted the curriculum of its "mother country". This was viewed negatively by the new government, which felt that vernacular education fostered only ethnic and national sentiments towards the respective "mother countries" of the population, instead of a Singapore national identity.

4. The Singapore government has been providing highly subsidised public housing for its population since the 1960s with the establishment of the Housing Development Board. Today, it continues to provide good quality subsidised housing to over 80% of the population. For a general discussion of public housing in Singapore, see Yeh, S.H.K. (ed.), 1975, *Public Housing in Singapore*, Singapore: Singapore University Press.

5. In 1989, the ministers expressed the need to take greater action in fostering the creation of a national identity in Singapore. They argued for a set of common values for all Singaporeans, irrespective of their ethnic backgrounds. This culminated in the tabling of a White Paper, which became enacted as legislation in 1991. See White Paper, *Shared Values*, 2 January 1991.

6. For a discussion of this, see Bass, J.R., 1973, *Malaysian Politics, 1968-1970: Crisis and Response*, University of California, Berkeley, PhD dissertation, Ann Arbor: UMI.

7. For a discussion of this, see Far Eastern Economic Review, 4 June 1987; 2 July 1987; 22 October 1987; 17 December 1987.

8. See Far Eastern Economic Review, 4 June 1987, pp. 9.

9. For a discussion on the origin of Liberation Theology, see Smith, C., 1991, *The Emergence of Liberation Theology*, Chicago: Chicago University Press.

10. See Far Eastern Economic Review, 22 October 1987, pp. 22-24.

11. In 1993, there were comments by the Indonesian government questioning the loyalty of its Chinese population over the issue of their increased investment in the People's Republic of China rather than in Indonesia.

12. For a critical analysis of this, see Haas, M., 1989, "The Politics of Singapore in the 1980s", in *Journal of Contemporary Asia*, 19(1): 48-77.

13. This was a report filed by the Internal Security Branch (ISB) and included in the annex of the White Paper.

14. See Kuo, E.C.Y., Quah, J.S.T. and Tong, C.K., 1988, *Religion and Religious Revivalism in Singapore*, Report prepared for the Ministry of Community Development, Singapore

CHAPTER 5

Buddhist Welfare
and Charity

INTRODUCTION

By separating the temple institution from the Sangha, the roles of the temple and the Sangha are now clearly defined. As a religious bureaucracy, the temple is now free to conduct both religious and secular activities within the legal confines. Today, the Buddhist temples are regarded as important providers of welfare services.

This chapter will explore how the temple takes on welfare roles and becomes an important welfare and benevolence provider. The cultural politics of religion is such that while the temple sees its welfare roles as strictly belonging to the moral dictum of its teachings, the State sees the temple as a legitimate space where the group of temple-goers can be convinced to take on the welfare roles. Through a series of Land Law and planning policies, the state indirectly transforms the role of the temple into an important welfare provider. In this sense, the religious space is partially turned into secular space for the less-privileged groups of people within Singapore society. The temple can thus be seen as a champion of the underclass, and it assumes moral authority over the citizens, albeit under the directive of the Singapore state.

TEMPLES AND DEVELOPMENT

Big and small Chinese temples of Buddhist, Buddhist-Shenist and Shenist origin are scattered throughout the island. It is possible to identify the temples according to their physical structures. A typical Chinese temple has an ornate brightly-painted tiled roof with upward-curving eaves. The temple is usually free standing, surrounded by a compound. A main shrine hall dominates the interior of the temple, housing the main deity and a pantheon of lesser deities. The back portion of the building is the kitchen area where food is prepared and religious paraphernalia is stored for use within the temple. Usually the temple has an upper floor that forms the private quarters of the monk, nuns and priests.

The main shrine hall and the adjoining shrine halls are public areas of worship. Any devotee or worshipper can enter and worship. The door to the temple is open during the day, every day, throughout the year. As long as they do not disrupt the tranquil environment, devotees or worshippers can stay in the shrine hall as long as they wish to pray, meditate or do nothing. The main religious services are held in the main shrine hall, and most active temples have some kind of religious function regularly, either on a weekly or monthly basis.

There are also private residences that are converted into small temples. These can be found in private housing estates. They are often not open to the general public. Usually they are smaller than a typical temple and their sole reason for existence is to provide a private space for the monks and nuns to concentrate on their spiritual cultivation. There are also isolated small shrines, usually by the wayside, under trees. The lay people who believe that a spirit lives in the tree usually erect a small shrine and worship the spirit.

In land-scarce Singapore, clever use of land becomes important. Land planning and land-use patterns are therefore awarded top priority. Since 1965, the Ministry of National Development's Land Planning Department and its subsidiary, the Urban Renewal Authority, have created intricate land-use patterns, rationalising land for residential uses, industry, commerce, tourism, parks and nature reserves. The Master Plan governed land planning and land-use patterns. The objective of this Master Plan was to regulate land development through land-use zoning, density and plot-ratio control, reserving lands for schools, open spaces, infrastructure facilities and other essential community uses (Ministry of National Development, Planning Department, 1985: 3). The Urban Renewal Authority (URA), formed in 1974, was empowered with the task of redeveloping the Central District. The introduction of the Land

Act of 1974 empowered the URA to acquire land from private landowners (with compensation) for redevelopment purposes (Wong and Ooi, 1989: 788-812).

Temples were thus not immune to this push for development. Tan Eng Liang, a Senior Minister of State for National Development, argued that "the resettlement policy is clear-cut, irrespective of religions, irrespective of owners and irrespective of organisations" (Kong, 1993: 30). Likewise, "temples, mosques or churches will have to give way to urban renewal or new development, unless they are of historical and architectural value" and few fit into this narrow criterion (Kong, 1993: 31). Thus, from 1974 to 1987, 23 mosques, 76 *suraus*, 700 Chinese temples, 27 Hindu temples and 19 churches were acquired, and their land used for public development purposes (Kong, 1993: 31). Although the affected religious institutions could apply for alternative sites through URA and HDB, not all of them managed to get sites for their temples. Increasingly, various temples combined their resources to lease one site from the relevant authority, the government viewing the situation thus: "it is not possible to have a temple for temple, a mosque for mosque, a church for church substitution. This is uneconomic, impractical and, in the limited land space of Singapore, impossible" (Kong, 1993: 31).

However, there were specific provisions for religious institutions and land was set aside for their construction. Kong provides an interesting argument concerning the arrangement of places of worship in Singapore. She argues that the provision of space for religious institutions to move to is akin to the provision of higher order goods and services in a town or city where such a move is based on the formula of efficiency and functionalism. Thus, in this context, "religious building sites are provided in the new towns as another amenity that sections of the population require" (Kong, 1993: 28). The government works to a standard formula in the provision of landed space for these religious institutions in HBD new towns. Every 12,000 dwelling units will be provided with one landed site for a church; every 9,000 dwelling units will be provided with a site for a Chinese temple; while for a site to be granted for a Hindu temple, there is to be one for every 90,000 dwelling units. This means that two or three new towns share a single Hindu temple.

On the other hand, the Muslims are to be allocated a site for a mosque in every new town. Part of the reason for this favourable treatment is because of the historical status of the Malays (for the most part, Muslims) and their claim to Singapore Island. Enshrined in the Constitution, the treatment of the Malays is clearly spelt out:

> ...recognise the special position of the Malays, who are the indigenous people of Singapore, and accordingly it shall be the responsibility of the Government to protect, safeguard, support, foster and promote their political, educational, religious economic, social and cultural interests and the Malay language. (Constitution of Singapore, 1985: 73).

In setting out lands for specific religious groups, the state has ensured that each group is given a share in the way of replacing the lost religious institutions proportionate to their population size except for the Malays who are assured of a mosque in each new town. Administratively, this is made easier since all sites for the construction of mosques are offered to the central governing body of the Muslim community, Majlis Ugama Islam Singapura (Muslim Religious Council, MUIS in short). The chief surveyor predetermines the cost of the site and is set about three or four times lower than the market value (Kong, 1993: 28). Likewise, the Indians have their Hindu temples assured, although shared between two or three new towns.

Theoretically, the Christian churches and the Chinese temples (Buddhist and Shenist/Daoist) are given the same treatment, with parcels of land allocated for their use. In reality, because of the number of denominations in existence, the parcels of land allotted to both groups are subject to competition within their respective Christian and Buddhist, Shenist/Daoist groups. For instance, within the Christian group, the Methodists, Charismatics, Catholics and other Christian denominations may compete for a religious site. This is also the case for the Buddhist and Shenist/Daoist group. This competition for scarce religious sites might result in conflicts within the groups. To solve this problem, the HDB runs a tender system with the highest bidder winning the land bid. Because of the high price for the land site, it has led to collaboration among different denominations of the same group. It is now a common sight for several groups of Chinese or Christians to share a religious site. For example: when the existing temples came under the urban renewal programme, five Chinese surname groups gathered together to purchase a religious site to house their patron gods. The site was purchased and built at a significant cost that was split among the five partners. At the altar of the main shrine hall, a shared deity, the Clear Water Ancestor (*qing-shui-zhu-shi-gong*) occupied the central position. He was the mythical ancestor of the five surname groups. He was flanked on the left and right by the other patron gods, the position of which was determined by drawing the *qian* (Anxi Association Year, 1986). In another case, two Christian denominations came together to purchase and build a church, sharing the premise (*Straits Times*, 1985).

In catering to the development of Singapore, the state, through its land planning and land-use policies, has indirectly restructured the spatial distribution of the religious institutions in Singapore. It has transformed small isolated temples into large religious complexes through the allocation of large plots of land. Because of the large expense as a result of the large temple size, the welfare and social recreational activities, only those temples with sufficient resources can continue to function. While there continued to be private religious residences, these are small in number and they usually do not cater to the general public.

With the scale of operation comes the scale of activities. The ideal is a multi-functional temple complex, which performs a variety of functions, both social and religious. A multi-functional temple may be defined as one that provides religious, welfare and recreational facilities under its roof. It is an institution for public worship where anyone may visit. It will be a place for mortuary rites and a funeral parlour, a crematorium, a collabarium for storing the urns of ashes of the dead and a memorial hall to house the ancestral tablets. It will also be a place of theological and scriptural education, with a library housing the Buddhist scriptures, a venue for religious seminars and classes for the teaching of the dharma to the public. Finally, it should ideally be a charitable organisation that runs a home for the aged, infirm and/or the handicapped.

The transformation to a large functional temple with welfare facilities often creates tensions between the monks and the lay members. Failure to compromise often results in the demise of the original temple. I illustrate this by the case study below.

A CASE STUDY: COMPROMISE OR NOT?

Two temples, Buddhist Temple A and Shenist Temple B, stood in a former rural kampong district. Temple A was a traditional village temple managed by a Buddhist monk. Temple B was a clan-based temple with regular religious activities for its clan members. Within this area, there were a few isolated thatched roof houses. The area was earmarked for redevelopment and almost all the former inhabitants were housed in a nearby housing estate, paving the way for development to take place. The surrounding land was acquired by the government and resold for private development into an upper middle class housing district.

The two temples were served acquisition summons by the Land Department, but because the temples stood outside the CBD and were not hindering the development of government projects, they could appeal to retain their premises. It was understood that the land would be auctioned to a private developer, so there were strong grounds for an appeal.

The two temples had an intimate relationship. Both were patronised by the same people from the clan associations. The monk from Temple A provided Buddhist-Shenist services to the laity. He also performed the last rites of passage for the dead, especially the rite of *gong-de*. He got on well and was supported by the clan members. He also recruited a reformist monk to teach Buddhist dharma, a move that is popular among the general public.

After receiving the acquisition summons, the two temples joined forces and appealed to the Land Department for it to be retained as a religious site, co-joining a large Buddhist temple and a nunnery in the vicinity. After several appeals, the request was granted if a large temple is built to replace the existing two small ones.

Plans for the new temple complex were drawn. A total of 10 million dollars was estimated for the project to cover the cost for the land, two main shrine halls, a library, an auditorium, a collabarium, a memorial hall, living quarters for members of the Sangha and a welfare home for spastic children. The question then was, who was going to pay for the construction? Should it be the monk, the clan members, or both? As a religious professional, the monk did not have the financial means and he was dependent on the wealthy clan members to help with the financing of the project. This financial dependence reduced the influence of the monk in decision-making.

A main point of disagreement was that of the identity and name of the new temple. The monk wanted to retain the name of Temple A but the clan members wanted to retain the clan temple name. According to the monk, a public Buddhist temple would attract more people, whereas a clan-based temple would only cater to the needs of the clans involved. Besides, the temple should follow the new trend demanded by the society and encouraged by the government, i.e., to establish a Buddhist and not a Shenist temple. The clan members, on the other hand, wanted to retain the exclusivity of the clan temple for the clan members. The inability to compromise resulted in serious conflicts with the clan members abandoning the project and looking for an alternative premise to house its temple. The monk was then left to find his own sponsors to finance the project. Because of the lack of patronage and funds, the project was abandoned and the land was taken by the government and sold to private developers.

Here we can see the tripartite relationship between the Singapore state, the Sangha and the laity in their attempt to restructure and reorganise temple structure. Negotiations and objectives are key factors in determining the success of a project. Whenever possible, the government will most likely permit the retention of the religious sites. However, this is often at a cost. In this particular case, the monk and his patrons had to fulfil certain criteria set down by the government – to construct a large multi-functional temple complex and to provide a home for the less privileged. The monk, on the one hand, had to acquiesce to the demands placed upon him by the state, and on the other hand, to meet the demands of the clan members. As the case study illustrates, the monk antagonised the clan members in his attempt to please the state. This led to the withdrawal of support from the clan members whose vested interest in preserving the clan identity and their patron gods is stronger than their commitment to Buddhism. To the clan members, a clan temple is not only a religious space but also a communal space, where individuals or groups of clan members could congregate and socialise, ensuring that the identity of the clan would be preserved. Anything falling short of this was not worth venturing. Thus, for them, the merger of Temple A and Temple B was not a worthy cause if its identity could not be retained.

THE TEMPLE AS A WELFARE SPACE

The development of the temple as a provider of welfare coincides with the varying strategies implemented by the Chinese community to cope with changes within the Singapore society. The strategies taken by both the temple and the Sangha have therefore to be seen within this wider context.

The relationship between religion and charity has been an intimate one. The Buddhist Sangha has, since its formation, taken on the role of a provider of charity and welfare for the less fortunate public. Much of its work in this area, because of its small scale, has generally gone unnoticed and unacknowledged by the general public, except for those who have been at the receiving end. In recent years, the Sangha and temples have formalised their charity work and provide and run welfare homes. Their work in this area is now being recognised by the general public and the State.

In this area, the State has consciously encouraged the religious institutions to play an active role in the provision of welfare facilities. The Singapore government does not subscribe to the theory of a welfare state – only in dire situations would the state assist those in hardship. The result is that only those in abject poverty are given monetary welfare handouts. As part of the state ideology of self-reliance, the government channels its resources to education, training, housing, public works and other ends which are beneficial to the whole community.

In the 1980s, this ideology of self-reliance was intensified, as the state encouraged different institutions and groups to assist the less privileged groups. The role of community organisations in charity and welfare work has been enshrined in the White Paper "Shared Values" to further encourage this form of communal commitment to the overall development of individuals, especially the less privileged ones. The "Shared Values" states that

> "We are seeking a balance between the community and the individual, not promoting one to the exclusion of the other... The need for the community to support the individual, and especially show compassion to the less fortunate, surfaced repeatedly in the discussions on Shared Values.
>
> One way Singaporeans can put society above self and show concern for others is by participating personally in this effort. Many Singaporeans volunteer to do community work. Many more contribute to community and welfare programmes. Such community efforts not only help in a practical way to solve the problems of the poor, but also strengthen the sense of togetherness, cohesion, and self-reliance of the society" (Shared Values, 1991: 7).

The roles to be played by the communities were further highlighted:

> The Chinese clan associations are good examples of community support. In the colonial period, they played a large role helping new arrivals to establish themselves, providing education for the children, looking after the sick, and even burying dead members who had no families here. It was not as though the individual members had any automatic rights to welfare, but the clan, and particularly those members who had done well, felt a strong social responsibility to help their brethren.

The Malays too have a similar tradition of "*gotong royong*", or mutual help. This is the way the community undertakes projects for the general good, or helps out particular individuals who are in need of support. Even today, many Malays still practise this "kampung spirit" in the housing estates, by forming welfare committees or Muslim benevolent organisations.

The Indians, like the Chinese, are organised in sub-ethnic groups: the Tamils Representative Council, the Singapore Ceylon Tamils' Association, the Singapore Kerala Association (for Malayalees), and the Singapore Khalsa Association (for Sikhs). More recently, the Singapore Indian Development Association (SINDA) has been formed to provide comprehensive social services to all Indian groups.

Such community support for individuals will keep Singapore a humane society. At the same time, it helps us avoid the dependent mentality and severe social problems of a welfare state as experienced in many developed countries (Shared Values: 7).

The vision outlined by the Prime Minister, Goh Chok Tong, is to develop a more compassionate society under the directive of the Ministry of Community Development, together with civic, ethnic, voluntary and community organisations.

As the religious organisations in Singapore progress towards the 21st Century, the challenge for them is to find a niche where they can justify their existence in a modern and compassionate society. To a certain extent, the finding of a new niche is necessary, as new generations of Singaporeans are presently questioning the value of religion in the modern Singapore society. Within the Chinese community, there is a high level of dissatisfaction and scepticism of Chinese religious syncretism. This has prompted the Buddhist temples and Sangha to search for new roles to legitimise their existence. This, together with the encouragement of the state, has resulted in a formalisation of the religious institution as a provider of welfare and charity.

Religious institutions have traditionally been the avenues of charity and welfare work. So, it comes as no surprise that they have taken on a renewed interest and expanded the scope of their welfare activities in response to modern demands. Within a Weberian framework, it is a "rational adjustment to the world". Since its early days, the Buddhist Sangha has been involved in various welfare projects. It is possible to divide its involvement in welfare and charity works into three phases. Phase One stretched from the post Second World War to post-independence years, coinciding with the economic and social restructuring of the Singapore nation-state. Phase Two stretched from the early 1970s to the 1980s, when rapid industrialisation and development took place. Phase Three started from the 1990s as Singapore became part of the newly-industrialised nations.

During Phase One, it was not uncommon for the temple to provide food and sometimes, temporary living space for those in need. This was particularly so if the temple became separated from clan associations and functioned as an independent entity. Members of the Sangha, especially the monks, also provided some form of counselling to those in need of a sympathetic ear. This was especially important in an immigrant society where there was an absence of facilities for this. So, the Sangha, as a neutral party, served this important role. To a certain degree, the temple and the Sangha can be seen as the predecessor of the modern day Chinese welfare system in Singapore.

The Chinese temple also served as a kind of "tea house" where the poor, the destitute and the social misfits could be assured of some kind of material support. The temple rarely turned away anyone who needed a bowl of rice or a cup of tea. Right up to the 1970s, there existed a sizeable number of beggars with no kin, no home and no means of meeting their basic needs as they were too old to work. They often relied on temples for food, and sometimes, for shelter. With economic restructuring and strong state discouragement of begging, the physically fit beggars were pushed into productive employment, while the elderly and handicapped were sent to welfare homes. Today there is no begging on the streets of Singapore, although there is a small number of beggars and a handful of physically disabled, all elderly men and women in their sixties and seventies, who station themselves in several big temples. On religious occasions, they line the temple and beg for cash from the devotees. The temples provide them with food, and they use the public facilities for bathing and cleaning themselves and, may sleep within the temple premises. Although several large temples have homes for the elderly, these beggars do not fulfil the criteria set by the government and cannot be admitted to the homes. Having no other alternative home and not being able to sleep in the street, the temples have allowed them to "live" within their compounds. If a beggar dies, the temple performs the death rites.

Apart from this, the temple and Sangha also provided tea to the general public. During the early years, when poverty was still the issue, there were many instances when workers and pedestrians could not afford drink or food during their course of travel from one part of town to the next. It was not an uncommon sight for temples to open their doors and provide refreshment to these needy people. Women especially benefited from this gesture, as virtuous women continued to be regarded as those who did not "expose themselves" in public places, thus psychologically preventing them from entering coffee-shops on their own. Visiting a temple for worship and accepting some refreshment there, however, was different. Women would often be seen in temples in twos or threes. Apart from worship, they also engaged in social interaction among themselves, chatting and exchanging news. This takes place even today, as the temple continues to be seen as a gathering ground for social interaction among women, and as it continues to be an accepted norm that they accept offers of drink or light refreshment from the temple.

During the early years, temples also set up tea-stands outside the temple gate and provided tea to passers-by that needed a drink. Often a big pot of Chinese tea and several teacups would be placed on the tea-stand. There would also be a basin of water to rinse cups. Since the 1980s, this facility has been discontinued. Today, people no longer use this facility, for a number of reasons. The economic environment and the subsequent rise in the standard of living mean that the Chinese could afford to buy their own drinks. Furthermore, the rise of the coffee-shop culture means that more men, and also women, patronise coffee-shops where there is social interaction among friends. The coffee-shop has, to a certain extent, replaced the temple as a place of social interaction, especially for men, although the temple continues to be an important place for women.

The temple also provides relief aid in emergency situations. This was especially so during the immediate post-independence years. From 1950s to early 1970s, the temples and the Sangha were involved in emergency work, providing funds, food, clothing and shelter to victims of natural disasters, especially floods and fires. Singapore has a tropical monsoon climate. During the monsoon season, heavy downpours resulted in massive flooding in low-lying areas. Prior to the construction of a comprehensive drainage system in the 1970s, flooding was a frequent occurrence. Many families, in both rural and urban areas, were affected. Fire was the other major hazard. As late as the 1960s, residential buildings, especially those in rural villages, were built primarily from wood and palm-leaves. It was not uncommon that a whole village burned to the ground as a result of fire. In the urban centres, badly-connected electrical circuits of old pre-war shophouses was the main cause of fire, and it was a frequent sight that rows of shophouses were ablaze because of these faulty connections. These fire victims needed relief aid to help them through their difficult moments.

While the State provided some kinds of emergency relief for these victims, it was insufficient. Much relief was left to private organisations. The temple played its role by rounding up its supporters and helping these victims. The temple and the Sangha rarely offered cash, which was often given by the state or large charitable institutions. They mobilised the devotees of the temple to provide aid and prepared communal meals for the victims. Sometimes its devotees would help collect used clothing and food items from the public and distribute them to the victims. Likewise, temples were also used as temporary shelters, along with schools and community centres.

The temple and the Sangha have shown themselves true to the Buddhist notion of compassion, ready to assist in relief work. The monks regard one of their primary responsibilities to be assisting others. In this way, the bodhisattva ideal is expressed in compassion and willingness to assist others. These monks state that "it is only natural that we help in whatever small ways we can"; "we exist for such purposes"; "we cannot isolate ourselves from the rest of the community"; "it was never the Mahayana Buddhist tradition to only shut ourselves away from the community and *xiu-xin*", and "how can we *xiu-xin* at ease when we know that there are so many who are crying out for help"?

The general public also responded positively to these relief efforts. Both the Shenists and Buddhists felt that it was right that the Sangha came out openly to assist the victims and to open their doors to them. They felt that public donations were important, as there were insufficient relief funds provided by the state. While the temples and the Sangha were not wealthy, they became rallying points where the public could place their donations, in cash and kind, and these rapidly reached the victims. They also felt that it was important that the Chinese community express a united sense of communalism and that the different dialect groups and clan associations gather together for a good cause. The temple thus reinforced Chinese identity and helped the Chinese to locate themselves within the wider community. By bringing the various groups of Chinese together, the temple cuts across the dialect and clan boundaries and allowed the different groups to interact with one another. It enabled the Chinese to go beyond their social networks and engage in wider social relationships. The breaking down of social barriers among the different dialect groups was also attributed to the Mandarin language, the common communicative medium among them. Some Chinese even mastered various Chinese dialects, allowing further social interaction among them.

THE TEMPLE AS A BENEVOLENCE HALL (*SHAN-TANG*)

Another important provision of the Chinese temple and its Sangha members is the establishment of the *shan-tang*, literally benevolence hall. When the early Chinese migrants arrived, they also brought along their understanding of the Chinese medical and health system, their understanding of illnesses and diseases, and their knowledge of herbal medicines and cures, heat therapy and acupuncture. The Chinese have continued to depend greatly on this knowledge in their treatment of a wide range of new tropical illnesses and diseases.

The benevolence hall functioned as a clinic where the Chinese physicians treated and dispensed herbal medicine. Some Sangha members were also trained as physicians. The benevolence hall is known as *shan-tang* because its aim is charity. Patients were treated by a trained physician, who could either be a Buddhist monk, a Daoist priest or a lay person. In temples where the monks were qualified physicians, the treatment was done by them. Otherwise, a trained Daoist priest or a lay person would be invited to treat patients on a voluntary basis. In this case, they received no payment but it was the accepted norm that those who were treated give small donations to the physician, often in the form of a red packet containing a small sum of money. During the early years, many of those who visited were extremely poor and the amount they contributed was only a few cents. This contribution to the physician was different from their contribution to the temple, which was incense for the gods, a gesture of appreciation and gratitude shown by grateful patients. While the monetary economy was beginning to take root within the immigrant community, there were also many social actions that did not demand payment in monetary form. Money was considered an important medium for exchanges of goods and services but it was culturally incorrect to offer money as appreciation for virtuous acts. Virtuous acts had to be repaid with "gratitude and feelings from the heart". However, the patients' red packets contained money.

After consultation, the physician would write out a herbal remedy for the illness and the patients would then visit a herbal shop to buy the herbal remedy. During the early years, when the *shan-tang* within the temple was also a herbal shop with a wide range of herbs, patients usually purchased the herbs there. At present, most herbal remedies have to be purchased from a traditional herbal shop (*yao-cai-dian*).

The *shan-tang* fulfilled its functions during the earlier years when the Chinese community was undergoing tremendous social and economic transformation. It has now become an institution belonging to the immediate past. The *shan-tang* that existed within the temple premises is no longer in existence. Some have disappeared along with the smaller temples that were victims of the urban renewal or development programmes of the 1970s. Others have shut down because of dwindling demands and competition from other forms of medical houses.

While the *shan-tang* has been an extremely important social institution, providing an essential service to a large majority of the Chinese and also to other ethnic groups, its position is gradually being replaced by others. As a benevolence hall, its role was limited primarily to those in need but as the Singapore society progressed, the Chinese community has accumulated more wealth and individual Chinese have experienced a rise in the standard of living and accrued substantial wealth, so there is less need to rely on welfare. Most people are now able to pay for the medical services they need, irrespective of whether they are Western or traditional ones.

BUDDHIST FREE CLINICS

However, an important reason for the disappearance of the benevolence hall is its metamorphosis into the modern Buddhist Free Clinic which continues to treat patients using traditional Chinese medicine. These clinics, with their bureaucratic organisation, employ updated technological knowledge, use modern equipment and have comprehensive services. They now provide alternative health care treatment to Singaporeans. In the future, the Sangha desires to establish a hospital based on the Chinese medical system of healthcare and treatment, which uses natural cures and medicines, in accordance with the present global trend towards alternative medicine, herbal medicine, acupuncture, naturopathy and homeopathy.

As early as the 1960s there were already plans to establish free clinics to provide medical treatment according to the Chinese medical system. One monk, Venerable Shong-Kai, with training in Chinese medicine, felt a need to provide such services to certain sectors of the Chinese population. Some of the elderly people told me that in the 1950s and 1960s they had very little knowledge of Western medicine and did not trust pills. They did not know what they were, and many felt that after taking the pills their illnesses had worsened, so they continued to rely on herbal remedies. Sometimes, they took both Western pills and herbal remedies at the same time.

The shift from *shan-tang* to free clinic indicates a move from an informal to a formal structure as dictated by the bureaucratic requirement set down in legislation and the expanding needs of the population. As a non-profit charitable institution, it has to formally register with the Registrar of Companies. As such, it is required to have a constitution spelling out its objectives and its trusteeship, executive council and administrative structure. Thus, the primary objective of the clinics is to "work for the welfare of the poor and sick. Patients, irrespective of sex, race and creed, who are in strained financial condition may be given Chinese medicine and treatment, free of charge". In line with Buddhist morality, the clinics do "not treat patients with venereal or infectious diseases or patients injured or wounded because of fighting" (Buddhist Federation Free Clinic Constitution).

The first Buddhist free clinic was established in 1969. This was an extension of the *shan-tang* concept, and the clinic was located within one of the earliest Chinese temples, Pu Toh See Temple, located amidst a large Chinese population. A new wing was constructed to house the clinic. The primary reason was to cut down on cost. Another consideration was to locate the clinic in a densely-populated Chinese district to facilitate access to the clinic. Pu Toh See Temple fulfilled this criterion.

During the early days, patients were given free treatments, and the needy were given free medicine as well. Today, patients are charged a nominal registration fee of $1 per visit with fees waived for those who request it. Likewise a nominal charge has been levied for the medicine with a waiver for those who request it. The number of patients using this clinic increased overwhelmingly from a mere 2,510 in 1969 to over 200,000 in 1974 and to over 400,000 patients in 1982. This increase has been viewed as a positive indication of the need to provide alternative medical care to the general population. The high demand has prompted the Singapore Buddhist Free Clinics to open up more branches. Today, the Singapore Buddhist Free Clinic has six branches (five clinics and one rehabilitation centre) under the central management of the Singapore Buddhist Free Clinic. Since its formation till today, it has treated over 12 million patients. Patients go there for acupuncture treatment as well as traditional Chinese medicine (http://www.sbfc.org.sg).

In its management board, the president is a monk and he is assisted by a team of lay people who look after the daily operation of the Singapore Buddhist Free Clinic. They include his deputy, secretary, treasurer, medical superintendent and several committee members. Two auditors audit the finances of the Free Clinic. The monk heads the presidency because he is the *paters familias* and his advice is sought on most decisions. In reality, it is the lay members who wield the most power and take charge of the daily operation and management. As a formal non-profit institution, it is accountable to the state and its members for its operations and activities. Both the state and the members can voice their satisfaction or discontent through various channels open to them. The state, through its Registrar of Companies and Ministry of Home Affairs and Ministry of Community Development, can prevent undesirable activities from taking place within the clinics by giving warning if it sees the clinic straying from its objectives. As a last resort, it can refuse the clinic a licence to operate. The lay community can also cast a vote of no confidence on the executive and branch committees if they are not performing their tasks. Likewise, they can also register their dissatisfaction by withdrawing their financial support.

Because of the need for public accountability, the State has systematically encouraged the formalisation of institutional structures among voluntary, benevolent, welfare and religious institutions. All Buddhist temples and the Sangha Council are now public institutions. The monks and nuns are often consulted for religious and moral matters. They can also be physicians if they are trained and qualified to do so. However, today, they are not involved in temple administration. During the early years monks were decisive in the management of the *shan-tang*, but this is not so presently. This check on the influence, strength and power of the Sangha is deliberate, as the state regards religion as a sensitive element and is cautious about its roles and activities. In encouraging religious institutions to provide welfare facilities and charity to the less privileged, the state is careful to ensure that the powers of the religious institutions are confined within a stipulated boundary.

As the government encourages private and religious institutions to contribute to charity and the welfare of its population, it also provides incentives for them. The Charities Act of 1982 provided fiscal privileges. An institution registered as a charitable organisation under the Societies Act (cao 262) before 1 January 1983 is entitled to tax exemption, including property tax as well as government subsidy.

As non-profit charities, the clinics operate on private funds generated mostly from public donations, and individual temples, monks and nuns often appeal to their adherents for donations. A handful of wealthy philanthropists are often counted on to give large donations to worthy causes of this nature. However, small sums ($5 to $200) usually form a constant pool of ready resources for operating and maintaining these clinics. Most temples organise an annual drive for donations for the clinics. Lay people also help to raise funds through personal ties and social networks with friends, colleagues and employers. Apart from this, the Singapore Buddhist Free Clinic raised funds from their annual and other events such as walkathon and their anniversary banquet and celebrations. They also issued charity vouchers and these can be used as presents or condolences in place of cash or wreaths (http://www.sbfc.org.sg). Since 1997, the Singapore Buddhist Free Clinic has become a member of the Health Endowment Fund under the Ministry of Health and it is now entitled to generous grants from the government to help run its welfare projects.

The funds are divided into two categories of use, and individuals and groups can donate to either category. The first is for the purchase of medicine and medical equipment; the second is for general uses. In the early 1970s, there was a shortage of money and the clinics could barely afford to provide free medical treatment and medicine. Instead of levying a fee, they appealed directly to the public for donations to buy medicine. Since then, the division has worked well for the clinics and has ensured a constant pool of money.

Philanthropy in Singapore has become a way for wealthy Chinese to gain social recognition and an elevation in status, and it is a common practice for welfare institutions to acknowledge large contributions by naming rooms and buildings after the donors. The Buddhist Federation recognises those who contribute more than $5,000 annually as life members, while those who donate over $100 are ordinary members. These two categories of donors have voting rights. But the Sangha fears that vested interests from a few individuals might tarnish the names of the clinics and the Federation, and that the welfare aspect of the clinics might be subordinated to the economic interests of large donors. They prefer small donors who would not have a controlling influence.

PROVISION OF WELFARE HOMES

Provision of welfare homes has now become an important function of the temples. This is particularly so since the 1980s when the state openly encouraged different religions in Singapore to provide welfare homes for the destitute and the less privileged. This is in line with the government's policy of encouraging "corporate welfarism" in the private sector to provide accommodation to less privileged persons for a fee paid by their families (Chua, 1982: 326-328). The immediate Singapore family is also taken to task for not looking after aged parents, culminating with the introduction of the Maintenance of the Elderly Parents Act, making it obligatory for children to look after their elderly parents (*Straits Times*, 26 August 1991). The government thus confines its assistance to counselling and encouraging certain activities. Its policy towards helping senior citizens is outlined thus:

> Elderly Singaporeans aged 60 years and above will increase from the present nine percent of the population to 11 percent in 2000, and to 26 percent in 2030. Senior citizens should continue to be an active and valued part of the community. We will encourage more Senior Citizens' Activity Centres, Senior Citizens' Clubs and other family-oriented programmes to be set up to help senior citizens remain active in the community.

> We will work with community and voluntary welfare
> organisations to provide community-based day-care, respite and
> residential care facilities for the frail aged. Over the next five years,
> 11 new homes will be built, increasing the number of residential
> places by 50 percent. (Goh Chok Tong, 1992: 31).

The 11 new welfare homes built by the government from 1993-97 have a capacity to house a total number of 1,500 aged and destitute. Criteria for admission was stringent and few gained admission. But this is inadequate. In contrast, there are over 40 residential homes run by voluntary groups. The government thus encourages temples to build and run welfare homes for not only the aged but also handicapped children. In an attempt to streamline welfare policies, some temple-based welfare homes now work in collaboration with the Social Welfare Department and only take in recommended inmates. These temples are provided with a subsidy by the state.

Several Chinese Buddhist temples have established welfare homes for the aged. They include the Tai Pei Old Folks' Home, attached to Tai Pei Temple; Evergreen Old Folks' Home, attached to Phor Khar See Temple (the largest temple in Singapore); and Singapore Buddhist Welfare Services Old Folks' Home. All three only admit elderly men and women on the recommendation of the Social Welfare Department and do not take in any others who come to them from other sources. Apart from these, the Metta Welfare Association, linked to the Golden Pagoda Temple operates nine centres providing care and welfare services.

These welfare homes conform to the guidelines laid down for voluntary welfare homes. The homes provide spacious accommodation, and are equipped with a gymnasium and/or a recreation room. A trained nurse is on service on a daily basis. The homes also organise handicraft sessions to help residents utilise their time productively. Religious services are conducted to cater to their spiritual development and the elderly are encouraged to attend and participate in prayer services. At the Tai Pei Old Folks' Home, there is an in-house clinic to take care of general medical needs. At the other two, voluntary medical practitioners make weekly rounds to check on residents. Those who are in need of specialist services are brought to hospital. Likewise, qualified staff including nurses, doctors, physiotherapists and teachers are recruited to help with the elderly and the autistic children in the homes and centres run by Metta Welfare Association.

EXPANSION OF WELFARE FACULTIES[1]

Since the 1990s, many Buddhist organisations have formalised their role as providers of various types of welfare facilities and services to the general public. Today, there are sixty such Buddhist organisations. Their welfare facilities and services can be broadly divided into three main types. The first includes community homes and centres that provide home and care facilities for the elderly and needy. These consist of homes for the aged; home and social services for the socially marginalised groups in the community, such as drop-in centres for recovered and recovering drug addicts; and residential homes and help services for the sick elderly, the aged and destitute female elderly and the needy. The second type of facilities and services include the provision of centres and services in health services and education, such as dialysis centres for kidney patients and day activity centres for the intellectually disabled. Some centres provide counselling, rehabilitation services, physiotherapy, occupational therapy services and support for patients affected by an array of illnesses including stroke, arthritis and other diseases, as well as the chronically ill. They also provide loan of medical equipment for patients from low-income groups. The third type includes the provision of educational facilities and services to the general community such as childcare and studentcare centres in various housing estates as part of Buddhist involvement in community care.

One of the key characteristics of present Buddhist organisations in their role as welfare provider is that each one is involved in the provision of a variety of welfare services. This is in contrast to the earlier Buddhist organisations which generally only provided one type of welfare service. An example is the Golden Pagoda Temple which operates the Metta Welfare Association (MWA). Under the umbrella of the MWA, there are nine affiliated centres which provide an array of services and facilities. In 1995, it established the Metta Day Care Activity Centre for the Intellectually Disabled. In 1998, it established the Metta Day Rehabilitation Centre for the Elderly and a neighbourhood Yu Neng Metta Student Care Centre One for the South East District. In 2000, it established the Metta Home for the intellectually disabled and Metta Hospice Care. In 2001, it further established Metta School for students with learning disabilities and another neighbourhood Metta Student Care Centre in the North East district. In 2002, a second Yu Neng Metta Student Care Centre Two was established.

In 2001, the MWA had 136 staff with an annual expenditure of $4.3 million, funded primarily by government grants, sponsorships and donations (Metta Welfare Association Annual Report 2001). Apart from this, the association, in conjunction with the temple, organised fund-raising activities such as the sale of Chinese New Year cakes, mooncakes and Christmas cakes; the Metta Charity Walk and Charity Draw; and the I-Charity golf and charity banquets. A second example is the Foo Hai Ch'an Monastery which, since 1994, established and operates the Ren Ci Hospital, the first hospital operated by the Buddhist community in Singapore. The monastery also established the Foo Hai Buddhist Cultural and Welfare Association which manages four welfare centres and facilities: the Aspiration Child Care Centre in Tampines, the Foo Hai Elderly Daycare Centre in Marine Parade, a childcare and studentcare centre in Bedok North and the Wan Qing Lodge Day Centre for the Elderly.

What motivates Buddhist organisations to expand their delivery of welfare services and facilities and becoming all-encompassing in reaching out to the socially less privileged and marginalised population is the vision of the monastic leaders and their interpretation of religious doctrine. The abbot of the Foo Hai Ch'an Monastery, Venerable Shi Ming Yi put it:

> ...Buddhism talks about compassion, and compassion should not
> just be a theoretical thing but it should be put into practice. So

putting it into practice through doing some social work, I believe,
is also a way for people to get to know Buddhism and to cultivate
compassion in us.

A second characteristic of present Buddhist organisations
involved in the welfare sector is their move towards transnational
welfare works. In the early years, some of the wealthier Buddhist
organisations would provide financial assistance to overseas Buddhist
organisations and poverty-stricken or natural disaster-stricken
countries on an *ad hoc* or needs basis. Today, some of these Buddhist
organisations have formalised their welfare roles on a transnational
basis. For example, the Foo Hai Ch'an Monastery has extended its
religious compassion to Sri Lanka. It is in the process of building a
welfare home called the "Village of Compassion" and training Sri
Lankans as care and management people. Venerable Shi Ming Yi has
also started Buddhist counselling services in Hong Kong. Likewise,
the abbot of the Golden Pagoda Temple, Venerable Shi Fazhao has
also been actively involved in transnational charity and welfare works
and helped with temple rebuilding in Thailand, Myanmar, Cambodia,
China, Nepal and Sri Lanka.

A third characteristic is that many of these welfare homes and
facilities are accessible to people and children from different ethnic
and social background. This is in contrast to the earlier welfare homes
that generally admitted only the Chinese. At the same time, their
workers and volunteers also come from different ethnic backgrounds.
For example, in the Metta Welfare Association, the supervisor of the
Metta Hospice Care and a senior staff nurse of the Metta Home are
Muslims. Likewise the principal of the Metta School is a Christian
and the vice principal is a Muslim. This fits neatly into the
government's push for a multi-religious and multi-cultural framework
for work and social life in Singapore.

A STRATEGIC STATE – RELIGION PARTNERSHIP

While the proliferation of welfare facilities and services organised by
the Buddhist organisations can be attributed to the Buddhist

understanding of compassion, it can also be argued that the actions of the state have facilitated their formalisation and expansion. Through the years, the state and religious organisations have developed a strategic partnership in the delivery of welfare services and facilities to the general public. The Singapore government has mapped out areas where welfare services and facilities are required and encouraged the religious institutions to take up the role as welfare providers. At the same time, it has laid out guidelines to ensure that homes and facilities set up meet state requirements which protect the interests of the elderly, the children and the socially disadvantaged Singaporeans under the organisation's care. For example, Metta School operates under the Ministry of Education (MOE) Special Education guidelines, with a proper school management committee and its curriculum needs to be approved by MOE.

Both human and financial resources are required to establish welfare homes and facilities. While it is often easy to encourage volunteers to perform community works, welfare home and services require both full-time work personnel as well as sizeable financial resources. There is a very small number of wealthy Buddhist organisations and temples, but most religious organisations on their own find it hard to have sufficient financial resources to start up and maintain these services. Given the fact that the state has actively encouraged these institutions to provide welfare facilities and services, it has established legislation to provide financial assistance to these organisations to help them in their welfare work.

Such religious organisations can apply for an annual grant from the government to help defray the running costs of these homes and centres, with the amount of grant given varying from institution to institution. One example is the Metta School for the intellectually disabled where a part of their funding comes from the MOE and another part from the National Council of Social Services (NCSS). Likewise, the NCSS provides grants to many welfare homes run by the religious organisations that are its members. Membership of the NCSS provides these organisations with legitimacy in the eyes of the state and facilitates their application for financial grants. At the same time, it legitimises their activities in the eyes of the general public. As such, many of these Buddhist organisations have become affiliated to this state bureaucracy, facilitating a workable state-religion partnership.

This state-religion partnership has both advantages and disadvantages. The key advantage is that the strict guidelines laid down by the government will ensure quality assurance in the delivery of care and prevent mistreatment and exploitation of the young, elderly and intellectually-disabled people. This is very important to ease the anxiety of their parents and relatives. However, one of the drawbacks is that these religious-based welfare centres and homes have to observe the tight guidelines laid down by the NSCC or the relevant government authorities. For example, the religious-based dialysis centres for kidney patients cannot accept patients above the age of sixty as it is the guidelines laid down by the National Kidney Foundation (NKF). As a result, elderly patients are known to have been rejected from such services and had to incur huge bills for their dialysis treatment in private clinics or government hospitals.

Apart from grants given to run homes and centres, the government also leases land at nominal prices to those religious institutions which want to build welfare homes and service centres; however, religious institutions need to raise their own funds to cover construction costs and internal furnishings. Likewise, the government also charges nominal rents in housing estates for the various centres run by these religious institutions as part of their community care projects. Depending on the size and scale of each home constructed by the religious institution, the overall cost can be a hefty sum of over several million dollars. Fund-raising by these institutions becomes a crucial and major activity to ensure the fruition of these building projects, which can sap the limited energies and resources of their organisations and steer their main attentions away from their welfare activities.

Policy Implications

Several viable recommendations can be made to ensure the continuation of the above strategic partnership between the Singapore state and the religious institutions:

(1) The state's encouragement and support for the religious institutions in their efforts to focus and expand the provision of welfare facilities and services need to be continued. This can be done by providing land for such purposes free of charge, so as to reduce the financial burden of these religious institutions, many of which do not have endowments but depend primarily on donations from their adherents and the public for such purposes.

(2) These centres should be allowed more autonomy in running the welfare facilities and services.

(3) There is a need for quality control but this can be achieved through an independent body and not necessarily through government-related institutions.

(4) The government can provide financial and other incentives, to encourage these centres to become even more multi-cultural and multi-ethnic in nature, given that all of them provide services to Singaporeans irrespective of ethnic background as a matter of principle.

(5) Given the growing transnational approach to the delivery of welfare services, the government might want to consider matching funds for such services for their effective delivery. This is particularly so as such religious organisations also act as goodwill ambassadors that enhance the image not only of the religious organisations themselves but also Singapore as a caring and compassionate country in the global setting.

CONCLUSION

By participating in the process of religious modernisation, Buddhism has consciously chosen a welfare niche for itself. In so doing, it establishes social legitimacy through its compassion for the population. This welfare niche is also carefully nurtured by the state. Thus, what we have today is a multifunctional Buddhist temple, with its existence intricately tied to the needs of the Singapore state and its people, and simultaneously serving as a sacred space and a welfare space.

It is thus possible to argue that the Singapore state and religious institutions, each with its own agenda, are able to forge a strategic partnership over the provision of welfare facilities and services for the benefit of the socially and economically less-privileged sectors of the Singapore population. Given that Buddhist institutions are searching for new roles in an increasingly globalised Singapore and the world, it is likely that Buddhist compassion as articulated in the provision of welfare facilities and services will take centre stage in years to come.

NOTE

1. The following sections reproduced from "Delivering Welfare Services in Singapore: A Strategic Partnership between Buddhism and the State" by Kuah-Pearce Khun Eng, first appeared in *Religious Diversity in Singapore*, edited by Lai Ah Eng (Singapore: ISEAS and IPS, 2008). Reproduced here with the kind permission of the publishers, Institute of Southeast Asian Studies, Singapore <http://bookshop.iseas.edu.sg> and the Institute of Policy Studies, Singapore.

CHAPTER 6

Experimenting with Religious Values as Asian Values

INTRODUCTION

> We see a society in Singapore where people with the ability can get rich quickly. Having got the money, unless they have solid values based on what the great civilisations espoused, they could waste their money. Heaven knows what they will do. They will not bring up their children properly. Sooner or later society will degenerate (Goh Keng Swee, quoted in *Straits Times*, 29 December 1981).

The belief that Singaporeans cannot be trusted to look after themselves is one important factor that pushes the government to intervene constantly in the welfare of its citizens. Critics have unanimously labelled the Singapore government as being "paternalistic". More specifically, its former Prime Minister, Lee Kuan Yew, acts as a Confucian patriarch, constantly looking over his shoulder to make sure that the nation he has largely created does not fall short of his expectations. Despite these criticisms, many of the older generation Chinese share his aspirations and fear that the younger generations are adopting undesirable "Western" values. Some feel Lee and his government have rightly echoed their concerns.

This perception is reinforced by a rapid rise in the nuclear family structure, the breakdown of the traditional family unit and a declining emphasis on family values such as filial piety and loyalty, which led to the introduction of the Maintenance of Elderly Parents Act. A sizeable group, about 20% of highly educated women, in the 40-44 age group remain single. Others have opted for careers and small families with one or two children (Kuah, 1997). Moreover, many young men and women are opting for cohabitation, thereby putting family and marriage, which the state considers as core institutions, at risk. Educated married couples are seen as not producing sufficient children to add to a (decreasing) pool of future talents. These have become major preoccupations of the government, which sees the introduction of Western liberal ideas as primary threats to the moral fabric of the Singapore society. It has thus appointed itself as the moral guardian and introduced "Asian values" for its citizens.

THE GREAT DEBATE ON ASIAN VALUES

In the late 1980s, in a search for an alternative paradigm to restructure the society, Lee Kuan Yew, the then Prime Minister, advocated the implementation of a set of Asian values. Subsequently, other Asian leaders, notably the Malaysian Prime Minister Mahathir Mohamad, have become strong advocates of Asian Values for Asian societies. Consequently, the debate on Asian Values began in fervour. To a certain degree, what they are advocating is that there is an Asian path to modernity in addition to a Western path.

The popularisation of a set of Asian Values for Asian societies has its roots in the rapid economic growth and the success story of the various Asian societies. The emergence of the four mini-dragons (Taiwan, Hong Kong, Korea and Singapore) and the various Asian Tigers (Malaysia, Thailand, Indonesia and Vietnam) from the late 1970s onwards have led Asian leaders to search for an explanation for the economic growth miracle. The first wave of growth that involved the mini-dragons of Taiwan, Hong Kong, Korea and Singapore has led Lee Kuan Yew to advocate the existence of a Confucian Ethic that propelled these so-called Confucian-based countries to succeed. The Confucian Ethic is characterised by a set of desirable work values namely diligence, loyalty, humanity, self-sacrifice, teamwork and co-operation. The central argument here is that the rapid economic growth in late Capitalism can only be achieved if the workers possessed the above mentioned values and because the Asian workers possessed this desirable Confucian Ethic, Asia experienced the so-called "Asian Growth Miracle".

Apart from proposing the desirable Confucian Ethic for economic growth, political leaders in Asia have also advocated the need to create a set of Asian values for the purpose of nation-building. At the forefront are again Lee Kuan Yew and his ministerial cabinet who consciously put forward a set of Asian values as part of their nation-building programme. In their attempt to create an acceptable set of Asian values, the Singapore team explored the various Asian religions and argued for religious values to be incorporated as part of the desirable Asian value system.

As Singapore was busy implementing and incorporating the desirable Asian and religious values as part of its nation-building programme, scholars and commentators in the Western world have criticised this move as a way that Singapore justified its authoritarian rule. As such, the advocacy and implementation of Asian values began to be interpreted as justification by Asian societies to continue with authoritarian and undemocratic way of government. The implementation of Asian values was then regarded as the antithesis to modern human rights concepts and practices (de Bary, 1998:3; Zialcita, 1999; Manan, 1999 and Surin, 1999).[1] Others however took a broader view of Asian Values and explored various Asian religions and their contributions to this debate (Cauquelin, Lim and Mayer-Konig, 1998). The crux of their debate is their support of an Asian value system as an alternative path to modernity. It is in this context that the Singapore government began to explore religious values as potential Asian Values and national values for its multi-religious population.

RELIGIOUS VALUES AS ASIAN VALUES

In searching for a set of Asian values, the Singapore state looks to the existing religious values that would be acceptable Asian moral values to its people. The Asian values should ideally allow the individual, family, school and other social groups, community and the nation to work towards a common aim: to create individuals with the desired values and a community with common values and goals. The values should also ideally assist in the political and economic development of the country.

The government aims to create an "Ideal Singaporean", embodying the desirable values. One way to establish this moral value parameter is to promote selected religious values as desirable values through public campaigns and education. This was succinctly expressed by Lee Kuan Yew in his letter to the Ministry of Education.

> The litmus test of a good education is whether it nurtures citizens who can live, work, contend, and co-operate in a civilised way. Is he loyal and patriotic? Is he, when the need arises, a good soldier, ready to defend his country and so protect his wife and children and his fellow citizens? Is he filial, respectful to his elders, law-abiding, humane and responsible? Does he take care of his wife and children and parents? Is he tolerant of Singaporeans of different races and religions? Is he clean, neat, punctual and well-mannered? ....
>
> We have a mix of immigrants from different parts of China, India and the Malay world. We have to give our young basic common norms of social behaviour, social values and moral precepts, which can make up the rounded Singaporeans of tomorrow. The best features of our different ethnic, cultural, linguistic and religious groups must be retained. The best of the East and West must be blended to advantage in the Singaporean. Confucianist ethics, Malay traditions and the Hindu ethos must be combined with sceptical Western methods of scientific inquiry, the open discursive methods in the search for truth. We have to discard obscurantist and superstitious beliefs and practices of the East....
>
> The greatest value in teaching and learning of Chinese is the transmission of the norms of social and moral behaviour. This means principally Confucianist beliefs and ideas, of man, society and the state (Lee Kuan Yew, 1979).

Various aspects of religious values can be harnessed to promote desirable behaviour to help with modernising Singapore and to counteract Westernisation. The Singapore state views with alarm an increasing number of Westernised Singaporeans with "the loss of faith in traditional religions" and understands that "many Chinese have given up Daoism, Buddhism or ancestor worship" (*Straits Times*, 12 Jan. 1989). The ruling elite fear that "the next generation is not growing up with the same outlook as their parents. Nor is it acquiring updated values, which their parents' generation have carefully thought out and imbued in them. As a society, we are absorbing ideas from outside faster than we can digest them, in danger of losing our sense of direction" (*Straits Times*, 12 Jan. 1989). The government feels the need to inculcate "a clear set of values, strongly held and shared by Singaporeans [which-sic] can help us to develop an identity, bond ourselves together, and determine our own future" (*Straits Times*, 12 Jan. 1989). The deputy Prime Minister, Lee Hsien Loong, outlined the promotion of an identity in three ways. First, to find common values which all can share; second, to preserve the heritage of our different communities; and third, to ensure that each community also appreciates, and is sensitive to the traditions of the others (*Straits Times*, 12 Jan. 1989).

Lee found the answer in Confucianism and other Asian religions. He saw that the Chinese community, in order to elaborate the abstract values of the National Ideology into concrete examples and vivid stories, must draw upon selected Confucian concepts for several reasons. First, it is the heritage of the Chinese part of the population. Second, it stresses the importance of placing society above self, a key value we want to preserve. And third, many Confucian ideals are still relevant to us. An example is the concept of government by honourable men, who have a duty to do right for the people, and who have the trust and respect of the population (*Straits Times*, 12 Jan. 1989). To him, "this fits us better than the Western concept: that a government should be given as limited powers as possible, and always treated with suspicion unless proven otherwise" (*Straits Times*, 12 Jan. 1989).

Clearly then, Confucianism can be made to contribute positively in assisting in the promotion of a national ideology among the Chinese sector of the population (if the emphasis is correct), for it has to be "revised to fit an urban, industrial society. Confucianism must be brought up to date, and reconciled with other ideas" (*Straits Times*, 12 Jan. 1989). For example, cited Lee, "in China, where traditionally family ties are paramount, this practice led to favouritism of relatives by officials. But in Singapore, we have adopted a clear separation between public office and official duty on the one hand, and private interests and personal obligations on the other. This has enabled us to run a clean and efficient bureaucracy, free of nepotism" (*Straits Times*, 12 Jan. 1989). Moreover, "traditional Confucian family relationships are also strictly hierarchical. Sons owe an absolute duty of filial piety and unquestioning obedience to fathers. Males take precedence over females, brothers over sisters, and the first born over the second and third son. But in Singapore, the parent-child relationship is more respectful rather than one of absolute subordination. Sons and daughters are treated more equally, because of family planning" (*Straits Times*, 12 Jan. 1989).

It is clear from the foregoing that the state intends to use Confucianism to further its interests. For example, a shortage of labour in the industrial sector has resulted in the state encouraging its female population to take on economically productive roles in the name of being good Confucian citizens, putting the needs of the nation ahead of individual needs. Furthermore, the ruling elite do not believe in a welfare state as in the West. It thus promotes the upholding of the family as the basic social unit of the society and filial piety in order that the young look after the elderly parents and uses the Maintenance of Elderly Parents Act as a punitive measure to shame the population into caring for their parents.

The state also enlists the help of the clan associations, Chinese Chambers of Commerce and the media in its efforts to promote Confucianism. Lee openly stated that "Chinese clan associations can help to preserve the Asian identity and values of Singaporeans by taking part in the formulation of a National Ideology" (*Straits Times*, 16 Jan. 1989). He wanted the clan associations "to play an active role, working with the government and grassroot organisations, to identify the core values, find ways to preserve the family unit, and cultivate the spirit of community above self" (*Straits Times*, 16 Jan. 1989). The mass media is also enlisted to write and give publicity to these values. In both the Chinese and English newspapers, a section has been devoted to the discussion of Asian and Confucian values. For example, the Chinese leading newspaper, *Lianhe Zaobao* (United Morning News) carried a regular Sunday column on "Culture and Society" where Confucian ideas were being discussed. Furthermore, the values are also being promoted in the various campaigns initiated by the state. Examples of campaigns are the "Respect your Parents" campaign and the "Productivity" campaign.

The state also sees Confucian values as important to the economic development of Singapore. In the 1980s, there were many discussions about the economic success of the newly-industrialised countries, known as the "Four Little Dragons" of East Asia, and politicians and academics attributed this success to Confucian values (Marishima, 1987; Leung, 1987). This view was also reflected by Lee Kuan Yew in his speech at the Conference on Global Strategies when he said that the Japanese, Vietnamese, Koreans and Chinese shared Confucian values of hard work and thrift. Furthermore, he said that these peoples "have learnt the valuable lesson that to make the greatest progress in the shortest possible time, it is necessary for a people to move in unison. And this implies the need to make sacrifices for the good of the country and its progress" (*Straits Times*, 29 Oct. 1988). Thus to Lee, Singaporeans cannot afford to be complacent and must preserve the five critical relationships stated by the Confucian philosopher Mencius: (1) love between father and son; (2) duty between ruler and subject, (3) distinction (sic) between husband and wife; (4) precedence of old over young; and (5) faith between friends (*New York Times*, 5 November 1988).

Apart from Confucianism, selected values found in major Asian religions have been adopted. The four main religions – Buddhism, Islam, Hinduism and Christianity – were seen as having the ability to provide readily acceptable values that will transform Singaporeans into the "ideal citizens" as outlined above. The state argues that:

> A major part of Singapore's cultural ballast will be the religious
> faith of its citizens. Religion is for many Singaporeans the source
> of their sense of morality, social duty, and concern for their fellow
> men. Religious faith is a constructive social force, so long as those
> practising a religion give full respect to other faiths, and do not
> use religion to pursue political causes... (Shared Values, 1990: 8)

A series of measures is taken to ensure that selected religious values are transmitted to Singaporeans at large. Religious institutions have been encouraged to educate their respective laity on the merits of the desirable Asian values and to translate these values into community actions. Individuals are encouraged to participate in these activities. A special programme called "Religious Knowledge" was introduced as part of the moral education programme for all secondary school students in 1984 – although this programme was abandoned in 1989. To ensure that the various religions co-exist amicably, the Presidential Council for Religious Harmony was formed in 1992 under the auspices of the President of Singapore.

IMPLEMENTING RELIGIOUS EDUCATION IN SCHOOLS

The belief that moral values have to be consciously learnt and taught constituted the basis for the introduction of Religious Knowledge in schools. Buddhist Studies, Confucian Ethics, Bible Studies, Islamic Studies, Hindu Studies and World Religions were introduced as options within the Religious Knowledge programme. Students were allowed to choose from the various options, subject to formal consent by their parents so as not to conflict with the religious beliefs of the individual family. Neither did it want to make it a convenient avenue for religious groups to proselytise. Thus, it laid out stringent rules governing the teaching of Religious Knowledge.

The various Religious Knowledge options taken by students coincided roughly with their ethnic backgrounds, thereby further reinforcing the ethno-religious mosaic of Singapore society. A further option on World Religions catered to those students who preferred a general approach. However, all the options sought to highlight a set of relevant moral values encapsulated in the Shared Values.

The streamlined approach to Religious Knowledge led to the writing of suitable textbooks for the Confucian Studies, Buddhist Studies, Hindu Studies and World Religions except Bible Studies and Islamic Studies. This task rested with the Curriculum Development Institute of Singapore (CDIS). In this way, a secular socio-functional approach to religion was expounded and Buddhist monks, Hindu priests and Confucian scholars were consulted on scriptural interpretation.

Expounding Secular Values in Buddhist Textbooks

By exploring the contents of the textbooks of these two (one for Secondary Three and one for Secondary Four), it is possible to spell out clearly the desirable moral values expounded by the state. The Buddhist Studies (BS) text stressed two main concepts: Four Noble Truths and the Eightfold Path in Buddhism. Doctrinally, the Four Noble Truths explain the causes of sufferings while the Eightfold Path delineates the way out of suffering. Placing these teachings in lay terms, Buddhist Studies translated these concepts into values such as self-reliance, tolerance, loving-kindness and compassion. For example:

> Because Buddhism respects the right of people to enquire freely and to choose for themselves, it is tolerant towards other faiths. Buddhism teaches one to live in harmony with all regardless of race or religion. This attitude of tolerance is particularly important in a society like Singapore where many races and religions co-exist. (BS.1: 3).

Making use of the concept of the Eightfold Path, Buddhism is extolled as not only teaching desirable virtues, but also right actions. Thus, there are three main categories of actions: those pertaining to the attainment of good conduct (right speech, right action and right livelihood); those that aim at mental development (right effort, right mindfulness and right meditation); and those of right understanding and right thought, that lead to wisdom.

> If one has respect for truth, one will avoid telling lies. When a person consistently avoids telling lies, his relatives, friends and associates will trust him and value his sincerity. But if a person lies for the first time and the lie is not detected by others, he may continue to tell more lies until it becomes part of his nature. He will eventually lose the respect and trust of others. (BS.1: 79).

In the textbook, right livelihood means avoiding trades that are detrimental to the individuals and the community at large. Five categories of harmful trades were identified. They include those dealing with weapons and firearms, the taking of life, the slave trade, intoxicants (especially the drug trade) and poisons. Other desirable values include filial piety, loyalty and those governing the proper role of women within a patriarchy. For example:

> Happy is the woman in this life who is a capable worker, courteous in her ways, who manages her servants well and guards her husband's wealth. Happy is she in the next life who is firm in faith, virtue, charity and wisdom. (BS.1: 102)

Apart from the cultivation of individuals in morality, values on interpersonal relationships and that of society are also important. The *Sigalovada Sutra*, one of the Buddhist scriptures, is used to illustrate the desirable values. It stresses six types of human relationships (parent-child; teacher-pupil; husband-wife; friends; religious teacher-disciple; and employer-employee) (BS.2: 21-24).

The parent-child relationship is considered one of the most important relationships within Singapore society. As the state continues to stress the importance of the family as the core institution for the stability of the society, the type of moral behaviour expected of parents and offspring becomes paramount. With the increasing number of young Singaporeans opting for the nuclear family, there is an increased number of elderly Singaporeans living on their own or sent to nursing homes. This has prompted the government to act on the issue of filial piety. In addition to giving housing priorities to those who opt to live with or in the same district as their parents, Religious Knowledge was implemented precisely to heighten the consciousness and responsibility of young Singaporeans in this area. This is how it is expressed in the text:

> There is happiness and harmony in the home when parents do their best in bringing up their children, taking good care of them and educating them, and when the children appreciate their parents' efforts in providing for their security and well-being. Filial love is a form of respect that children have for their parents. A child may express his gratitude and respect towards his parents by:
>
> (i)   supporting them
> (ii) taking upon himself the duties that they have to perform
> (iii) protecting the family property
> (iv) preserving the family honour
> (v)   making offerings in honour of them and transferring merits to them after their death, [i.e. ancestor worship - sic]
>
> The feeling of parents towards their children is one of tender compassion. Parents protect their children and wish them well. Parents can guide and help their children by:
> (i)   restraining them from unwholesome behaviour
> (ii) teaching them moral values
> (iii) providing for their education
> (iv) helping them to make a good marriage
> (v)   letting them inherit the family wealth at a proper time (BS.2: 21-22)

Likewise, the reinforcement of the roles of parents is highlighted in what the state considers to be important for young Singaporeans. Marriage is an important priority in face of the progressive increase in late marriages and singlehood (Kuah, 1997:36-70). The other area

205

of importance is the relationship between husband and wife. Here again, the increasing divorce rate, separation and cohabitation are seen as major factors that undermine the foundation of the family. Also, in the more traditional Chinese family, the father remains a patriarch until his death. This has often created ill feelings between the patriarch and the sons, and at times has accentuated sibling rivalry because of the fight over family wealth. One way is to encourage the proper division and the relinquishing of wealth at the appropriate time. The state again reminds the respective parties of their duties in this area for the overall stability of the nation.

Likewise, Confucian Ethics (CE) was introduced as another option of Religious Knowledge, aimed at both the Chinese and non-Chinese, since it was introduced as a universal ethical value system with timeless quality. The teaching of Confucian Ethics has the following objectives: "(1) to inculcate Confucian values in the students; (2) to assist them to grow up and lead meaningful lives as upright moral citizens; (3) to make them aware of their cultural and moral heritage; (4) to help them understand the importance of self-cultivation; and (5) to enable them to understand the historical development and modern relevance of Confucianism" (CE.1: preface).

Similar to Buddhist Studies, Confucian Values emphasises the importance of self-cultivation, the process of achieving desirable values, and the various types of human relationships (parents-children; brothers-sisters; husband-wife; friends; and citizens-state). Confucian ethical values of humanity, wisdom, courage, righteousness, propriety, trust, loyalty and compassion are also consciously taught to the students. The textbooks also inform us of the rights and duties of individuals through illustrations using traditional Chinese folk tales. The fear that Chinese culture is fast losing its adherents to Western values made the teaching of Confucian Ethics all the more intense and urgent in the minds of the government leaders and functionaries. These values are illustrated as thus:

> How should we as children behave towards our parents?
> Parents, naturally, are concerned over the welfare of their children.
> They love them, bring them up and provide for them. It is,

therefore, only natural and right that children in return love, respect and take care of their parents, especially when the parents are old and most in need of their support. In other words, it is the duty of children to treat their parents with respect and love in their daily life. This is *xiao* or filial piety.

...It is only courteous and considerate that we inform our parents where we are going and when we shall return so that they do not worry about us unnecessarily. When we see our parents busy with household chores, we could offer to help in whatever way we can...

There are, unfortunately, some people who leave their parents when they are old and need their care and attention most. Instead of looking after their own parents, they find excuses to send their parents to homes for the aged. Can people who behave so irresponsibly be entrusted with other duties and responsibilities? Surely, those who do not care for the well-being of their own parents cannot be relied upon to work for the well-beings of others. (CE.1: 99-101).

Attempts to integrate Confucian values with everyday living and with the values of the state – including the values of the work place and the values of multiculturalism, basic rights and duties, and compassion and care for others – are taught to the students:

Confucians consider that "within the Four Seas all men are brothers". They uphold the principle of universal brotherhood where one should "overflow in love to all" and not merely to one's relations and friends. If we treat all people with the same respect and love just as we treat our brothers or sisters, the world will surely be a more peaceful and happier place to live in. To achieve this, we are recommended to be tolerant and forbearing: "The cultivated person honours the able and virtuous, and bears with all". (Analects XIX: 3). Even though the cultivated person respects ability and virtue, he also accepts all others in society. The Confucian ethical system then, is very tolerant of other cultures and systems of moral or religious belief (CE.2: 120).

207

Selecting Buddhist Studies and Confucian Ethics – Parental Choice

Among the Chinese students, Buddhist Studies[2] and Confucian Ethics[3] were the two most popular options. At school, the Buddhist Studies and Confucian Ethics programmes attracted substantial numbers of students. The nomination of a religious studies programme by individual students was in the hands of the parents and not the students. As religious affiliation continued to be seen as closely tied to ethnicity in the wider society, the Ministry of Education adopted a cautious approach to the issue of choice. The students were not given a choice for fear of offending the parents. The Ministry was also wary of attracting the hostility of the various ethnic groups should the students be allowed to choose a religious programme outside their own religion without parental consent.

In 1983, the Ministry of Education conducted a survey of the choice of religious studies made by the parents for their children for 1984. Over 30% of the parents chose Buddhist Studies, making it the most popular option with Bible Studies capturing 20% of the students. One can attribute the popularity of Buddhist Studies to the desire of many parents to retain cultural continuity. By talking to many parents, I gathered that they feared that, with rapid modernisation, their children would reject many of the traditional Chinese values and practices that they hold to. The introduction of Buddhist Studies and Confucian Ethics were thus viewed favourably by the Chinese as they saw in it a legitimate means of reviving their cultural identity. In 1989, Buddhist Studies attracted 44.4% while Confucian Ethics attracted 17.7% of Secondary Three students (Kuo, 1996: 306). It was likely for the foreseeable future that most Chinese parents would opt for Confucian Ethics and Buddhist Studies for their children had the programme not been prematurely abandoned in 1997.

The writing of the Buddhist Studies and Confucian Ethics textbooks, amidst the voluminous number of books on these two subjects, may seem somewhat superfluous. However, within Singapore's political culture, the significance of rewriting the textbooks cannot be underestimated. These textbooks provide the students and general population with the state's version of Buddhism and

Confucianism, thereby allowing the state to propagate its values through the indigenous religious ideological system. This version of Buddhism and Confucianism is based on pragmatism and rationalism and ties in with the state's goals for a modern rational Singapore society: values that express acceptable moral values, emphasise economic development and political adherence (Kuah, 1990).

EDUCATING SCHOOL TEACHERS FOR THE RELIGIOUS KNOWLEDGE PROGRAMME

Apart from streamlining the textbooks for the religious knowledge programme, the Ministry of Education also produced teachers' guides and trained teachers for the Religious Knowledge programme. The writing of the teachers' guides was undertaken by the Buddhist Team of the Curriculum Development Institute of Singapore (CDIS), which is part of the Ministry of Education. This is to ensure that teachers were taught the appropriate way of teaching various religions to the students. While teachers were encouraged to participate and take up teaching responsibility in religious education, it was often the school principals who would assign the tasks to selected teachers.

(i) Buddhist Studies Teachers' Guide

The Buddhist Studies Team also produced the teachers' guide for the Buddhist Studies. This was not unusual. All planned teaching material produced by the CDIS came in a threefold package of text for students, guidebooks for the teachers and audio-visual materials to supplement the verbal teaching. The teachers' guide provided a step-by-step instruction on how to deal with the subject. The object is to standardise the method of teaching and the elaboration of the content of the course so that it can be taught identically and effectively in all schools. The guide instructs the teachers to articulate the aims of each chapter at the start of the lesson. The use of pictures and slides is recommended for exposing the students to the content. The teaching and the discussions, the guide enjoins, are to have a pragmatic orientation. The teachers should first discuss the text and the topics on Buddhism, and then follow up by highlighting the desired virtues and values. The teachers, at their own discretion, should try to link their lessons to the real-life environment. As an illustration of the last, for instance, in teaching that Buddhism stresses self-reliance, the teacher may ask the students questions like this: "How could one get good examination results?" The answer to be generated from the class should be, "By depending on oneself"; or "Why should we donate to a charitable organisation?" The answer should be "Because it shows compassion and loving-kindness".

Although the teachers are permitted to draw relevant examples on their own initiatives, it is generally required of them that they will not stray away from the guide. A rationalisation for conformity in this teaching advanced by the Ministry of Education is that Religious Knowledge classes should be confined strictly to the teaching of the religion and its values and that they should not be used for proselytisation. The Ministry argues that this is important as the students taking Buddhist Studies might belong to a different religion. To ensure that they do not convert, the students are not allowed to conduct religious prayers or rituals in the sessions. Moreover, they are not allowed to bring in any religious paraphernalia used for worship into the classroom. The teaching is intended to be secular at all times. Knowledge and not faith must be transmitted.

For the same reason, the teachers and schools were not allowed to organise tours to any of the places of worship. This last prohibition was withdrawn when both the schools and the public protested about the extreme character of the regimentation. The arguments raised by the protesters in the media were that the best way a student could get knowledge was through interaction with the religious organisation and the religious personnel. The students could learn the values from the priests as they see them put into practice. The teachers were then allowed to organise tours to the Chinese and Hindu temples, churches and mosques but only for educational purposes. During the visits, the students were not to be given religious instructions by the priests or members of the lay congregation, nor were they allowed to participate in the religious activities. In practice, these were religoius tours where the students were taken to the temple and given the names of the gods and deities in it, were briefed on the history of the institution and if it ran a welfare home, taken to it especially to emphasise the social relevance of it to the nation. The students were lectured on the moral values put into practice by their teachers but were not permitted to attend sermons or discussions.

(ii) Recruitment of Teachers for Buddhist Studies

At the initial stage of the Religious Knowledge programme, it was very difficult to recruit teachers for training in the Buddhist Studies. While some teachers have some understanding of Buddhism, many knew very little of the scripture and the philosophy. Not knowing what was in store, the teachers were apprehensive of teaching Buddhist Studies. Many Chinese teachers told me that the Buddhist Studies had a low status among the teachers and at the Ministry of Education. Some told me that in the educational circles Buddhism was tolerated but Christianity was favoured because of the perceived high-class status of the latter. Some of the teachers were apprehensive that if they participated wholeheartedly in the teaching of the programme, it would be held against them in some way. When I probed them further about the anti-Buddhist environment at school in general, they said that they were not disadvantaged by their personal beliefs. Nevertheless on a personal level, many are caught in a dilemma because of the low esteem Buddhism commanded in the school environment. On the one hand, as educated individuals, they felt embarrassed at holding to a faith that has been defined and occasionally condemned by some people as irrational and superstitious. So most teachers avoid public displays of their faith, keeping it for home. On the other hand, they were unwilling to convert to Christianity. I found that to many teachers, fence-sitting was painful. Many teachers resisted recruitment to training Buddhist Studies passively. Few Buddhist teachers volunteered for the training initially, preferring to teach secular subjects.

As the schools were required to send in their quota of teachers to be trained in the Religious Knowledge courses, some heads of schools took to drafting the teachers into undertaking training. In some schools, this aroused dissatisfaction and complaints over arbitrary selection. There were numerous cases of complaints by teachers who were Christians and who were forced into teaching Buddhist Studies. Some who resented it told me that had they agreed to teach Buddhist Studies, their reservation about the worth of Buddhism would have prejudiced their teaching of the subject. Some of the teachers of Buddhist Studies told the students in the classroom that they did not belong to the religion. I wrote in my notebook the following account of how a teacher conducted the Buddhist studies in her class:

> The teacher, a woman in her thirties, told me that she began the first Buddhist Studies class by telling the Secondary Three students that she is not a Buddhist but a Christian. She was instructed by the principal to take the Buddhist Studies class and was not given a choice.
>
> She started her lesson by outlining the course structure, telling the students that she would keep closely to the textbook. She then instructed the students to open the book at the first chapter. She began her lesson by reading the introductory paragraph of the chapter and followed it with an explanation of the meaning of the paragraph. She continued in this style of teaching, reading sub-sections namely "The relevance of Buddhism", "The spirit of free enquiry", "self-reliance", "Loving-kindness and compassion" and "Buddhism and science".
>
> She approached each sub-section with meticulous care, making sure that she thoroughly explained the meanings to the students and yet at the same time continually distancing herself from the religion. In her explanation to the students, she constantly said things like "Buddhism shows people how to grow into maturity and wisdom so as to help understand themselves and the world in which they live"; "Buddhism teaches one to develop one's mind so that one finally sees life as it really is"; "Buddha encourages people to investigate the truth of His Teaching before accepting it"; "Buddha discourages blind practice and superstition"; "Buddhism stresses the need for self-reliance and individual effort"; "Buddhism respects the right of people to

enquire freely and to choose for themselves" and "Buddhism recognise that all living beings are equal".

In the course of teaching, she was careful and constantly asked the students whether they understood the passage or not. One of the students asked, "Teacher, Buddha taught us all the good things and values, but what about you? Why are you also not a Buddhist since it is such a virtuous religion?" She did not reply.

Most of her statements were a repeat of what she had been taught during the training or from the textbook. She is a good teacher and tries hard but obviously resents having to teach something for which she has no empathy. We spoke at length about her experience in the teaching and she remarked:

> I felt very uncomfortable teaching a subject of which I have not only very little knowledge and which I am a non-believer. I felt as if I am cheating the students. You have heard them asking the question why I choose not to be a Buddhist. I really felt embarrassed. I wish I could drop the teaching and get back to teaching Mathematics."

After the initial unhappiness, the Ministry of Education instructed schools to select appropriate teachers of similar faith or those with empathy to the various religious knowledge programmes. The schools were encouraged to rely on volunteers and where the number of willing teachers fell short of the required number, the schools were instructed to fill the quota after consent from the teachers before submitting their names for the training programme.

To assist in the project, lectures and seminars were organised to introduce the teachers to Buddhism. The newspapers also helped in the publicity through a regular column on Buddhism and other religions so that the teachers, parents and the general public have additional teaching material. On an individual basis, teachers in some government schools also organised religious study groups to further understand the religious knowledge that they were teaching. They also formed a joint association for those involved in Buddhist Studies which aimed "to deepen the knowledge of the various aspects of Buddhism especially Buddhist philosophy, Buddhist psychology, Buddhist art, Buddhism and Science and to exchange information on Buddhism". The group met regularly but informally. Most discussions were confined to general topics and to a reading and elaboration on specific Buddhist scriptural discourses. There were no rituals involved. The meetings took the form of group discussion.

The Buddhist Studies Team and some of the officials from the ministry associated with it were supportive of Buddhism and its adherents. Buddhist monks were invited by the Buddhist Studies Team to help in the training programme for teachers. The Buddhist Studies Team, by co-opting the monks into the programme, had been able to raise the status of the Sangha in the eyes of their colleagues from other departments, the Buddhists and the non-Buddhist public. Such opinions as I gathered generally were favourable to the work of the team.

(iii) The Training for Syllabus

There were two parts to the training in Buddhist Studies again designed by the Buddhist Studies Team of CDIS. The first part was concerned with imparting information on Buddhism. The second part dealt with the method of teaching the course. The first part was structured in a way that enabled the trainee teachers to have an overview of the Buddhist philosophy as well as the actual values, which were used for moral education. The Team was also responsible for inviting outside speakers to help in the training course and included the monks and educated lay Buddhists. However, it was the team members that did most of the teaching. The course was conducted in the English and Chinese languages in order to assist the teachers to acquire proper articulation in the language medium in which they would teach their students.

The programme was conducted over a period of ten weeks, focussing on a new theme at each session. It was a training programme that imparted the purpose and scope of the course and how Buddhism could be made relevant to the ideological goals of the Singapore State. While the monks assisted in the dissemination of scriptural knowledge, the team members lectured on the relationship between Buddhism and secular living, focussing on the relevance of Buddhism to a modern society and its relevance to the culture of Singapore.

The teaching content was both selective and pragmatic. Only those aspects of Buddhism that were of immediate social relevance, as defined by the Ministry of Education, were included in the teaching. The teachers were continually instructed to take a "rational and ethical" approach to Buddhism. The course was aimed at providing sufficient information so that the teachers could respond to the epistemological queries arising during the course of their teaching of the subject.

The second part of the training course was designed to instruct the teachers on the teaching of the subject and the use of the textbook. For this part of the training, the teachers were divided into small groups. Teachers from the neighbouring schools were grouped together and the courses were conducted at a number of schools after hours. The team members led these sessions. The teachers were expected to read the textbook and the teachers' guide in advance. During discussions, CDIS members explicated the contents to ensure that the teachers knew with certainty that the moral themes and not the theology were the key themes to be taught. This training lasted for four sessions and the teachers were expected to attend all the sessions. After which, the teachers were deemed as qualified and returned to their schools to teach Buddhist Studies.

(iii) Monks and Nuns as Teachers

Members of the Sangha were invited to teach Buddhist theology to the teachers. Since 1983, two English-speaking Theravada and two Chinese-speaking Mahayana monks were invited to help regularly in the training of the teachers. The inclusion of the monks in the teachers' training programme was welcomed by all. Only six monks were involved in the training programme for the teachers. In general, the monks and nuns were seen as unsuitable to teach Buddhist Studies in schools. One reason given was that they were inexperienced in classroom teaching. There was also argument over the academic qualification of these monks and nuns as most of them did not attend secular schools for their education. The fact that some of the monks were erudite Buddhist theologians and scholars of Chinese history and culture who formally studied at monastic institution of higher learning away from Singapore was not recognised by the Ministry of Education. The Ministry stated that only properly trained teachers with a further training in Buddhism could teach at the schools.

Yet two schools in Singapore engaged a Buddhist monk and a nun respectively for their Buddhist Studies moral education classes. The first was a Catholic mission school, which had a programme of religious studies for their students going back to the period before independence. The principal of the school was a Catholic priest and a well-known protagonist of religious pluralism and tolerance in Singapore. In the interest of his students, most of whom practiced Chinese religion, he undertook to provide Buddhist Studies in addition to Bible Studies. He engaged a Theravada Buddhist monk to teach in the Buddhist Studies programme.

The Manjusri Secondary School, the only Buddhist-mission secondary school, has a Buddhist nun teaching Buddhist Studies since its establishment in 1984. The school taught its own Buddhist Studies programme to all its students from Secondary One onwards. The Buddhist nun taught the Secondary One and Two students but was not allowed to teach the state-sponsored Buddhist Studies as part of the moral education programme to Secondary Three and Four students. The Secondary Three and Four students were taught by a properly qualified teacher trained with the CDIS.

The appointment of a Buddhist nun as a Buddhist Studies teacher had only been approved by the Ministry of Education because of the strong backing from the Singapore Buddhist Federation and a public outcry over the discriminatory attitude of the Ministry when it first dithered over giving the permission. The Buddhist Federation, in a long correspondence with the Ministry, persistently argued that the Buddhist school must be treated on par with other Christian mission schools and should be given the freedom to appoint its own staff for additional religious studies.

"SHARED VALUES" REPLACING RELIGIOUS VALUES

In 1988, Prime Minister Goh Chok Tong, suggested developing a national ideology for all Singaporeans. Two years later, the White Paper for "Shared Values" came into being, with its objective to help "to evolve and anchor a Singaporean identity, incorporating the relevant parts of our varied cultural heritages, and the attitudes and values which have helped us to survive and succeed as a nation".[4]

The "Shared Values" consist of five central values namely: (1) nation before community and society above self; (2) family as the basic unit of society; (3) regard and community support for the individual; (4) consensus instead of contention; and (5) racial and religious harmony (Shared Values: 10). The idea behind this is to ensure that these values are universal, so that all ethnic groups will be able to subscribe to them. Furthermore, all ethnic groups are encouraged to use religion to highlight these shared values. For the Chinese majority, Confucianism and Buddhism have become the focal points for the transmission of these Shared Values. While emphasising that Confucianism is not a subterfuge for imposing Chinese values on minority communities, the state nevertheless argues for the relevance of selected Confucian ideals as relevant to Singapore society.

The Chinese Chamber of Commerce and Industry, the Singapore Federation of Clan Associations, the numerous clan and surname associations, and all the Buddhist temples supported these two programmes and initiated related activities to support this move. The Chinese Chamber of Commerce and Industry and the Singapore Federation of Clan Associations provided financial sponsorship for conferences, workshops and public discussions on this topic. Likewise, support was also given by the Chinese newspapers, especially the *Lianhe Zhaobao* (United Morning Newspaper), with regular columns devoted to this topic. Buddhist temples' newsletters also carried discussion on this issue. There was excitement throughout the Chinese community and concerted efforts were made by them to promote Buddhism and Confucianism.

However, this movement suffered a setback when the government decided to withdraw its support in 1990, which led to the abandoning of the Religious Knowledge programme. An important reason lies in a government-commissioned report on religious activities in Singapore. In 1989-90, this report, which comprises a series of six reports on the study of religion, was released. The study found that there had been a strong resurgence of Christianity, and to a lesser degree of Buddhism, in the 1980s. The authors warned that intense religious proselytisation and the religious revivalist fervour could result in inter-religious conflicts if the religious revivalism was not handled cautiously. The authors also pointed out that "the introduction of religious courses has a significant impact on the present and future religious development in Singapore", recommending a "systematic study be conducted to assess the long-term effects of the Religious Knowledge programme on the Singapore society" (Kuo, 1996: 307). In 1990, Tony Tan, then Minister of Education said "One fundamental change has taken place. Unlike 1982, there is today a heightened consciousness of religious differences and a new fervour in the propagation of religious beliefs" (Kuo, 1996: 307). As a result of this report, and the fact that religion has always been treated as a very sensitive issue in the multi-religious Singapore society, the government abandoned the Religious Knowledge programme of seven years and toned down the link between Asian values and religious values. From 1990 onwards, Religious Knowledge became an optional subject for all Secondary Three and Four students. As a result of this, few students have chosen the course, preferring academic courses.

Although religion is still considered an important idiom in promoting desirable Asian and moral values, only the communities concerned are involved with imparting religious values to their members and adherents, with the state playing a side role. However, the state continues to keep vigilance over the conduct of the activities of the religious organisations, with the Maintenance of the Religious Harmony Act providing the framework, ensuring that religious leaders keep within the accepted boundary.

CONCLUSION

The experiment for promoting religious values as desirable Asian values was a shortlived experiment. When the state found a more viable set of values as expounded in the "Shared Values", the religious knowledge programme was dropped in favour of the "Shared Values". However despite this, the Religious Knowledge programme has enabled school students to study and understand the teachings of Buddhism and Confucianism as pragmatic and rational religions, without religious prejudices. Furthermore, it has rekindled the interest in Buddhism among the general Chinese population. In this regard, the Religious Knowledge programme has indirectly aided the spread of Reformist Buddhism, especially among the younger Singaporean Chinese.

The movement has also managed to gain support from various Chinese social organisations. The Chinese chambers of commerce, clan associations, Chinese newspapers and temples have been the main supporters of this movement, with supporting activities ranging from scholarly conferences to religious and cultural activities. Even as the state shifted its policy from religious values to a set of secular "Shared Values", Reformist Buddhism, which has already gained momentum, continued to flourish and attract members. Today, the Reformist Buddhists continue to promote Buddhism as a pragmatic and rational religion. They considered it as a modern religion and ready to take on challenges posed by other religions, especially Christianity.

NOTES

1. For a recent discussion on this, see the special issue of *Sojourn* on "Asian Ways: Asian Values Revisited" Vol. 14(2), 1999.

2. An extended discussion on the Buddhist Studies Programme can be found in Kuah, Khun Eng, 1991, "State and Religion: Buddhism, Moral Education and Nation-Building in Singapore", *Pacific Viewpoint*, 32(1): 24-42.

3. For an argument on Confucianism in Singapore, see Kuah, Khun Eng, 1990, "Confucian Ideology and Social Engineering in Singapore", *Journal of Contemporary Asia*, 20(3): 371-383.

4. *Shared Values* was presented to the Parliament and passed in Legislation in 1991.

Towards a Reformist Buddhism

Towards A Reformist Buddhism

INTRODUCTION

In the process of religious modernisation, the state, the lay community and the Sangha have engaged in various strategies to speed up the process of change. Each group modernises the religion according to its own agenda. Despite the differences, they have all worked towards a singular goal of promoting Reformist Buddhism as a modern religion.

In Shenist practice, it is the ritual that takes centrestage; but in Reformist Buddhism, it is the Buddhist ideology that is the key concern for the adherents. Reformist Buddhism adopts various scriptural tenets from the different Buddhist traditions to answer contemporary needs. Its primary focus is not on the attainment of enlightenment. It is more concerned with this-worldly needs, and it argues that near salvation can be attained in this world and in one's lifetime. Monkhood is only one path to salvation. The other path is to pursue various spiritual and socio-welfare activities to attain this-worldly salvation. Reformist Buddhism is seen as a modern religion that focuses not only on the Buddhist doctrine but also on the socio-cultural and welfare aspects of the society. It is a scriptural religion as well as a social religion, and provides time and space for members to interact in a religiously and socially intimate way. At the same time, it is also a compassionate religion, in that it cares for the socially less-abled and less-privileged people both within Singapore and abroad. It therefore appeals both to the younger as well as the older generations of Singapore Chinese of all classes.

(a) Central Tenets of Reformist Buddhist Teaching

Although Reformist Buddhism adopts various aspects of scriptural knowledge from the different Buddhist traditions, there are key tenets that it expounds to its members and the general public. The key scriptural tenets are (i) the doctrine of causation, i.e., the Four Noble Truths; (ii) the theory of Karma, Rebirth and Merit-making; (iii) Morality and Ethic; (iv) Buddhist Work Ethics; (v) Compassion and Humanity; and (vi) the Eightfold Path. The central idea behind the selection of these various Buddhist teachings is to enable the followers to understand the meaning of life through the Buddhist understanding of suffering and the ability of individuals to reduce the level of suffering through their own actions in both the religious and secular spheres. Let us explore briefly the key Buddhist teachings.

(i) The Doctrine of Causation

Doctrinally, early Buddhism's "Discourse on Causal Relations" expounded on two themes, that of causality and that of the causally-conditioned phenomenon (Kulapahana, 1976: 26). These themes run through all spheres including psychic, moral, social and spiritual (Kalupahana: 27). There are four main characteristics of causation: objectivity, necessity, invariability and conditionality. These can be tested throughout the life process (Kulapahana: 27).

The theory of causation explains how suffering comes about and how one can be released from the cycle of suffering or *samsara*. Suffering is the result of craving. As human beings, we succumb easily to the temptations of material things and sensual pleasures and crave them. Craving leads to attachment. But when we fail to get hold of them or lose them, we become unhappy. Craving and attachment are the result of ignorance. We therefore need to be conscious of our thoughts and actions in order to eradicate our cravings and attachments. Eradication will free us from desire. This theory of causation is commonly known as the Four Noble Truths. It teaches us that our suffering, which is the result of craving, is the result of our ignorance of the above facts.

In explaining the events that shape the world – the good and the bad, happiness and sadness, wealth and poverty and others – the theory of causality alludes to the fact that all material things, social processes and human emotions are impermanent and are all unsatisfactory. To cling to them can only cause suffering (*dukkha*).

At the level of mundane living, our worldly existence creates needs, wants and responsibility. We need food, shelter and clothing for our basic survival. The social institutions that we have created compel us to be responsible social beings and to ensure the perpetuation of the family and society. The state requires adherence to rules and order so that the society as a whole may live in peace and harmony. These serve to bind us deeper into the social structure of the society we live in.

Our very social existence with all these attachments and responsibilities, in the Buddhist teachings, is thus the very cause of our suffering. Both result in suffering. Happiness and sadness are two aspects of the same process. The only way out of suffering is to move out of the this-worldly cycle. In short, as long as we are in this world, we cannot escape suffering. The best we can hope for is less suffering. The Eightfold Path provides the way out of suffering. It involves adopting right views, right aspirations, right speech, right actions, right livelihood, right exertion, right mindfulness and right concentration.

(ii) The Theory of Karma and Rebirth

A second important aspect of the Buddhist teaching is that of karma and rebirth. The three factors that cause karma are external stimuli, conscious motives and unconscious motives (Kalupahana: 47). Human beings are subjected to external influences in the physical, social and spiritual realms and these influences produce a variety of feelings and actions. There are positive and negative feelings and actions. The negative ones include greed and hatred and the positive ones include compassion, kindness and helpfulness (Kalupahana: 47). All these feelings and actions are the causes of an individual's good or bad karma (Kalupahana: 47).

In Buddhism, it is karma that causes all individuals to suffer. Karma is believed to be caused by intentional actions of the body, speech or mind. In every action, there is a cause and an effect. Good actions result in happiness while bad ones result in suffering. There is long-term and short-term karma. When the effect of an action is felt in the same lifetime, it is know as short-term karma. When the effect is felt only in a later life, it is known as long-term karma. It follows that when an individual performs good deeds, the person will be assured of a good karma, either in this life or in subsequent lives. Thus, the individual is responsible for his or her present and future state of life.

It is also karma that determines whether an individual is born as a human or some other being. There are six realms of existence in the Buddhist cosmology: the human, heaven, azuras, animal, hell and pretas planes of existence. The aspiration in spiritual development is to ensure that individuals will be reborn as humans. Therefore, it is important to accumulate merits to ensure a good karma. A good karma is the result of a person's store of merits in his or her past lives and good deeds and actions in the present life.

One way to ensure a good karma is to perform merit-making and accumulate merits. In most societies where Buddhism is practised, merit-making has developed into an elaborate institution. Alms giving is the most common form of merit-making and the monks, by the act of accepting alms, allow the giver to accrue the desired merits. In most societies, merit-making goes beyond alms giving. Other meritorious acts include wholly or partly financing temple building and temple repairs, becoming a monk oneself or having a son become a monk, and observing Buddhist holy days and the five precepts. Giving and receiving are absolute and inalienable reciprocal acts.

In most Buddhist societies, the amount of merit one receives is dependent on the types of contribution one makes to the Buddhist cause. For example, in Thailand, giving alms to the monks is considered an important and essential act of merit accumulation, but it is not ranked as highly as financing the construction of the temple, which provides for a higher level of merit accumulation. Other means of acquiring merit include performing charity and welfare works, observing religious rites, and cultivating proper personal development and behaviour (moral and ethical values). Merit-making is therefore important for individuals to ensure good karma and serves as an insurance policy for the present and future.

Another aspect of merit-making is the transferability of these merits to deceased ancestors, which ensures that they will have a speedy rebirth as human beings. In Theravada Buddhist societies, it is a common tradition for one son of the deceased to assume monkhood on a temporary basis in order to transfer merits to the deceased parent. Among the Mahayana Buddhist societies, it is the full-time monks and nuns who perform merit transfer to the deceased.

For the Buddhists in Singapore, merit-making takes place in the temples. In the Buddhist temples, monks and nuns transfer merits to the dead through special prayers on a daily basis, and also on special occasions. Prayers and food are offered to all sentient beings. Some Mahayana temples also have a memorial hall housing the soul tablets of the dead. A fee is charged for the space and services provided for the dead by the monks and nuns. The practice of placing the ancestral soul tablets in the Buddhist temple is a fairly recent introduction in Singapore. It started in the early 1970s and has steadily gained popularity. This change is attributed mainly to the change in the economic status of women. As Chinese women move out of the domestic sphere, goaded by higher educational achievements and the rapid economic and industrial development that has established greater job opportunities, they have less time to tend the domestic altar. Once the momentum has been set, it became a fashionable trend for people to leave their ancestral soul tablets in the temple after the death of their ancestors. At the Mahayana Buddhist temple, there is also a small shrine containing a soul tablet placed outside the shrine hall and dedicated to the wandering souls.

There have also been numerous cases where the ancestral tablets were removed from the domestic altar and placed in the temple. One common reason given by the informants was that they did not have sufficient time to care for the dead ancestors, so in order not to neglect their responsibility, they placed them in the temple where the monks and nuns would take better care of their ancestors. Another reason for this trend is attributed to the religious faith of the adult children of the dead. Those who have converted to Christianity or other religious faiths deem it inappropriate for them to perform ancestral worship or be involved in any Chinese religious rituals. This is especially so among the Christian fundamentalists. There is also a small number who no longer have faith in Chinese religious practice and openly declare themselves as having no religion. They place their ancestral tablets in the temple in order not to contradict their non-religious status. The most important reason of all is that majority of Chinese Buddhists understand the significance of karma and thus many prefer to place the ancestral tablets in the temple to facilitate merit-making by the monks and nuns.

(iii) Morality and Ethics
Another central piece of Buddhist teaching that the Reformist Buddhists focus on is Buddhist moral ethics. There are five groups of vices, namely: (i) the taking of a life, both of oneself and of others; (ii) taking what is not given; (iii) wrong indulgence in sensual pleasure; (iv) falsehood; and (v) indolence consequent on the use of intoxicants (Kalupahana: 58). Reformist Buddhists are required to translate these virtues into everyday practice. The virtues are interpreted as not to kill, not to lie, not to drink, not to commit adultery and not to steal. There are different views among the Reformist Buddhists on the extent to which these Buddhist values can be interpreted to suit modern living. For example, the first precept, not to kill, has been translated in different ways variously. The fundamentalists interpreted it to include the killing of all living forms, including insects, animals and people. They argue that in Classical Buddhism, the monks were required to have a net or muslin bag and strain water before drinking it. This was to prevent them from consuming living insects and hence violate the precept not to kill. They were expected to show compassion by driving away, rather than killing, insects such as mosquitoes and wild animals when they were wandering in the forest. Today, Reformist Buddhists apply this rule to their food consumption. Thus there is restriction to a vegetarian diet. Some of the Reformist Buddhists also associate this rule with the present animal rights movement, by defending animal rights. By linking Buddhism with the animal rights movement, they hope to put their faith to action, thereby linking the

sacred with the secular. They also hope that such actions will raise the profile and credibility of their Reformist Buddhist movements as modern and trendy in the eyes of the local and global communities. Another matter here is that of mindless and violent killing for pleasure, as in hunting and in warfare. Here, the Reformist Buddhists openly denounce such practices and are very vocal about warfare carried out by different groups in the world.

A second rule is not to engage in sexual misconduct. Monogamy has become an entrenched norm in modern society but without much success given the rampant infidelity committed by single and married people. The conjugal relationship between a man and a woman is seen as important for the stability of the family as a core social institution. Buddhist morality dictates that a man or woman should not conduct extra-marital relationships. Almost all agree that this should be strictly followed. Many see it as a test of one's religious conviction, moral cultivation and will power. For those who have erred, their advice is to stop and to repair the damaged marriage and family. Likewise, they argue that single men and women should not indulge in sexual relationships, but they argue that it takes great human energy and consciousness to veer away from this temptation. After all, Buddha himself was tempted throughout his life by this. At present, the spread of AIDS has further strengthened their argument for the need to observe Buddhist teaching on morality. They are active in participating in the fight against the spread of AIDS by extolling their members to uphold this value. While sexual promiscuity is not condoned, about half of the respondents feel that there are exceptional cases. They feel that one should not stigmatise a person for his or her act of prostitution. This is especially so if a woman has no other recourse – say, if she is divorced and unemployed, with a family of young children to look after. But they stress that this should only be a temporary option.

The third rule is not to lie. The Reformist Buddhists argue that this rule is subject to relative interpretation. If to tell a lie would lead to conflict resolution, then it is an acceptable act. Most agree that it is acceptable to tell a "white lie" if no harm is caused.

The fourth rule is not to steal. The majority of the Reformist Buddhists feel that it is important to adhere to this teaching.

The fifth rule is not to drink. Drinking is often viewed as a bad habit leading to addiction. Some argue the causal link between drinking and marital and family disharmony, social discord, violence, and child and wife abuse, but half of my respondents see social drinking as acceptable. Heavy drinking, which can lead to unruly behaviour, is less than desirable, while alcoholics are not only undesirable, but encouraged to go for treatment.

(iv) Buddhist Work Ethic

Another Buddhist teaching is that of hard work, honesty and loyalty to one's occupation. However, occupations that encourage cheating and dishonesty are less desirable. The Reformist Buddhists regard professions such as law and commerce as likely to compromise morality. But many also accept that such professions are part of modern life and development and lead to modern comfort, and as long as those who are in these trades treat other people fairly, they should not be penalised by the Buddhist community. The Reformist Buddhists also argue for more compassion and understanding in the workplace, and that superiors have the responsibility to look after their workers. An ethical workplace is a place where the management treats the workers fairly in terms of remuneration and working conditions.

(v) Compassion and Humanity

The Reformist Buddhists also want every individual to express compassion and humanity for fellow human beings and other living things. They feel that it is important to have kind thoughts and believe that only with kind thoughts can kind actions, such as giving donations to help the less privileged sector of the population, be generated.

(vi) The Eightfold Path (*Aryio Atthangiko Maggo*)

By understanding the Four Noble Truths, a Buddhist is in a position to direct himself or herself out of a life of suffering. This is done by practising the eight moral virtues laid down in the Eightfold Path (Kalupahana, 1976: 59). These eight moral values are right view, right thought, right speech, right action, right living, right effort, right mindfulness and right concentration (Kulapahana: 59). In following the Eightfold Path, the ultimate aim is the elimination of all desires – physical, sensual and material – and to reach a stage of selflessness and ultimately the cessation of all future births. The final goal is nirvana.

By observing and practising these Buddhist teachings, the Reformist Buddhists are now engaged in the process of self-cultivation of an inner-worldly mysticism, which they believe will lead them on the path towards enlightenment.

(b) Organisational Structure

The Reformist Buddhist movement is not a single movement, directed by a centralised organisation with an integrated programme. Rather, it is a series of activities carried out by lay Buddhist groups with participation from Reformist monks. Most of the lay Reformist organisations have organisational structures similar to that of a temple. The main difference between the Reformist organisations and the temple structure is that the place of worship and activities is often a residential or office building instead of a religious building. Furthermore, they are registered as secular societies with the Registrar of Societies instead of as religious institutions, although their activities are both religious and secular in nature. These Reformist Buddhists do not hold allegiance to a specific Buddhist tradition, as they want to do away with labels. Many openly claim a non-partisan status and prefer the name of Buddhayana, a name reflecting their focus on Buddha and Buddhist teaching. Many Buddhist temples provide space for the members to carry out their reformist activities

A lay Buddhist organisation is formed when several individuals spearhead its formation, focussing primarily on Buddhist scripture. Each Reformist group sets its own agenda and organises its own activities. On some occasions, groups may jointly organise religious activities, an example being the joint activities held on Vesak Day, a designated public holiday for believers of Buddhism.

The Reformist Buddhist organisations are of two types. The first type is the informal lay Buddhist organisation, in which a few like-minded Buddhists come together and practise meditation and Buddhist dharma. It does not have a formal bureaucratic structure and a business address. Often, activities are conducted in the home of one of its members. When the number of members has grown substantially, the members might decide to form a lay Buddhist organisation and formalise their activities, create a bureaucratic structure and register with the Registrar of Societies as a non-profit religious institution. It must then have a formal constitution and an executive committee. Alternatively, it may be registered with the Registrar of Companies, in which case it will function as a company, subject to the operating rules governing business corporations. In both cases, it will have a formal structure with an executive committee and permanent business address to conduct its activities.

By forming lay Buddhist groups and promoting doctrinal Buddhism among the younger Chinese, Reformist Buddhists have consciously changed the religious practices and landscape of the Chinese in Singapore. Whereas in the past many younger Chinese were passive participants in Chinese religious syncretism, today many are active participants in the Reformist Buddhist activities. There are numerous lay Reformist Buddhist groups operating in Singapore today. Below are some examples.

(i) Singapore Buddhist Youth Fellowship (SBYF)
The Singapore Buddhist Youth Fellowship was formed in 1984. Its aim is to gather personnel and material in order to help propagate Buddhism in Singapore and to set an exemplary Buddhist lifestyle.

All members must be active Buddhists who are expected to contribute substantially in time – and, if able, money and skills – to aid the Buddhist cause. All members must show singularity of purpose. A full-time worker is called a *dharmacari* (literally, "practitioner of dharma", in the Pali language). There are several *dharmacari* in the organisation. In addition, there are numerous Buddhist friends (*mitra*). The *dharmacari* and *mitra* are formally admitted into the lay order in an initiation ceremony. During the initiation, they are required to take the SBYF pledge to "help all those who are interested in their personal development, and aim at making possible the discovery of the highest ideals of the Buddhist teachings".

The aim of the SBYF is to create a conducive environment to personal spiritual development. This is reflected in the types of activities embarked upon by members of SBYF. Its philosophy is to be self-sufficient economically in order to be free to pursue their spiritual course without financial constraints. So, instead of relying on public donations, they have established economic enterprises to ensure a steady flow of funds into their organisation. In the area of spiritual development, members are required to cultivate their mental health through meditation, scriptural study and fellowship interactions (including outdoor camps and spiritual retreats). They are also expected to engage in "Right Livelihood" so that their economic pursuits benefit the society instead of being merely the pursuit of material wealth. The SBYF has started a "Right Livelihood" project involving the sale of books and tapes and the publishing of literature on Buddhism.

From Beginners to Committed Buddhists

The path of cultivating the Buddhist faith for a beginner and becoming a committed Buddhist is divided into several phases. SBYF aids the beginners on their paths to becoming committed members. The public is first exposed to Buddhist teachings through the mass media, public lectures, bookshops and their library. These are the initial contact points between the interested public and the SBYF members. The SBYF members are most concerned about publicising their activities to the public.

When individuals have shown interest in Buddhism, they are encouraged to attend courses run by the SBYF. Subsequently, if they show signs of greater interest, they are encouraged to attend interaction camps to familiarise themselves with the dharma and to involve themselves with the various social activities of the SBYF. They are then encouraged "to develop spiritually through the practice of meditation and participation in dharma discussions". Often, these are accompanied by weekend spiritual retreats. Regular courses are also organised for the purpose of deepening an individual's commitment to Buddhism.

Having gone through this training, new members are encouraged to proceed to the second stage, in which they are encouraged to attend advanced training and specialised courses in meditation to develop further religious skills. By this stage, the members are considered sufficiently knowledgeable and "spiritually ready to make a commitment to become a *mitra*". A *mitra* is a lay person who has committed himself or herself to Buddhism and the Buddhist cause. He/She continues to observe rigorously the Buddhist precepts in his/her daily life and to engage in spiritual development in the form of meditation on a daily basis. While he or she continues to lead a secular life, a large part of leisure time is taken up by spiritual development. In the words of one respondent, "the time is now utilised in a spiritually productive manner". The length of training required to become a *mitra* is dependent on the individuals themselves. On the average, it takes about five years of learning, exploring and questioning for a person to become convinced and make a commitment to live the life of a *mitra*.

Having reached this stage of spiritual commitment, the *mitra* can proceed to an advanced stage of lay commitment, and if he or she so wishes, can become a *dharmacari*. A *dharmacari* is a Buddhist working full-time for the cause of Buddhism. He or she works for the SBYF but receives no salary. Instead, he or she is given a small stipend for personal needs. The aim is to rid oneself of material wants – a *dharmacari* does not engage in moneymaking activities. He/she may or may not be married, although he/she leads a lay life, wears no robe and has no physical or diacritical marks, as a monk or nun would. In short, a *dharmacari* attempts to lead a semi-monastic life within a secular environment.

The idea of encouraging committed members to become *mitra* and *dharmacari* within the SBYF is to establish a core group of lay Buddhists committed to the promotion of Buddhism on both full- and part-time basis. Although the recruitment of *mitra* and *dharmacari* is a very slow process, those who are involved are confident that they can attract a sufficient number of committed Buddhists to their cause.

The SBYF has other plans to be put into action. One of their main goals is to be financially self-sufficient, by establishing the "Right Livelihood Project" to promote ethical business. Officially launched in 1984, the project took off with the establishment of a trading firm called Syarikat Periagaan Mandala, which has three subsidiaries: the enterprise Nirvana deals with books and stationary; Nirmita trades in audio-visual and copying equipment; and Bistar trades in computer hardware and software. The parent company also undertakes the publication of leaflets, brochures and books on Buddhism, which are distributed free to the general public.

Those members involved in the enterprise are volunteers and have to abide by the rules laid down in the *Mitra* Code of Conduct, which stresses values such as responsibility, generosity, communication, ethics and personal development. Many members feel that they should develop and diversify their commercial arm in order to further expand their activities and hence the movement.

(ii) Buddha Sasana Buddhist Association

Another group of Buddhists has founded a lay organisation that focuses on the scripture and on meditation. They call themselves Buddhayana Buddhists in an attempt to eradicate the traditional divisions within Buddhism. Their informal organisational structure appeals to those who do not like rules and regulations. There is very little restriction on their religious and spiritual pursuit. Members are encouraged to participate in the organisation's activities. This association is loosely organised, consisting of three linked religious units each specialising in one aspect of Buddhism: meditation, dharma and chanting. Each unit has one or two core members who are experts in the area. Members can choose to participate in one or all of their activities, and tend to move from one unit to another freely. The association invites visiting Tibetan monks, on a short and semi-permanent basis, to act as their religious mentors. These monks teach meditation to the members, give dharma lectures and conduct religious services with elaborate rituals in the Tantric tradition to the members and public.

The meditation unit has two lay leaders who lead the group in Buddhist meditation. There are about nine core members who gather together regularly to meditate and discuss their own meditating skills and development. Each member has been doing meditation since the 1970s. Some started off with yoga meditation, others with the basic breathing method and the rest with the visualisation method. When the group gathers for meditation, it is each according to his/her own style and method. This variation allows for a good discussion after their practice. The group meets once a week in the evening. Members are also friends. Apart from meditation, they socialise with one another. Among them are two doctors, one lawyer, two businessmen and four teachers. Three are women, two of whom are the wives of the two doctors. The third woman is an independent participant. All came because of the relaxed atmosphere.

A second unit is the dharma discussion unit. Here, the central focus is on learning the Buddhist teaching, the dharma. Most of the participants in this unit are young adults, in their late teens and twenties. There is a large number of college and other tertiary students in this unit. Many are attracted to Buddhism because they want to know more about the dharma and the friendly atmosphere of the place. The members in the group are very sociable and helpful, and very encouraging to newcomers. In contrast with the meditation group, these young members are full of vigour, enthusiasm and activity. Many of them come from families that practised Shenism. They have few ideas about Buddhist teaching prior to joining the dharma group. Most have been encouraged by their friends to join the dharma discussion unit. A few were drawn to Buddhism during their university days, when they first attended the unit out of curiosity and eventually become convinced members. This is also an informal group, open to all interested in pursuing the dharma. Although there is a core group of members, at any one time there are always new members present.

There is no set curriculum for dharma discussion. Usually, members decide on one text and discuss the meanings within the text. At other times, certain Buddhist concepts might interest them and they might discuss them during their weekly meeting. There are also occasions where they discuss the relevance of Buddhism in everyday life and in contemporary society. The members look towards the Buddhist teachings as a principle guide to solve their moral and ethical dilemmas and to justify their actions. For instance, among the un-married Chinese female students and workers, the increasing tensions of modern day romance, courtship, pre-marital sexual relationships and cohabitation have created pressure for them to conform to the prevailing norms. Many have found that Buddhist teachings provide a major excuse to adopt a more conservative stance on this issue.

A third unit is the chanting and prayer unit. This unit appeals to those who have more familiarity with Shenist practices, especially older women, but there are also some younger men and women who are keen to learn the Buddhist chants and prayers, which are chanted in a musical fashion with the help of various liturgical instruments so that they can participate in the chanting during their weekly religious services. To them, to be a Buddhist is not only to understand the dharma and meditation – it is also important to participate in religious services on a communal basis. Besides, they do not wish to be left out of religious activities in which all their friends and other members are able to perform.

(iii) A Foreign Buddhist Sect – Singapore Soka Association

Apart from home-grown lay Buddhist organisations, there are also foreign ones. One of the most active groups is the Soka Gakkai Buddhist Sect that appeared in Singapore some 30 years ago. The Singapore Nichiren Shoshu Buddhist Association, a branch of the Nichiren Shoshu Soka Gakkai Sect of Japan, has a rigid and highly-bureaucratised structure, with a tightly controlled centralised management.[1] Today, it is known by the name Singapore Soka Association. Its central committee has full authority over the running of the Singapore branch, but is responsible to the sect's head office in Japan. It divides Singapore into various neighbourhoods and each subgroup is responsible for recruiting members from the local neighbourhood districts. Its members are divided into groups based on age, sex and occupational criteria. Thus, there are groups for young men, young women, boys, girls, married men and married women. There are also separate groups for schoolteachers and manual workers.

Since its inception, members have embarked on aggressive proselytisation (*shakubuku*) which has led to a rapid rise in membership.

The converts swear allegiance to the new faith and formally eschew all other religions. They must destroy all other religious icons and images, including the ancestral tablets of their households. This approach has alienated many Chinese, who regard the sect to be as disruptive to family values as the fundamentalist Christian groups. Some do not accept it as Buddhist. It is commonly known as the "Japanese religion". Recently, in its attempt to attract younger Chinese, and recognising the hostility created in the households, the sect has taken a moderate approach. The iconoclasm is now voluntary. The conflict is somewhat lessened by the policy of converting whole families instead of just individuals.

The earlier Nichiren Shoshu Buddhist Association has been successful in attracting members from the working class primarily because of its simple theology and ritual. This consists of the daily recital of the two short chapters of the Lotus Sutra in Chinese and the mantra in Japanese called "*Namyo-ho-renge-kyo*". Members are also taught the teachings of the founder of the sect. Not unlike Shenism, the sect focuses on this-worldly achievement of its members and the total reliance on the mystical power (*myo-ho*) of the Lotus Sutra to satisfy daily needs, especially its ability to cure illnesses through faith healing. Its members are taught to have total trust in the Lotus Sutra, the sect's founder and its leaders, who "are knowledgeable in the Lotus Sutra". Members are expected to participate in all the association's activities and to be seen regularly in the premises of the association. While not listed within its constitution, it has become an unwritten code that members tithe or at least donate very regularly to the association. Members are expected to purchase all their religious paraphernalia from their internal shop. This is primarily because all the ritual items are Japanese in form. The association is not unlike a total institution in its firm control over the socio-religious (and other) aspects of the lives of its members.

(iv) A Lay Sangha

Following the example of the Friends of the Western Buddhist Order,[2] a lay Sangha was formed in the 1980s by a group of lay Buddhists. Its main objective is to establish an institutional framework for committed lay Buddhists who have chosen to lead a monastic life without ordination or constraint on their actions by the Sangha Council. At present, there are some 20 lay preachers working for the Buddhist cause. Compared to the ordained monks, these lay preachers have a liberal approach to religion. They continue to hold full-time jobs and are therefore financially independent of others for support. Apart from this, they spend all their energies, time and resources in promoting Buddhism. Their social position among the orthodox Buddhists remains anomalous. The ordained monks and nuns do not regard them differently from the lay members, even though some monks recognise and approve of their religious fervour. Among the Reformist Buddhists, they are held in high esteem. As the Nichiren Shoshu group has demonstrated, lay preachers have the potential to become powerful and influential leaders and organisers. Lay proselytisers have a greater potential for attracting people to their association, lifestyle and views towards Buddhist enlightenment.

(c) Main Activities

The main activities of the Reformist Buddhists fall into the religious and the secular domains. Within the religious sphere, there are six main types of activities, namely: (i) propagating Buddhist scriptural knowledge to the general public; (ii) encouraging general participation; (iii) nurturing a group of committed Reformist Buddhists; (iv) performing missionary work and engaging in subtle proselytisation; (v) putting faith into real life practice and action; and (vi) legitimising Vesak Day as a public holiday. Within the secular domain, the Reformist Buddhists support numerous socio-cultural and welfare activities.

(i) Religious Activities

The first act among the Reformist Buddhists has been to teach the general public the differences between Shenism and Buddhism and to correct the negative perception of Buddhism in the eyes of the younger Singaporean Chinese. They do this by organising public lectures and seminars for all people. In temples and lay Buddhist organisations, there are now weekly talks and lectures given either by Reformist monks or lay Buddhist scholars. Furthermore, many Buddhist temples and societies also organise regular dharma classes to enable members to discuss Buddhism among themselves. Each dharma group consists of lay leaders and members who usually get together on an informal basis in the evenings or weekends to discuss dharma. Within each group, there are often one or two members with some knowledge of Buddhist scriptures to lead the discussion. In some temples, a list of discussion topics is posted in advance to the public.

In Singapore, Buddhist scriptures written in Classical Chinese, Pali, Sanskrit and Tibetan can be found. Because of language difficulties, many Buddhists do not read the texts but read books on Buddhism written by either monks or lay scholars. One task of the Reformist Buddhist movement is to make available Buddhist literature and books to the lay people. Reformist groups have undertaken to print booklets, pamphlets and books on Buddhism and distribute them freely to the public. Sympathetic publishers and owners of printing firms have printed them free, and, since the early 1980s, there has been a proliferation of materials on Buddhism in both the English and Chinese languages. These pamphlets and books have been placed in all Buddhist temples for individual consumption and distribution. Members are also encouraged to dispatch information to family members, friends and colleagues. The idea is to spread Buddhist teachings to the general public.

Other activities that the Reformist Buddhists organise are public lectures and seminars. Lectures are often held in temples and lay Buddhist organisations. In recent years, the number of listeners ranges from 50 to over 100 or more. Occasionally, several Reformist groups jointly organise public lectures on a grand scale by inviting well-known foreign scholars and monks to speak. Often, such lectures are held in a large public auditorium, with advertisements in local newspapers to draw attention to them. Such lectures are often well attended and attracted large crowds, sometimes totalling more than 1000 people.

A third activity is the performance of Buddhist rituals, which include chanting, meditation and prayer. Group chanting is considered to be of special importance. For the Reformist Buddhists, this ritual activity will create the right atmosphere for spiritual development. Chanting in a temple or in a group enables the participants to develop religious companionship. In some temples, chanting groups are organised to teach newcomers the techniques of chanting. Although this practice is most popular among the elderly, it is also gaining popularity among the young.

Meditation is another method of cultivating faith. Numerous meditation groups have sprung up in Singapore and are most popular among the younger Reformist Buddhists. Meditation classes, either taught by monks or lay Buddhist meditation experts have also been organised for the general public. Meditation is regarded by many as a way of relaxation and as a form of psychotherapy in a highly stressful society like Singapore, and appeals predominantly to the young and to professionals.

On special religious days, the temples and lay organisations also organise prayer services for the members and public. Individual temples and lay groups emphasise different types of ritual and prayer activities. Some have special purification rites (*xiao-zai-fa-hui*), others pay homage to certain Buddhist deities, emphasise the chanting of different sutras, or liberate animals. Some temples organise spiritual retreats for the members, during which they observe the five precepts and the eight vows. The observing of the five precepts and eight vows are two recent introductions into the lay practice, which prove to be popular with both the old and the young Buddhists. These retreats are occasions where individuals participate in personal spiritual development in a communal way. Usually, a retreat lasts for three to four days. The participants live in the temple for the duration and adhere to a strict religious programme including lectures, meditation and chanting.

Another area that the Reformist Buddhists have put much effort into is establishing viable commercial activities for the organisations. Becoming financially independent is an important part of the Reformist Buddhist Movement. Many Buddhist temples today continue to depend wholly on contributions and sponsorship from the lay community for their activities. From the 1980s onwards, several Reformist Buddhist organisations have initiated and established business enterprises of an ethical nature – an example being the Singapore Buddhist Youth Fellowship discussed earlier.

As many of the Reformist Buddhist activists are as much involved in self-education and reinterpretation of the Chinese religion as in proselytisation, access to Buddhist scriptures and literature is considered by many to be vitally important. A Buddhist Library was opened in 1984 by a group of enthusiastic Reformist Buddhists. Initially, the books were donated by other Buddhists and by the temples. The library is situated in rented premises in one of the shopping centres in a working class suburb. The cost of maintaining the library is borne by a few supporters. Volunteers act as librarians. Members of the public may either read the books in the library or borrow them. Talks and seminars are held in the library, and it is a popular place, with its regular talks attracting a sizeable group of Buddhists. Today, many temples and lay Buddhist organisations have small libraries with books made available to the members and the general public on request. When the Religious Studies programme, of which Buddhist Studies was one subject, was implemented in 1984, these libraries became resource centres for students.

To enable better access to Buddhism, several bookshops selling Buddhist books and paraphenalia have been set up. The managers of the bookshops discussed below told me that their aim is to encourage Singaporeans to explore Buddhism. They also told me the venture is an attempt to put Buddhism into practice by engaging in ethical business, where part of the profits earned go to help with various religious and welfare activities.

The first bookshop was opened in 1982 by a Theravada monk and three lay Buddhists. Prior to the opening of this bookshop, there were few books on Buddhism on sale to the public. The bookshop sells mostly English language Buddhist books and scriptures. It is managed and run by volunteers to minimise cost. A second bookshop was opened by five lay Buddhists in 1984. This second bookshop has a wider range of books catering to diverse interests. There are the

Chinese language books imported mainly from Taiwan and Hong Kong and some English language books from Sri Lanka, although a majority of them are imported from Western sources and are written by Western authors. The range of topics covered in the second bookshop is wider. Books on meditation, Buddhist education, philosophy and psychology and psychotherapy can be found in the bookshops. Since then, non-Buddhist bookshops have also devoted a section to books on religions and provide a wider selection of books on Buddhism to the general public.

Apart from making Buddhist literature available to the general public, the bookshops also serve as an informal advertising channel where various Buddhist activities, talks and seminars are advertised. Often the volunteers who mind the shops engage the potential customers in conversation on Buddhism and then encourage them to attend the Buddhist talks and activities. It is also at the shops that many pamphlets and booklets bearing Buddhist teachings are handed out freely to potential Buddhists. In fact, a sizeable portion of my informants told me that they first got to know of scriptural Buddhism in this way.

Another main concern of the Reformist Buddhists during the early years of the movement had been to raise the status of Buddhism within the wider Singapore society. To ensure that Buddhism is recognised as an accepted religion within Singapore society, it needed to be treated the same way as the other religions. In Singapore, public holidays were granted to the Muslims, Christians and the Hindus for their celebrations, but this was not the case for the Buddhists until the 1980s. The Reformist Buddhists and the Sangha argued for Vesak Day, the day of Buddha's Enlightenment, to be made a public holiday in Singapore. This has been granted, and today it is a public holiday. The Reformist Buddhists argued that by granting Vesak Day as a public holiday, the status of Buddhism would be level with that of Christianity, Islam and Hinduism. The Christians celebrate Christmas and Easter, both public holidays. Likewise, Hari Raya Haji is a designated public holiday when Muslims celebrate their religion. Deepavali is a Hindu religious occasion and is also a designated public holiday. Making Vesak Day a public holiday exemplifies the ethno-religious balance that the State wishes to impose on the population.

(ii) Cultural, Civic, Educational and Welfare Activities

The Reformist Buddhists have also responded enthusiastically to the various government campaigns that align with their Buddhist teachings. Support is given to the various campaigns, such as "Respect your elders", "No smoking", "National Heart Week", "National Productivity Week", "Two (children – sic) is Enough" (revoked in recent days), "Speak Mandarin", "Keep the Environment Clean and Green" and "Total Defence". Over the years, Reformist Buddhists have gradually weaved these government campaigns as part of Buddhist moral teachings. Thus, Buddhist teachings are used to promote the various campaigns and values that the secular state wants to promote. In this sense, Buddhism is made socially relevant to the modern secular state. Thus, one often hears:

> "Buddhism teaches one to respect one's health, which is why we stress a vegetarian diet which is low in fat and cholesterol";

> "Buddhism also teaches us not to drink so that we will not get into fights and unruly behaviour, which is part of the five main precepts that are observed by the Buddhists";

> "Buddhism teaches us not to gamble, tell lies and engage in promiscuous acts, which points to the values of honesty and social responsibility and to a stable family"; and

> "Buddhism teaches one to be responsible, and this means hard work and added production for the good of one's family and the nation".

The desire to be socially relevant has made the Reformist Buddhists consider their role as a provider of welfare facilities for the less privileged groups in Singapore society. Reformist Buddhists are now directly involved in secular charity and welfare work.

Members are encouraged to give donations and to provide labour for the various temple homes. Over 85% of my informants have contributed or donated some money to the charity homes on a regular basis. The amount donated ranged from a few to several thousands dollars. Donations are made several times a year, although some Buddhists told me that they try to pledge a small sum on a monthly basis for this purpose. Many consider the donations as "a practice of giving and as a way to cultivate loving-kindness in us". While some of my informants donated directly to the homes, many in fact donated through their temples. It has become a common practice in many temples today for the Reformist Buddhists to undertake to collect donations for the welfare homes. This collection often coincides with a religious function, from which the proceeds are used for charitable purposes. While the temple stresses good deeds and accumulation of merits through such acts, many donate because they want to help less privileged people. Few mention that they want to accumulate merits to improve their future births or even their present lives.

Reformist Buddhists have also taken a direct interest in providing labour for the numerous welfare homes. Volunteers are recruited to perform menial tasks such as the cleaning of the inmates' quarters and general cleaning, and to help in the preparation of meals. Many Reformist Buddhists perform these chores on a regular basis. Various temples and lay organisations have organised their members to assist in the cleaning tasks. Housewives who are able to make some time and can cook often undertake the preparation of meals. It is also a common practice for Buddhists to visit the welfare homes to provide company and entertainment to the inmates. In fact, this latter task has been taken on by the youth groups of most temples. Many of the Buddhist youths find it "socially responsible to take care of the old men and women who had no kinsmen or were forsaken by their children." In some temples, the youth group moves to different homes each week so as to cater to a wider group of inmates. In others, they only visit one home regularly. Apart from visits, the youth group also organises outings for the inmates of the homes.

In line with the national campaign to "Respect your elders", most temples hold their own campaign to honour their senior members. Apart from being respectful to their senior members, youth groups also organise special functions, such as a banquet and cultural night, for senior members and the elderly from nursing homes in an attempt to establish goodwill within the neighbourhood. The Buddhists feel that there is a need to reach out to the wider community.

Reformist Buddhists also provide material goods and some money to the homes and individual inmates, and it has become a common practice for them to undertake to provide the homes with food or amenities. Often, some wealthy businessmen undertake to make contributions because they have benefited from the assistance of the monks associated with the homes and have long-standing relationships with the Buddhist community. Some of these businessmen are also recognised Buddhist leaders. Apart from this, it is not uncommon for the Reformist Buddhists to organise and collect donations on a regular basis from their fellow Buddhists. Cash donations are collected and used to purchase small personal items (such as towels, soaps and toiletries) which are presented as gift baskets to individual inmates on occasions such as Vesak Day and Chinese New Year.

The provision of welfare services to the community represents one of the most important tasks undertaken by the Reformist Buddhists to project themselves as socially relevant, thereby legitimising their standing in the eyes of the Chinese, the Christians, other religious groups, and, above all, the state.

Another area in which Reformist Buddhists have been much involved recently is education. They enthusiastically supported the government's policy of introducing Religious Studies into the school curriculum. Over 95% of my informants were overjoyed over this proposal. Many felt that it was a good policy. They believed that religious education, more specifically Buddhism, would be good in training the students to become socially responsible citizens with the right types of moral and social values. Many were also overjoyed by the decision of the government to include both the Buddhist Studies and Confucian Ethics courses into the Religious Knowledge Programme.

With the adoption of Buddhist Studies as one of the religions in Religious Knowledge, the Buddhist community hastened to do their bit. The Singapore Buddhist Federation, which is a Federation of all Buddhist organisations, undertook to establish a Buddhist mission school for secondary students in 1984. Up until 1984, there were only two Buddhist mission primary schools, which had been built in the 1960s by the Buddhist community. Since then, education has been given priority. The new secondary school, Manjusri Secondary School, has attracted favourable responses from Buddhists since its start and enrolment has been high. This has prompted talk of setting up more schools under the auspices of the Singapore Buddhist Federation in the future.

(d) Buddhist Fellowship

Finally, the Reformist Buddhists are also very keen to promote both spiritual and cultural activities to their members. Apart from the different religious units – meditation, chanting and scriptural study, many lay Buddhist groups organised different cultural activities for their members. Some run cultural and religious tours for their members and this has become a popular activity for many of them. Cultural and religious tours to Buddhist and non-Buddhist countries and cities such as Thailand, Hong Kong, Taiwan, Burma, Sri Lanka and Nepal have now become an integral part of the Reformist Buddhists' agenda to widen the knowledge of their members. Some of these religious tours have involved as many as two to three hundred members. Others organise social outings, cooking lessons, flower arrangement, choir and dancing classes.

In organising all these activities, the Reformist Buddhists have taken into consideration the religious, social and recreational needs of the members and have attempted to reform the temples and lay Buddhist organisations so that they may become places where the religious meets the social. They have also attempted to provide fellowship for their members so that such fellowships may form a tight socio-religious network to further bind the members together. It is this attempt to incorporate social and cultural elements into Buddhism and make religion socially relevant to the people that is the hallmark of Reformist Buddhism. To a large degree, Reformist Buddhists are now selling a spiritual lifestyle package to the public and those who find it relevant to their needs will buy it while others will go shopping around for alternative packages on the market.

EFFECTS OF REFORMIST BUDDHISM

The full impact of Reformist Buddhism within the Chinese community in particular and Singapore society in general can only be realised with the passage of time. Since the 1970s, the movement has gathered great momentum, and its impact has been felt throughout the Buddhist community in Singapore. The fact that the Buddhist elite group was formed partly to compete with the Christian elite has gained it acceptance among passive members (nominal Buddhists). Through the sociological changes wrought in Singapore, the latter has become aware of the fact that it is their Chinese orientation which is now being expressed by the Reformist Buddhists. In this expression, they see a challenge to the power-holders and their Christian supporters. By aligning themselves with the Reformist Buddhists, they seek to fight the old battles. While the Christian elite and their supporters have claimed victory over colonialism and are now seeking modernisation (Westernisation), the Chinese masses want cultural decolonisation and a vindication of "Asian Values" however they may be considered.

In preaching Reformist Buddhism, the Buddhist counter-elite in effect has created a new cultural space for the Chinese population. The encroachment by Western, social libertarian values and its religious components in all spheres of life and through multiple institutions and arenas (schools, work place and mass media) has led to a feeling of cultural insecurity among many Chinese. Chinese religion and its institutions, in particular, are being constantly challenged by these Western institutions.

Furthermore, Chinese religion has also been a direct target of criticism by the state. As I have discussed earlier, the state has been arguing for a "rational" and "scientifically-based"' religion which would curb "superstitions" and "occult practices". Among other things, because of this active disapproval, Chinese religion in its traditional folk form is losing some adherents. Nominal Buddhists are the products of the secular education system that teaches reason, logic and rationalism as opposed to faith, belief and supernaturalism. The cultural nexus that exists between Reformist Christianity (and perhaps all post-reformation Christianity) and rationalism has made it possible for Christians to be both religious and modern. Christianity has a niche in modernity. Such a niche is now being created by the Reformist Buddhists who want it to be both a Chinese and Buddhist space. In defining Reformist Buddhism and reshaping Shenism into part of Chinese culture, the Reformist Buddhists seek to rejuvenate the cultural elements that go along with it.

At the religious level, Reformist Buddhism has legitimised the process of rationalisation and bureaucratisation. Reformist Buddhists see the separation of the spheres of social existence into the sacred and profane as an inevitable part of Reformist Buddhism. According to them, reintegration takes the form of a lay Sangha which complements and at times, replaces the traditional temple and the ordained monks. They argue that these two processes will not diminish the religiosity of the people but rather bring it out from the home into the wider public social arena through secular attendance at public meetings and active participation by the followers.

Finally, the Reformist Buddhists have also attempted to integrate state ideology into the Buddhist ideology, thereby playing a supportive role to the various policies initiated by the government. In this sense, Reformist Buddhism has not only undergone a process of secularisation and rationalisation, but also a process of politicisation. The extent to which Reformist Buddhists engage in cultural politics is clearly seen by their active participation and their roles in supporting numerous governmental policies. To a large degree, this is facilitated by the separation of the temple from the Sangha structure. The actions of the state have allowed the temple and the lay Buddhist organisation to participate more actively in the secular sphere without the involvement of the monks, or without being hindered as the Sangha would. Thus, modern Reformist Buddhism takes into consideration the religious and social needs of the people as well as the political needs of the state.

NOTES

1. For a discussion of the Soka Gakkai Sect in Japan, see White, J.W., 1970, *The Soka-Gakkai and Mass Society*, Stanford: Stanford University Press.

2. For a discussion on the Friends of the Western Buddhist Order, see Subhuti, D., 1983, *Buddhism for Today: A portrait of a new Buddhist Movement*, Norfolk: Elements Book.

CHAPTER 8

Members and Their Religiosity

INTRODUCTION

Today, the changing profile of the Singapore Chinese population with its local-born, second and subsequent generations have found much of the Chinese syncretic religious practices less meaningful to their religious needs. While recognising the functional aspects of Shenism, they found it irrelevant to their quest for individual spiritualism and salvation. These younger Chinese are searching for a religion that will fulfil their spiritual needs. They seek a canon of religious teachings that encompasses a set of moral-ethical values and a spiritual excursion into the world of theodicy, eschatology and soteriology. They thus look to other religious organisations that will provide them answers to their quest for spiritualism. At the same time, they also look towards a priesthood (in our case, the *Sangha*) that is well-versed with the scriptures, erudite in their doctrinal exposition and charismatic in their public communication. Apart from fulfilling their spiritualism, these younger Chinese also expect the religion to take on relevant social roles. It is expected to be sympathetic and charitable to the under-privileged and marginalised groups of people including the aged and people who have been abandoned by society at large. These young Chinese found their quest of spiritualism in Reformist Buddhism.

This chapter will profile Buddhist membership found in Singapore and the changing religious needs of a younger Singapore Chinese population. It will also explore their position and influence within the Chinese religious community.

MEMBERSHIP PROFILING

The 1990 Census survey found that 31.8% of household heads surveyed are Buddhists and 23.8% are Shenists (Chinese traditional beliefs)/Daoists (Department of Statistics, 1994: (6):63). However, the 2000 Census survey groups religion according to resident population, reflecting the trend towards an individual-based belief instead of a household-based belief system. This reflects a growing trend towards regarding religion as a personal and private affair where individuals are free to choose their own religion. The 2000 Census shows that there has been a rapid increase of Buddhists in Singapore and a rapid decline in Daoism/Chinese traditional beliefs. Within the Chinese community, 54% of the Chinese are Buddhists while only 11% are practitioners of Daoism and Chinese traditional beliefs (Department of Statistics, 2001 (2): 112). Wee categorises believers of Canonical Buddhism and Chinese religion into three categories namely the "unambiguous Theravada and Mahayana Buddhists who are aware of Buddhist theology, non-differentiating 'Buddhists' who make use of both Canonical Buddhism and Chinese syncretic religions and unambiguous practitioners of Chinese syncretic religions" (Wee, 1976: 169). Today, this categorisation continues to hold true among the members even though the trend is to become a pure Buddhist.

(i)   Shenist-Daoist-Mahayana Buddhists

Many Chinese practise Shenism and Mahayana Buddhism. This is particularly so among the older practitioners. In my survey, those who practised Shenism are from the higher age groups. Over 70% of those in the age group 50 years and above visited both the Shenist/Daoist and Buddhists temples. Over 65% of these practitioners are women.

The main characteristic of the Shenist-Daoist-Mahayana Buddhists is the predominant use of the various Chinese dialects. Individual worshipping is done mostly in the dialect spoken by the worshippers. So, when the elderly women and men prayed to their god, they said their prayers in their own dialects.

At the same time, the priests and the monks also conduct their rituals in dialects. Consultation with the monks and priests is also done mostly in dialect. Many of them would consult a Daoist priest or a spirit-medium when they encounter some serious problem or a crisis. Often, they would go to a Buddhist temple first to pray and ask for assistance. When this fails, they would then consult the spirit-medium for help. The most common problems include mundane domestic affairs, illnesses, emotional and pyschological problems, and social and marital discord.

A second characteristic of the Shenist-Mahayana Buddhists is the nature of their worship. There is no obligation to worship regularly. Individuals visit the temple when the need arises. They can visit as often as they need or not at all. Although these temples conduct regular religious services, *fa-hui*, there is no obligation for the practitioners to participate in the service. In fact, individuals often request ritual services without personally attending these ritual services. Participation is purely on a voluntary basis. It is therefore not surprising that the 1990 Census shows that 62.3% of the Buddhists and 66.5% of the traditional Chinese believers/Daoists visited the temples only occasionally. This is in great contrast to the Christians and the Muslims where over 50% of their adherents make weekly visits to the church and mosque respectively (Department of Statistics, 1994 (6): 69).

A third characteristic is the multiple temple visit system conducted by the practitioners. The practitioners are not bound to one temple. It is very common for individuals to visit different temples for different purposes to help solve their religious and mundane problems. This form of multiple temple-visit is a common practice. Here, the believers simply request a ritual service and pay a fixed sum for the service. A popular temple is one where many people participate in their ritual services. As such, many temples do not have members but believers, *xin-tu*. Of the 260 respondents, over half said that they have visited different Shenist and Buddhist temples and paid for the services. Temple membership is, in fact, a recent invention. With Reformist Buddhism, there is an increasing push for the adherents to become members of a Buddhist organisation. Here, membership is through formal application and one becomes a member through the payment of a subscription fee.

It is possible to argue that the Shenist-Daoist-Mahayana Buddhist boundary is an extremely flexible and elastic one. It can incorporate everyone in it. No one will be excluded. One can also move in and out of it readily. As there is no need to declare one's status and participate actively in the temple's various events, it is assumed that most Chinese are in fact Shenist-Mahayana Buddhists unless they have declared otherwise. In a way, this falls neatly into the ethno-religious categorisation that the Singapore State has imposed from above where 67% of the Chinese are believers of Shenism/Daoism and Buddhism (Department of Statistics, 2001 (2): 112).

(ii) Mahayana Buddhists

The Mahayana Buddhists constitute the largest group of Buddhists in Singapore. Over 90% of the Chinese are Mahayana Buddhists. The reformist-minded ones are consciously rejecting Shenist practices and concentrating instead on the Buddhist practices. In this process of religious rationalisation, the individuals experience a high level of inner tension, having to choose between the two categories of Buddhism. According to Weber, depending on the level of tension and the resolution sought, a radical religious ethic can develop. But for most of these Mahayana Buddhists, while they attempt to be more Buddhist, there are also occasions where they practise Shenist rituals.

To differentiate between a Shenist and a Mahayana Buddhist, a Mahayana Buddhist is asked to take the vow of *san-gui-yi*. This is a vow of paying homage to the Triple Gem (Buddha, Dharma and Sangha) administered by a monk. Upon entering the Buddhist community, new members are given a Buddhist name, *fa-ming*. This name is only used on special occasions. By becoming a Buddhist, they acquire a new identity and often this provides them with the incentive to participate regularly in Buddhist activities. They also join formal membership of one or more Buddhist organisations. They are expected to participate in temple activities, contribute financially and assist the temples in their activities whenever possible. Most donate small sums regularly. They are also expected to attend temple activities on a regular basis. About 60% are in the age groups of 50-59 and over 60 years, 20% are aged 30–49 years and 15% are in the age group 20-29 years.

Most members attend a religious service on a weekly basis. They participate in chanting and reciting sutras. Different sutras are chanted on different occasions. The common ones chanted weekly are Amitabha Sutra, *O-mi-to-jing* and Repentance Sutra, *Da-bei-zhou*. On the birth anniversary of other buddhas and bodhisattvas, their repective sutra would be chanted. On other occasions, the sutra selected is dependent on the monk and the perceived needs of the Buddhists. These elderly women and men often learnt the wordings of the sutras through repetitive listening and memory. Many of them do not read or write. In recent years, most of the sutras are recorded on tape, which could be readily purchased from Buddhist bookshops or from the temples. This has made learning easier. Sutra recitation, recited in a melodious tune, usually lasts an hour. Many elderly women also recite these sutras, especially *O-mi-to-jing* and *Da-bei-zhou*, on a daily basis at home.

They also participate in the monthly religious service, *fa-hui*. Most temples organise this service. The most common religious service is the purification rite, *xiao-zai-fa-hui*. There would be chanting of the sutra and the performance of the purification rites where individuals and family members could, through the rites, purify their karma and accumulate merits and improve their karmic status. This is an especially popular rite among elderly women.

As these Buddhists become more involved in Buddhist activities and come to understand more of the Buddhist teachings, they are encouraged and gradually reduce their participation in non-Buddhist religious activities. They are also dissuaded from consulting spirit-mediums and from engaging in animism. They are urged to remove the Chinese syncretic religious icons and statues from their home altar. A majority of these Buddhists now have only a home altar devoted to the Buddhist deities and their ancestors. But this does not mean that they have thoroughly rejected the Chinese syncretic religious and Daoist practices. Some continue to consult the gods, deities and spirit-mediums when the need arises.

255

To the Mahayana Buddhists, there are several attractions to becoming part of the formal Buddhist community. One main attraction is the serene nature of the practice. Some elderly women informed me that as they progressed in age, they want peace of mind and Buddhist practices provide them with this. To some, they feel that they have fulfilled their social responsibility to their husbands (where they no longer have sexual relations) and adult children. At this stage in their life, they have leisure time and no longer wish to spend their time dashing around, going shopping or buying expensive things. They also no longer wish to be bound by materialism. What they really want is peace of mind and they found that temple-going and sutra-chanting provide a calming effect. Most chant every morning for an hour or two. At the same time, their primary preoccupation is the accumulation of merits and improving their karma. Through chanting, they engage in the path of spiritual cultivation. They feel secure that they are playing a role in charting their own salvation and are hopeful of a blissful afterlife in the Western Paradise, *qi-le-shi-jie*.

Related to this is their view on the Daoist practices, especially that of trance, bodily mutilation and occultism. During their old age, many find these practices violent and disturbing. The excitement and violent effects that they enjoyed earlier on no longer appeal to them. They argued that these were needed in time of difficulty and most have consulted the Daoist priests on occasions during their younger years. At present, they avoid going to the Daoist temples unless there is no alternative.

Several aspects are to be noted here. First, the shift from Shenism to Mahayana Buddhism is a gradual process. Second, the stability of the socio-political and economic environment in post-independent Singapore liberates them from the worries of mundane living and allows them to concentrate on their individual spiritual pursuit. Along with this is the religious re-orientation of these practitioners as a result of the efforts of Reformist Buddhists as well as a shift in the religious needs of the Chinese. At the individual level, Mahayana Buddhism fulfils their spiritual needs better than Shenism.

However, as Luckmann argues, the contemporary religious landscape is one that has shifted from an institutional-based to an individual-oriented type of religion. At present, there is clear evidence that individuals, in their religious pursuit, are drawing divisions between the ethical and the theological elements of their practice. While the social and ethical elements continue to assume importance in the community, the individuals are concerned with only the theological parts that answer their spiritual needs. Luckmann argues that it is these theological parts that are now being confined to the private individual sphere, resulting in a privatisation of religion (Luckmann, 1967). In Singapore, the Mahayana Buddhists are also being caught in this process of religious privatisation and secularisation. The shift away from syncretic Mahayana Buddhism and a return to Buddhist fundamentalism has now assumed an important focus in the practice of the Mahayana Buddhists.

(iii) Theravada Buddhists

Within Theravada Buddhism, there is the Singhalese Buddhist tradition serving the Singhalese community. The second is the Thai and mainland Southeast Asian (Cambodian and Burmese) tradition where the monks come primarily from Thailand and cater largely to the Chinese population. Many go to the Thai Theravada Buddhist temples to ask for help and a variety of favours as they would in a Shenist temple. Thai monks in Singapore have a reputation of being good in magical acts. They are therefore consulted for very specific purposes. This group of Chinese who consult Thai monks do not often see themselves as Theravada Buddhists but as Shenist-Mahayana Buddhists.

There is also a small group of Chinese Theravada Buddhists. These are the Straits Chinese. Since the 1950s, a small group of the Straits Chinese had adopted Theravada Buddhism and participated in Theravada Buddhist religious activities. They built their own Chinese Theravada style temple and invited a Singhalese monk to run the temple and be their spiritual guardian. These Theravada Buddhists are formal members of the temple organisation. Individual households and individuals become members through membership subscription.

The main characteristic of this group is that the main language of communication is English and Malay. The religious services are conducted in the Pali language and communications between the monk and the laity are in Malay and English. Among its members, Malay and English are used. Malay is most common among the elderly members and English is spoken by the younger members. Malay was traditionally the mother-tongue of the Straits Chinese and this has continued till today. Today, the members speak a mixture of Malay and English.

A second characteristic is the regular weekly attendance of the members. 85% of the members attend the weekly service. On most occasions, all family members will attend the service together. Thus, it is not uncommon to find members of different generations attending the religious service together. In most cases, parents and children will go to the service together. There are also several households where three generations of grandparents, children and grandchildren attend the service together.

A third characteristic is active participation by the members. While the monk is the head of the temple, the temple is run by the laity themselves. The members handle the administration and all the mundane aspects of the temples. Apart from this, the elderly men and women are also actively involved in various aspects of temple work. The men busied themselves with temple religious affairs while the women busied themselves with the preparation of food for the monks and the laity.

A fourth characteristic is their interest and their understanding of Buddhist teaching. Most of them have been taught the Buddhist dharma by the monks and they are therefore relatively well versed. Among the younger members, 95% have attended the Buddhist Sunday School for several years where they learnt the Buddhist teaching. In recent years, the Theravada Buddhists have joined the Reformist Buddhist movement to promote scriptural Buddhism to the public.

iv) Reformist Buddhists

The Reformist Buddhists are not homogenous. Broadly speaking, there are Mahayana and Theravada Reformist Buddhists. Within the

Mahayana Reformist Buddhists, there is now an increasingly influential subgroup based on the Tibetan tradition. They call themselves the Tibetan Mahayana Reformist Buddhists. However, increasingly, Reformist Buddhists prefer to be known as non-sectarian in their approach. They call themselves "Buddhayana" to signal their adherence to non-sectarianism.

A Reformist Buddhist explains his involvement in the following way:

> My own extended family is very involved in Buddhist activities. My two nieces are ordained as nuns. Since young, I was exposed to Buddhist teachings and have developed an interest in it. My search for esoteric knowledge has kept my links with Buddhism alive. As a medical practitioner, I did not see much contradiction between my faith and my practice.
>
> If I have been exposed to ritualism when I was young, I would probably have rejected Buddhism and become either an atheist or a Christian. I find it hard to accept a "god-created" world and see Buddhism as a far more superior answer to my quest for knowledge and more significantly, to be able to carry out my own search and research using the Buddhist notion of existentialism in the company of my colleagues.

To him, implicit in this rejection of a god-created world is also the rejection of the notions of superior versus inferior, authority and subordination. Many literate middle-class Buddhists told me that as Buddhists they reject the notion of an omnipotent and omnipresent God and believe that the achievement of personal soteriology through self-effort to be superior to other beliefs where an individual must rely on other beings. Being highly successful in their careers and with good families, they all exude a measure of confidence and self-control over their this-worldly attainment. Whether it is in this-world, or in the afterlife, they wish to preside over their own destiny instead of being subordinated to the whims of higher beings. This emphasis on self-reliance can therefore be seen as a projection of their this-worldly achievement into the other-worldly expectation. In a sense, they have opted for what Weber terms as "the path of mastery", i.e., asceticism. To Weber, it is the mastery over the worldly aspects of individual life and social conditions that is most favourable for the development of a new religious ethic. He saw Ascetic Protestantism as an attempt at the mastery of the world where an individual fulfils his religious commitments through secular activities in this world (Weber, 1958).

Their choice of practice is very much determined by their understanding and interpretation of Buddhism, which is shaped largely by their intellectual background. They are able to read books on Buddhist philosophy, psychology and the like with much ease. Through the Buddhist texts and books, they are able to focus on those Buddhist teachings that they feel are relevant to their needs and put them into practice. They hope to encourage others to follow them through their exemplary behaviour. Through their own effort, they have embarked on a gradual process of restructuring the Buddhist practices, placing emphasis on the dharma and meditation. Their practices appeal to like-minded educated professional Chinese. This process of rationalisation and restructuring of Buddhism therefore has a class overtone attached to it. It is thus not surprising to see an increased number of middle class and younger people attracted to the Reformist Buddhism.

The Reformist Buddhists are relatively new to scriptural Buddhism, enthusiastic and committed to the cause of promoting Buddhism to the general public. This type of lay Buddhist organisation has gained momentum among the younger and better-educated sector of the Chinese community. In my survey of the five lay Buddhist organisations with 260 respondents, over 70% of the members belong to the 20-40 years age group, about 15% are less than 20 years old with the remaining 15% over the age of 50 years. This is in contrast with the believers of Chinese syncretism where over 70% of those who visited the temples are 50 years or more in age. Furthermore, over 80% of them have at least 10-12 years of secondary education while another 12% have tertiary education. This is again in contrast with the believers of Chinese syncretism where over 70% have less than six years of education, with another 15% having 10-12 years of education.

Of the informants, over 30% have come into contact with Reformist Buddhism for less than five years. Another 45% know of Reformist Buddhism for over five years. 15% are involved in it for five to seven years. And 10% are involved in it for over ten years. However, 90% of them have participated in Chinese syncretism, either actively or passively prior to joining a lay Reformist Buddhist organisation.

Unlike the Chinese religious syncretism that attracted over 90% of elderly women to participate in the ritual services, the Reformist Buddhist movements have attracted a more equal proportion of men and women. Over 35% of its members are men. Of them, over 70% are in the age group 20-40 years old. Another 20% are from 40-50 years old. About one-third of them are actively involved in organising activities and 80% actively participated in one or more of the activities, which include dharma discussion, meditation, chanting, prayers and rituals.

Another finding is that the Reformist Buddhists can be divided into two main groups, namely the English-speaking and the Chinese-speaking groups. Each group establishes its own lay organisation to cater to the members' own needs. Although the majority of these Reformist Buddhists are bi-lingual, the post-colonial divide of English and Chinese education continued to have an impact on the way these lay institutions are organised. Those who considered themselves to be Chinese-speaking formed their own group and the English-speaking members formed one too. In this case, it is their most common language of communication that divides them into Chinese-and-English speaking and not their educational background. Thus, a person who has been educated in an English-medium school but speaks Chinese most of the time would consider himself Chinese-speaking. The reverse is also true. Today, although most schools have switched to the English-medium of instruction, this trend continues. The divide between whether a person is English-and-Chinese speaking depends primarily on his/her family and social environment. When a family chooses to use predominantly the English language as a medium of communication, then, English would become the "lingua franca" of that family, influencing all members of the family. In many families, it is a mixture of English, Mandarin and dialects. However, the individual may choose to use whichever language he or she feels most comfortable with.

In a post-colonial Singapore society, language continues to reflect the social status of the individuals. English continues to be the language of the elite and thus those who join the English-speaking lay organisations too assume a higher status. However, with the state policy of speaking Mandarin, the language has been elevated in status in recent years. As such, the Chinese-speaking lay organisations are also finding a niche for themselves in competition with the English-speaking organisations. These two organisations differed greatly from the temples practising Chinese syncretism where dialect is the idiom of communication. Within the temples, one dominant dialect would be used while the believers and practitioners often used their own dialect to communicate with others. It is not uncommon to hear three or four dialects spoken in one conversation depending on the members present.

Among the Reformist Buddhists, although there are some cases where members move freely and attend activities of the various lay Buddhist organisations irrespective of the language divide, many however attend one lay Buddhist organisation and participate actively in it. They attend the activities regularly and at times, help with organising other activities. Of them, about 40% attend the activities two to three times a week, 50% attend the activities and services at least once a week and the rest attend less than once a week.

The language divide also reflects on the socio-economic status of the members. It is found that the English-speaking members are mostly likely to consider themselves as middle and upper middle class. A survey of their occupations found that 15% have professional qualifications, 30% have technical qualifications, 20% have management qualifications 30% secretarial and clerical skills. At the professional level, there are doctors, engineers, computer analysts and teachers. There are also managers and management personnel, as well as technical personnel who work in big factories. Among the women, a majority of them hold occupations as clerks and secretaries in the private sector.

Among the Chinese-speaking Reformist Buddhists, about 50% regard themselves as middle class and another 50% see themselves as coming from the lower middle class background. Among those who regarded themselves as middle class, 65% come from a business background. Most of them have small and medium-sized family businesses or business partnership with others. The other 35% are in managerial, technical and service positions. For those who see themselves as lower middle class, they are in technical, clerical and secretarial positions.

(v) Nichiren Shoshu Buddhists

A discussion on the Buddhist profile will not be complete without mentioning a foreign Buddhist sect, Nichiren Shoshu, that has gained substantial members and made inroads into the Buddhist religious landscape in Singapore. One important aspect of change within the religious sphere among the Singapore Chinese is that a number have become disenchanted with Shenism altogether and accepted a different religious paradigm, in this case, they find their religious needs in a new sectarian group (Wilson, 1982). Nichiren Shoshu in Singapore is seen as a new Buddhist sect as it expounds the following characteristics: exclusive membership, monopoly of religious truth, operates as a lay organisation, equality among its members, voluntary membership, sanctions against members, absolute loyalty and acts as a protest group (Wilson, 1982: 91-91).

Since its establishment in the 1970s, the Nichiren Shoshu Buddhists have expanded greatly in number in recent years and attracted many young Singaporean Chinese. At the initial stages, it recruited mainly from the working class. Today, a large majority of its members continues to be from the lower socio-economic group. In recent years, they are also recruiting from the higher socio-economic groups.

Their rapid expansion is due to three main factors. First, they embarked on very aggressive proselytisation, which saw their number treble in ten years. A second reason for its expansion lies in the way it expounds its theology. The main focus of the practice rests with the chanting or recitation of two short chapters of the Lotus Sutra (*Namyo-ho-renge-kyo*). Members are required to conduct daily recital of these two passages at home. They are also required to attend similar functions in the temple on a weekly basis and participate in other social activities, of which there are many. Apart from this recitation, they are also taught the writings of their president, Ikeda, contained in several volumes written by him and the articles and commentaries of the official newsletter, *Seiko* of Nichiren Shoshu. The explication of the writings is done by the group leaders and members are expected to accept the teachings in a dogmatic manner. While members are encouraged to seek clarification and discuss the teachings and their attempts to put them into practice, members are discouraged from questioning the doctrine and its relevance. In short, the teachings of Master Ikeda Daisatsu are absolute and have to be regarded as the Truth by its members. No doubt is entertained. Much of their efforts went to service this end to ensure that its members understand and accept the doctrine as given to them.

The numerous social activities ranging from cooking and flower arrangement lessons for housewives to organising musical and dance groups for the younger members are means to attract people to their sect. The social aspect of the sect is an important factor in their proselytisation effort. The emphasis is not only on religiosity. But social aspect in fact grew out of the post-war needs of the Japanese where many Japanese suffered an identity crisis after their defeat in the war. In Singapore, rapid development and modernisation has brought about social disintegration and anomie among some sectors of the population. In organising these social activities, Nichiren Shoshu has managed to bring groups of people together in a socio-religious environment. This attempt to establish some form of communalism among varied people has been a successful point in their proselytisation efforts. Besides, the organisational framework which sub-divided their members according to their occupations and socio-economic status has proved to be significant not only in attracting but retaining its members within the sect. In this way, it helps to establish a series of networks of people within the wider institutional framework and ensures loyalty from them.

The Lotus Sutra and a Japanese version of Buddhism is not dissimilar to Mahayana Buddhism which makes it easier to be accepted by the Chinese. Furthermore, the central emphasis on the mythical power of the *daimoku* serves to lure people into the faith. It concentrates and relies totally on the mystic power, *myo-ho*, of the Lotus Sutra. To achieve their mundane goals, to solve problems and avert calamities, members need only to rely on this mystic power which can be called upon through their unfailing chanting of the *daimoku*, at least twice daily, but as often as need be. Apart from this, other Buddhist scriptures and practices are undesirable. The Lotus Sutra is regarded as the pinnacle of the Buddhist scriptures and Nichiren Shoshu is entrusted with the task of delivering this teaching to the world.

The mystic power of the *daimoku* is especially potent for curing those with terminal illnesses. Some members have attested to the mysterious disappearance of incurable illnesses once they have full trust in the mystic power and chant the *daimoku* regularly. It is the perception of this power that draws in a number of those who are seriously and terminally ill in the hope that the mystic power would perform the miraculous act of healing. Some of my informants attested to the efficacy of this power, informing me that their illnesses and those of their close relatives, ranging from perpetual aches to cancerous lumps diagnosed as incurable, have mysteriously disappeared after they began chanting the *daimoku*.

Those who joined the sect are expected to participate actively in spiritual discussion after the *daimoku* session where they inform the group of their spiritual development and the mystic power they experienced in solving their problems, be it an inter-personal relationship, health issue or others. Likewise, they are expected to report on their involvement in the social activities of the sect. This kind of open dialogue ensures that members practise religiously what is expected of them. It also enhanced their belief in the practice when positive results are noted.

At present, the sect has sought to further expand its membership and to legitimise its existence within the Singapore society by organising its members to participate in cultural performances during the National Day Parade, the Vesak Day Celebration and other cultural events. By adopting a high profile status and portraying itself to be socially relevant, with a lucid coherent ideology and a well-organised membership, it hopes to compete with other religious faiths and the reformist Buddhist groups and attract members. So far, while it is able to attract a substantial number of members from the lower socio-economic status groups, it has yet to make much headway with the professsional class who found the religious ideology overly simplistic and their practice and expectation too dogmatic.

THEIR RELIGIOSITY

In my survey, it has been found that the Reformist Buddhists have a high level of religiosity compared to the Shenists, which is comparable to the Protestant Christians. The display of religiosity is regarded as important among the Reformist Buddhists. They measure their religiosity in the following ways. First, they give daily offerings of incense. Second, they learn the dharma. Third, they participate in the ritual services in the organisation or temple. Fourth, they practise meditation, chanting or both. On the first and fifteenth days of the lunar month, offerings of flowers, fruits and food may be given to the Buddhist deities.

It is also found that the Reformist Buddhists see that becoming a Buddhist is a conscious act on the part of the individual. To become a Buddhist, one has to be admitted into the religion and take a vow of Triple Gem, *san-gui-yi*, and invite a Buddhist monk or nun to be his or her spiritual master, a rite of passage called *bai-shi*. In this vow, an individual becomes a Buddhist by declaring his acceptance of the teachings of Buddha, Dharma and Sangha. It also implies that the new member would abide by the Buddhist code of conduct and pursue Buddhism ardently. His entry into the Buddhist community is recorded in the registry of the temple where he or she takes the vow. The member is also given a Buddhist name where it would be used in all activities related to Buddhism. He is also given an identity card with his Buddhist name written on it. Having become a formal member, on religious occasions, the new Buddhist is required to put on a black robe, *hai-qing* and for those who have taken in addition the eight precepts, a brown robe. This is to differentiate the Buddhist members from the temple-goers. They can then position themselves in front of the shrine hall during the religious services.

Among the lay Buddhists, some do not take on a spiritual master. Instead, to them, they become a Buddhist by joining a lay Buddhist organisation and pay a formal subscription. Thus, formal membership is a new feature of Reformist Buddhism. One can be a member of several Buddhist organisations. In the survey, over 40% of the Reformist Buddhists are members of more than one organisation. Membership into the organisation entitles one to use the facilities of the organisation, especially the Buddhist texts. It also enables one to participate in all activities, although non members are also permitted to participate in them. Membership often implies that the members wish to become active members in the organisation by becoming involved in the organisational aspects of temple activities.

These Reformist Buddhists range in age from 10-50 years old. 85% of them belong to age groups 20-29 and 30-39. A small number are in their 40s. Among them, a number of the women reformists hold positions of responsibility within the movement. In terms of educational background, 48% have ten years of education, 37% have 12 years of education and 13% have a tertiary education. The other 2% have technical and vocational education. About 50% of members are English-educated and English-speaking and 50% Chinese-educated and Chinese-speaking. Of those with a tertiary education, 75% are English-educated and English-speaking. However, all are also bilingual.

Among them, they perceived their socio-economic status differently. 73% of the English-educated and English-speaking considered themselves as middle class. They have professional jobs e.g, doctors and engineers. Others include managers, technicians, teachers, clerks and secretaries. Most are from a relatively wealthy social background. On the other hand, 52% of the Chinese-educated and Chinese-speaking considered themselves as lower middle class, working in the technical and service sectors. About 13% are professionals in engineering and computer industries, and 30% in business who see themselves as belonging to middle class.

Over 75% of the Reformist Buddhists become Buddhists because of influence from friends, colleagues and family members. Through friends and family members, they become exposed to dharma lectures and discussions. They are introduced books on Buddhism and a different set of Buddhist practices. Many are attracted to scriptural Buddhism because of what they perceived to be the rationality of the Buddhist dharma, the fellowship they experienced within the Buddhist groups and the new ritual practices especially meditation.

The Reformist Buddhists regard the physical display of their practices as important expression of their religiosity and commitment to Buddhism. Within the home, all have an altar devoted to either one or more Buddhist deities. 55% of the respondents have more than one statue placed on the altar. Their choice of deities (Skyamuni, Amitabha, Matrieya, Guan-yin or others) is one of individual choice. They do not worship nor do they display other Chinese gods and deities at home. All agreed that it is proper to display the ancestor tablets and pay respect to their ancestors. Being a Buddhist does not mean that one should reject all aspects of traditional Chinese beliefs, especially those with ethico-moral overtones. But it is important to the reformist Buddhists to differentiate between the two. To them, this is an open acknowledgement of their religiosity.

Their attendance in Buddhist services and their home practice is another way of reflecting on their religiosity. 81% have attended the Buddhist services in the temple at least once a week. About 20% go to the temple more than once a week. At the temple, they engaged in dharma discussion, sutra recitation or meditation with fellow Buddhists. 95% attend special religious functions. Another distinct characteristic is that all are members of a Buddhist organisation. The establishment of an institutional kind of membership is regarded as an important move. This distinguishes them from the casual temple goers.

Religiosity is also measured according to their personal ritual performance. 95% give offerings of incense to the Buddhist deities, recite the sutras, meditate or read the dharma on a regular basis. Some perform these rituals daily. In traditional religious practices, women (often the mother) are the main practitioners both at home and in the temple where they give offerings of incense to the gods and deities. In contrast, the Reformist Buddhists are active participants in all these aspects.

FOCUSSING ON INDIVIDUAL SPIRITUAL ENLIGHTENMENT

These Buddhists see religion as playing two important roles. The first is the functional role where religion is used to answer their immediate this-worldly needs. The second role is that religion provides answers on suffering, morality and salvation. In anthropological terms, it provides answers to theodicy, soteriology and eschatology.

Some seek out those Buddhist temples with monks and nuns who are erudite in the exposition of Buddhist teachings to learn the dharma and participate in the religious activities. Others are being encouraged by relatives, friends and neighbours to attend these services. Through time, they form a tight network to reinforce each other's commitment. They would attend the services together and encourage each other to participate actively in them. However, among them, there is very little or no coercion to attend or participate. There is an unspoken understanding that whenever one of them is busy with family commitment, the rest would continue to attend the activities and keep the other informed of the events.

Enlightenment means different things to different people. To the Mahayana Buddhists, they want to be able to reach the Western Paradise, *qi-le-shi-jie*, in their afterlife. Failing to make it, then they want to be reborn as human beings. Among the Theravada Buddhists, there is a general recognition that spiritual cultivation is to reduce one's bad karma and be reborn as human beings. To most of them, nirvana is but a dream. They feel that there is no possibility that they could attain nirvana. What they want is a peace of mind and upon death, know that they would not be suffering as a *preta* (hungry ghost) or in the netherworld. The main focus for these two groups is to accumulate as much merits for themselves and for their dead relatives through merit-making. They therefore involve themselves actively in those religious activities that would allow them to accumulate merits such as contributions to construction of temples, presentation of robes to the monks during the Kathina (Offering of Robes to Monks) Ceremony, Vesak Day, Qing-Ming Festival, Hungry Ghost Festivals and welfare works organised by the temples. For the Reformist Buddhists, near enlightenment can be achieved in this life if they followed the Four Noble Truths and the Eightfold Path. Ultimately the belief that "there is Buddha in every heart" serves to encourage all to engage ceaselessly in spiritual cultivation.

CHAPTER 9

Competing Claims of Modernity and Class Identity: Christianity versus Reformist Buddhism

INTRODUCTION

In Singapore, a person's religious identity is closely linked to one's class identity. Among the four main religions in Singapore, Christianity is seen as a high class religion and those who identified themselves as Christian are by association from the middle and upper classes of society. This link between class and religion also has its roots during the early years of British colonial rule and this link continues to play an important role in contemporary Singapore.

This chapter will examine the competing claims of modernity and class identity of two religious groups – Christianity and Reformist Buddhism – and how they used these claims of modernity and class identity to compete for membership within the Chinese community.

CHANGING RELIGIOUS LANDSCAPE

Since the late 1970s, the presence of numerous Christian evangelical groups such as the Billy Graham Crusaders, Pentacostalists and Charismatics has resulted in aggressive proselytisation in Singapore, something that was not seen during the earlier years. Their success in attracting members of the public to their activities and their increased membership has resulted in heightened tension among the various religious groups and upset the ethno-religious balance between these evangelical Christian groups and the established religions. At the same time, there was also the emergence of Islamic Fundamentalism in Singapore. The rapid growth of various religious groups has prompted the government to take a close interest in their activities. Likewise government-commissioned research on religion has also come to the forefront in an attempt to understand religious revivalism in Singapore (Kuo, Quah and Tong, 1988).

Aggressive proselytisation coincided with a period of rapid economic and social change in Singapore. Such changes have resulted in a reassessment of the religious and spiritual needs of the younger Singaporeans. In a survey conducted among university students, it was found that the Chinese students had begun to question the usefulness of traditional Shenist religious practices (Nyce 1972: 30). One reason for switching from one type of religion to another is the existence of a cultural crisis where the norms, values and beliefs of the religious system that the individual was brought up with are no longer relevant to the needs of the individual (Wuthnow 1979). One form of cultural crisis has been associated with the increasing rate of intercultural marriages. In a study done by Tamney and Hassan (1987), it was found that intercultural marriage was the most common reason for young adults switching their religion. In most such cases, one partner was already a member of a particular religious group and the spouse felt obliged to switch his or her religion. Another reason for religious switching is the desire of individuals to belong to a higher status group. A third reason is the perception of Shenism as "old fashioned" and "irrelevant" to modern needs. A common perception of Shenism is that it is "an elaborate ritual system of meaningless practices" which provides no answer to questions of salvation, a "superstitious practice seeking to manipulate the divine forces for this-worldly and material well being" of the worshippers, and a religion of the dead.[1]

This dissatisfaction with the existing Chinese religious landscape has provided fertile ground for the Christian evangelists to proselytise and convert a substantial number of younger Singaporean Chinese. The rate of conversion has alarmed many of the Chinese, among them the older generation Chinese parents and the Buddhist community including members of the Sangha.

CHRISTIANITY'S CLAIM TO MODERNITY AND UPPER CLASS IDENTITY

In contemporary Singapore, Christianity is seen as a "modern" and "rational" religion and appeals to the young and middle and upper class professionals. Christianity has been seen as a superior religion because of the Church's focus on education and welfare work. Among many Singaporeans and Christians, it is the Western model of modernity that they adhere to.

Christianity's claim to modernity has its roots in British colonialism. In 1821, two years after the founding of Singapore, the first Catholic missionary arrived and introduced Christianity into the colony (Sng 1980: 2).[2] The first church was completed in 1939. Since then, missionaries of both Catholic and Protestant denominations have arrived and built more churches and spread the Christian faith. Along with the building of churches, many Christian mission schools were also built. After World War II, the first Christian seminary was built and completed. During this period, the English-speaking missionaries focussed on the provision of education to the people and provided homes to the orphans and homeless. These orphans and homeless who were adopted and cared for by the Christian missionaries became the first group of Christian converts. There was also a small group of Christians who were products of inter-marriage. These were the Straits Chinese, who formed the Malay-speaking congregations (Sng 1980: 123). A third group of Christians was formed among Chaozhou-speaking Chinese migrants who brought along their Christian faith when they first emigrated to Singapore from the counties of Puling, Jiyang, Chaoyang and Shantou in Fujian Province (Clammer 1991: 70). Others were converted because of poverty and they became "rice Christians". The formation of a Chinese Presbyterian Church led by Chinese pastors also led to a small increase in conversion among migrants. Between 1881-1900, only 500 new converts were baptised (Sng 1980: 103). Since then, Chinese dialect-based churches have been established to facilitate and encourage conversions among migrants (Sng, 1980: 105). Apart from education and welfare, the Church became involved in the eradication of various social vices, such as opium smoking and gambling, and provided medical aid to both the needy and the general community, thereby challenging the role held by the Chinese clan associations and temples.

In the aftermath of British colonialism, from the 1950s onward, the number of Chinese converting to the Christian faiths increased gradually to take advantage of the English-based education provided by the church. The lack of schools for the 140,000 school-going children created great demand for Christian mission schools as they had gained a reputation as "academically good schools" with good English education necessary for good careers. Chinese parents were therefore willing to send their children to these schools. After Singapore attained independent status, English, which is one of the official languages, became the functional language not only for cross-cultural communication among the ethnic groups, but also for the commercial and industrial sectors. It is also the key language of the civil service. As such many of the graduates who themselves were Christian converts were recruited into important positions within the civil service. An increasing number of Christians also became very successful in different professions and in business.

In post-colonial Singapore English language continues as the language of the civil bureaucracy, and it is today one of the four official languages promoted by the PAP government. Unlike the Malay, Chinese and Tamil languages, English is seen as a global and neutral language that cuts across ethnic boundaries, and its link with Christianity takes on the same meaning: Christianity is seen to cut through all ethnic lines. It is the only religion that does not have an ethnic boundary in the local context and its members come from all major ethnic communities. Other people's perception of this group, with English education, English-speaking skills and a Christian faith, is that it has a non-ethnic status and a modern image based on professionalism, a status that is coveted by the young professionals whose desire is to break away from ascriptive status to achieved status.

Today their children attend Christian mission schools – 62% of Protestant Christians and 81% of Roman Catholics are English-educated (Department of Statistics 1994 (6): 35). Christians also have a higher educational attainment than the national average: 23% have a secondary and upper secondary education. It was found that 40% of university and college graduates called themselves Christian in 1990 (Department of Statistics 1994 (6): 35). A substantial number of them have also received tertiary education in a Western country.

Given their educational background and professional training, these Christians are over-represented in professions like the law, medicine, and education, and at the higher levels of the civil service. They also dominate the public administration and large private transnational corporations. They also form a sizeable group in management, administration and technical sectors, and they are seen to dominate in the political arena, as some politicians openly declare their Christian faith.

These young Christians also live in luxurious private housing. Out of all the Christians (Catholics, Protestants and evangelical Christians), 26.5% live in private housing, including bungalows (single standing houses), semi-detached (duplex style houses) and terrace houses (Department of Statistics, 2001: 110),[3] thereby reinforcing their middle- and upper- class status. About 77% of Protestant Christians and 81% of Roman Catholics see themselves as middle-class and another 10% Protestant Christians and 5% Catholics see themselves as belonging to upper-class status. By comparison, only 55% of Buddhists/Daoists/Shenists regard themselves as belonging to the middle-class status (Clammer, 1985: 35). Today, 16.5% of all Chinese are Christians (Department of Statistics, 2001 (2): viii)

Christianity is thus often associated with power, both in the private and public sector. The fact that some politicians have openly proclaimed their Christian faith has led many to link it with political achievement and dominance. Christianity in Singapore is thus associated with wealth, social status and power.

From the 1970s onwards, to increase membership, church leadership was localised, with more Chinese bilingual priests and pastors entering the various churches and assuming religious leadership. At the same time, various Christian groups have embarked on an active recruitment process to attract members from different class backgrounds. Their efforts have been facilitated by the development of Housing and Development Board (HDB) new towns (Sng 1980: 62).

Today, Christian churches and its members are seen as "modern" and "upper class" with a good English education. The church is seen as a "rational" and "compassionate" institution, embarking on socially relevant and welfare activities that benefit the wider community. In a post-colonial Singapore, while the effect of British colonialism has long ago been diminished, the process of re-orientalising the Orient continues to play an important role in establishing the image that the West *inter alia* Christianity is superior to the indigenous belief system.[4] Christian missionary churches continue to teach the young that Chinese religious ritual practices and idolatry are superstition. This perception has found its way into the wider Chinese population and made Shenism not only unpopular but also undesirable.

In modern Singapore, being modern and urbane are important criteria for measuring one's social status and success. The definition of a modern individual is one who has a good education; is English-speaking and bilingual, or preferably trilingual (with another European language); is a well-paid, high-positioned professional or civil servant; lives in a private condominium, preferably semi-detached; and drives a luxury car. Such a person is positively middle class and, as mentioned, many of the Christians fall into this category. Thus, the Christians enjoy a "superior" and "modern" status in comparison with the rest of the population and are often seen as equivalent to the "old gentry elite group".

The non-Christian Chinese feel that they are placed in a disadvantaged position because of their socio-economic background. Many see themselves as belonging to the lower middle and lower social class strata. They tend to be in non-professional jobs – the majority in technical jobs, in the lower levels of administrations, or in secretarial or manual jobs. There are also others who are in business and trading and are wealthy by Singapore standards. However, they are not seen as having similar status to their Christian counterparts because of their lack of professional and educational qualifications. Most such businessmen and traders have some knowledge of the English language, and some are fluent in it. Many are also bilingual. They are seen as lacking urbanity and social grace in comparison with their Christian counterparts.

A third factor for Christianity's appeal to the young and educated is its claim to religious truth. Since colonial times, Christianity has proclaimed itself to be the deliverer of religious truth. This is in contrast to Shenism, which does not focus on and teach a religious doctrine. Among believers of Shenism, ritual practices are more important than religious ideology and many Chinese are not concerned with the religious ideology. The Christians, on the other hand, focus on biblical teachings and Christian rationality. The relative lack of ritualism is one aspect that appeals to the young and educated. A second aspect is the focus on individual religiosity where Christianity answers the spiritual needs of the individuals. This is in contrast with Shenism that fulfils the socio-functional needs of the community. A third aspect is the focus on Christian fellowship where members of a Christian fellowship group not only provide religious, but also emotional, psychological and social support for its members. This is especially important in the Singapore context where many young Christians do not have the support of the family when they convert to the Christian faith. Thus, the community of the faithful has, in fact, become a surrogate family for these young members.

A fourth factor is Christianity's approach to conversion. Many Christian groups embarked on aggressive proselytisation. Since the 1980s, Singaporeans have been introduced to a variety of Christian sects and cults that have emerged in Singapore. The Mormons (Church of Latter Day Saints), Pentacostalists, Charismatics, and Jehovah's Witnesses are a few of the more aggressive ones. There are also numerous Student Christian groups including the Campus Crusade, Navigators and Varsity Christian Fellowship, which are all engaged in active and aggressive proselytisation to convert young Singaporeans to their faith.

This aggressive proselytisation has encroached on the religious preserves of the established ethno-religious traditions. Young

Christian evangelists between the ages of 20 and 30 – some only in their late teens – preach, cajole and also harass those who refuse an audience. Often, they preach Christianity as the only true faith, branding others heathens and devil worshippers. This approach of claiming one's religious superiority and exclusivity, at the same time attacking the faith of others, has led to distress among those who have encountered these evangelists and has led, correspondingly, to dissatisfaction by established religious groups over Christian evangelical actions. There have been complaints over what has been regarded as religious harassment and blasphemy.

Most of these Christian denominations are charismatic. The religious activities of many of them include services that emphasise proactive forms of worship including speaking in tongues, waving of hands in the air and loud prayer sessions, conducted in the belief that the participants are having personal communion with God. This is a search for a religious system that can provide an answer to the question on personal salvation.

Finally, various evangelical Christian groups that are based in Singapore have sent their members to proselytise in all public places. Aggressive proselytisation can be found in schools, homes, workplaces and even in public parks; and it is not uncommon for students to preach to their fellow students in schools. The peer pressure in schools proves, at times, too strong for some of the students, who end up becoming converts and preaching to others.

The Christian activities, namely biblical study, church camp, fellowship and social outings, which are both religious and recreational, are more in line with the modern needs of these converts and serve to attract youngsters, by providing them with a sense of sociability, communality and social identity. As a result of these factors, there has been a rapid growth in the number of Chinese Christians – from 10% by the 1980s (Department of Statistics 1994 (6): 3) to 14.3% in the 1990s (Department of Statistics 1994 (6): 3) and 16.5% in 2000 (Department of Statistics, 2001 (2): viii).

However, there is competition and tension among the various Christian groups in Singapore. Since colonial times, there already existed competition between the Catholic and Protestant churches.

Today, a rise in a number of new Christian sectarian and evangelical groups has resulted in intense competition among them. The official census divides Christians into two main groups – "Catholics" and "Other Christians". Following the official categorisation, we find that the "Other Christian" churches are growing at a much faster rate than the Catholics because they employ aggressive methods of proselytisation to attract and convert members to their denominations.

METHODS OF PROSELYTISATION BY CHRISTIANS

A spectacular manner in which the evangelists have sought to convert is through a series of well-organised evangelical campaigns. Since the 1970s, campaigns such as "The Billy Graham Crusade", "Here is Life" and "I've Found It" religious movements have become the benchmarks of aggressive proselytisation. Most of these American-based mass evangelical movements have the financial and human resources, often fuelled by enthusiastic new converts, to stage protracted campaigns to attract conversion. They usually cover the mass media, buying up advertising space in print and electronic media as well as on billboards and buses to advertise their image. They also organise evangelism in public places. In Singapore, the National Stadium, which has a seating capacity of over 60,000 people, is a most sought-after venue. With massive advertising campaigns, these sessions often attract huge audiences and the stadium is often fully packed. Many go because they themselves are Christian, but there are also many who go out of curiosity and end up being captivated by the charismatic performance of the evangelist, with some converting on the spot and others doing so shortly after. There are often reports of mass conversion during campaigns of this nature. One informant said that he was so touched by the sermon, feeling that God was talking through the evangelist to him, that he converted instantly.

While this is one spectacular way of pushing Christianity into the forefront in Singapore, with pomp and fanfare, another more durable way, which ensures the bulk of conversion, is proselytisation on a one-to-one basis. Often, it is the young and the new converts who provide a ready force to carry out such a time-consuming and difficult task. It requires dedication and commitment, and one is guaranteed of many failures. The young ones are often encouraged to take up the challenge as a test of their own commitment to, and faith in, their new religion after a brief training period. They are required to proselytise from door-to-door, in public places, in parks, in eating houses and hawker centres – engaging people in dialogue, preaching the gospel and persuading the unwary and the curious to accept Jesus Christ as their personal saviour and Christianity as their faith. It is also not uncommon for them to involve friends, relatives and family members in debates on the topic.

I quote below, from my notebook, a typical encounter I had with two Mormon women in the Botanical Garden in 1984.

"I was approached by two girls about twenty years old when I was resting after a jog. They walked towards where I was seated and greeted me. They called themselves members of the Church of the Latter Day Christ and asked me whether I had a little time to spare. When I asked them what I could do for them, they sat down on the same bench, one on each side. X first engaged me in the conversation, asking me whether I had heard of the Mormon Church and how much I knew of the faith. When I replied that I knew very little, X expounded the Christian doctrine to me, focussing on my status as a sinner, and God as the Supreme Being and Jesus Christ as the Saviour. X constantly referred to the Bible and quoted from it substantially to give the reasons why I should be a Christian. Following this, Y took over and explained to me the origin of Mormonism and the functions and activities of the Church.

As I seemed eager to know about the religion, they invited me to their church and told me that many of my puzzles would be answered by one of their church elders. At the end of our conversation which lasted about an hour, I was invited to say a prayer with them. They prayed that I would soon be part of them. I was also given The Book of Mormon and some pamphlets.

As we were walking to a nearby hawker centre for a drink, I asked them how they had got involved in the service of preaching to the public. X replied that she was an overseas student at a liberal arts college in Hawaii which is run by the Mormon Church. There in Hawaii, the college strongly encouraged its students to proselytise and be of service to God. It became very evident to her during the second year that almost all her classmates took a year off to serve the Lord. She too signed up to proselytise in her home country, i.e., Singapore in 1984. She would resume her studies in 1985. Y said that she was introduced to Mormonism in 1981 by a colleague at work. She worked as a secretary in a trading firm. Since then, she has been very active in the church activities, particularly in the Youth Section. The church constantly exhorted everyone to preach to colleagues, friends and members of the family. She had several successes in bringing friends to the church and converting them into Mormons. Because of her zeal, she was approached by the main committee to take on "full-time" preaching for a year and to partner X who was then returning to Singapore for missionary work.

Both of them were given a flat to live in and a monthly stipend of S$800 and allowances for travelling, etc by the church.

When I asked them for their motives for preaching, X replied that it was their moral duty to serve the Lord. Y added that they wanted all Singaporeans to know the True Gospel and not be led by the heretics, especially the non-Christians.

When asked where they normally stationed themselves to carry out their duty, they replied "anywhere with a crowd". They especially liked the gardens and parks because, "most of them (the people) are often in a relaxed mood and are more likely to listen to what we say. Besides, there is always a large number of single persons who are out jogging and it is easier to talk to them than a group". Another of their favourite place is outside public libraries, but not inside it. This is mainly because they find it easier to talk to the students who are more receptive than the general adult population to their ideas. They also told me, they visited shopping centres, hawker centres and amusement parks.

They also informed me that while the church encouraged its members to take on a year's missionary work on a full-time basis, it strongly urged everyone to engage in some form of proselytisation among friends and colleagues. They told me that members are encouraged to bring in at least one new person to the church each month and be "of personal service to the Lord."

I had another encounter with lay Christian missionaries. This time, it was two Pentacostalists who came knocking on our door. Again I quote from my notebook.

"M and N first introduced themselves and asked for some of my time. After inviting them in, M, on seeing the family altar housing the Buddhist images and ancestral tablet, remarked, "Your family must be bai-shen".[5] When I replied in affirmation, she said, "So was my family previously, but now they are all Christians like me". N added, "It is your moral duty to bring them out of this mess of superstition. And you must act fast".

They proceeded with an introduction to the Christian doctrine and the wonders of Christianity. At the same time, they exhorted me. N said, "You must not be passive, your family and their future depend on you. You are the only person who can save them from suffering in hell and I think you should accept Christ now". They told me to invite Christ into me there and then and said that they would be only too pleased to teach me the prayer for the purpose. They offered to say the prayer together with me, which I politely declined. My mother who is a devout Buddhist would have been distressed.

I asked them how and why they chose my family. They replied that it was the church committee members who did the allocation. They worked in pairs and each pair was given a street to cover, often near their home. As they were students, they carried out preaching during the school holidays, but also sometimes, on weekends. They told me that working members were encouraged to spend one night each week to do this service.

When asked of their aim in preaching, they replied, "To spread the gospel and to preach to those who know very little or have not heard of the truth. Above all, it is our duty as Christians to do so".

When asked about their success, they replied, "It is important to make people aware of Christianity first even if they appear disinterested. Our duty is to try to persuade them to attend one of church functions, once there at the church, the church elders will be able to tell them more of the wonderful things of Christianity and they will surely join us".

Later, when asked about the success of their door-to-door campaign, they moaned, "It is very hard. So far, you have been the only person who really sat and listened to us. Many families, on hearing that we are Christians, tell us that they want to have nothing to do with us. We are only trying to help them yet they do not seem to understand. We just don't understand them at all."

This is how proselytisation was carried out from the late 1970s to present day. Many of my Buddhist informants also encountered similar experiences from those that I have recounted above. The Christian evangelists usually went prepared with a standard way of informing the listeners of their present state as sinners, followed by their need to receive Christ as their personal saviour. At this point, the evangelist usually asked the listeners about their religious status. If the listeners had another religion, they would condemn their practices as false. Evangelists were also taught stock approaches to counter stock responses if the non-believers showed hostility to their initial aggression. Since the 1990s, most proselytisers have adopted a less aggressive, yet still persistent approach in their conversion efforts.

In 1986, aggressive proselytisation has led some churches in Singapore to report a marked increase in church attendance and in the actual number of conversions, measured by the numbers of baptisms done. One church claimed a tenfold increase in the number of converts, receiving a total of 3,500 new converts in one year.

One of the most common methods is to proselytise to a single person in a public place. It is not uncommon for the evangelical Christians to engage unwary visitors in parks and gardens, shopping centres and other public places in conversation on Christian theology. While proselytisation is carried out among strangers, a more common form is preaching informally to friends, colleagues and family members. Often Christians will discuss their faith with friends and colleagues and persuade them to attend church services. Many of my Buddhist informants have encountered such experiences.

A third method is the formation of small fellowship groups within the public housing estates. These groups act as contact points for those interested in knowing more about Christianity, either on their own initiative or after receiving pamphlets or being introduced by the proselytisers. Each group, numbering about ten people or more, has a leader. Often addresses and telephone numbers of the contact person or persons are posted on public notice board in the public housing estates to facilitate communication between the interested parties and the group leaders.

A fourth method is to proselytise in schools. Traditionally, in Christian mission schools, the students are exposed to Christian gospels during their Religious Studies programme that is part of the formal curriculum. The priests or ministers also give regular sermons to the students. This is still the case in Christian mission schools. However, since the 1970s, proselytisation has also become very visible in non-Christian government schools. Although teachers and outsiders are barred from carrying out proselytisation in schools, it is impossible to stop students from preaching to their school friends. This has intensified, and it is extremely common for Christian students to distribute the Bible and preach to fellow classmates and schoolmates. Many Christian churches subtly encourage their younger members to preach to their friends in schools. Most of my young Buddhist informants told me that they had been approached by their classmates to attend church, and when they told them they were Buddhists, the older Christian students proceeded to tell them that there is only one true religion, Christianity. It is also not uncommon for some students to hold informal Bible study sessions in school and encourage the non-Christians to join in. Thus, a sense of fellowship experienced within these Bible study groups appeals to some students. While it is a formal policy of all schools to instruct students to refrain from proselytisation, it is difficult to effectively police this. Because of the organised nature of the Bible study group, this form of activity cannot be seen as spontaneous. Rather, it can be seen as a deliberate policy on the part of the church to encourage its young adherents, who are constantly reminded of their moral duty to their Church, to proselytise to their fellow classmates.

At the tertiary institutions, Christian students are even more active and aggressive in their recruitment processes. Numerous student-based Christian groups adopt an "all out policy" to recruit new members. Apart from organising an array of activities including seminars, talks, camps and retreats, members constantly engage new and old students in discussion, cajoling them to join their Bible study group. They target individual non-believers and invite them to seminars and talks given by prominent clergy.

Within the university hostels, proselytisation is carried out with even greater vigour. In one instance, a senior staff resident complained that her hostel functioned like a Christian seminary, pointing to a large part of the notice-board space that was taken up with Christian messages and posters bearing Christian messages stuck in all public rooms. Each night, four or five Bible study groups would be busy discussing Christian theology. There is also serious tension between the Christians and non-Christians with some students complaining that they were ostracised by the Christian students for adhering to other religions and they felt threatened.

A fifth strategy adopted is to distribute large quantities of pamphlets bearing the Christian message to the general public. It is now a common sight to have Christian volunteers stationing themselves in shopping centres, bus stops and MTR stations, parks and gardens distributing pamphlets of this nature.

A sixth method used is direct mailing. Today, 85% of the total population live in Housing and Development Board (HDB) flats and the mailboxes are located on the ground floor of each block of flats. Usually Christians living in the housing estates undertake to drop these pamphlets into the mailboxes of the residents living in the estate. There is no shortage of volunteers here. Although this is an easy method of putting gospel messages to the individuals, the effectiveness of this method in relation to the conversion rate remains a question to be answered.

In pursuing this course, the Christian churches have also sought to incorporate secular messages into the Christian teachings. They especially attempt to integrate government policies and campaigns into their gospel. By supporting the government campaigns on various social issues, they attempt to legitimise and rationalise their gospel teaching by bringing the secular into the religious and the religious into the secular. Hence, they now support campaigns like the "National Productivity", "Respect your Elders" and "Total Defence" campaigns. They hope that through incorporating these, they can win more hearts.

COUNTER-CLAIMS BY REFORMIST BUDDHISM

The intensity of Christian proselytisation has affected many aspects of the life of an average Singaporean. It has also brought individuals into actual contact with the Christians. While some have decided to give Christianity a try, others have rejected it outright. Yet others feel harassment and intimidation and resent the aggressive evangelical approach.

Within the Chinese community, Reformist Buddhism has emerged to challenge *Christianity's claims* to modernity. There are several factors that make it modern in the eyes of its adherents and the general population. The first is the focus of Reformist Buddhism, which is on scriptural teaching. Here it adopts scriptural tenets from the different Buddhist traditions to answer contemporary needs. Its primary focus is this-worldly spiritual and secular needs. It also argues that near enlightenment (nirvana) can be attained in this world and in one's lifetime. The pursuit of spiritual knowledge through participation in welfare and charity works are essential for merit-making in order to increase one's good karma.[6] Thus, to the Reformist Buddhists, religious truth is a combination of spiritualism and social welfarism.

Like the Christians, the Reformist Buddhists have also incorporated secular activities into their agenda. They actively

286

support numerous government campaigns. In addition, encouragement by the state and a desire to be socially relevant have made the Reformist Buddhists consider their role as a primary provider of welfare needs for the less privileged groups in the Singapore society by directly involved in charity and welfare work. It has become a common practice for the Reformist Buddhists to collect donations for welfare and charity causes. In this area, they not only have expanded but routinised their charity work as compared to the traditional Buddhist groups.

Another method to counteract the flow of members to Christianity is to encourage active participation and conversion. Like the Christian counterparts, they also embarked on proselytisation. But they refrained from proselytisation in public places such as the shopping malls, parks or along the streets. They encourage their members to proselytise among friends, family members and colleagues and to persuade them to join their activities. One of their strategies is to establish Buddhist networks of friends. They distribute pamphlets on Buddhism to friends and colleagues and engage them in discussions on the Buddhist teaching. Friends and those who have an initial interest in Buddhism are encouraged to attend talks and seminars and participate in other Buddhist activities. They also encourage their friends, family members and colleagues to attend their fellowship and functions. By not proselytising publicly, they have so far avoided antagonising non-believers. This subtle proselytisation has been effective in encouraging more people to attend their activities.

In my survey of 260 Chinese between the ages of 15-40, it was revealed that over 65% called themselves Reformist Buddhists and they have engaged in some form of conversation on Buddhism with their family members, friends and colleagues. Most of them found it easier to talk to those who were practising Shenism. Among the Christians, however, they found it easier to expound Buddhism to the Catholics, but they avoided openly inviting the Christians to abandon their belief. A small group of Christians have attended Buddhist activities, read Buddhist scriptures and reconverted to Buddhism.

Many Shenist and non-members are also attracted to Buddhist fellowship. The Reformist Buddhists are encouraged "to reach out" to their friends and others, and are told to bring family members and friends along when attending Buddhist fellowship. Following the Christian example, the Reformist Buddhists have established fellowship groups. Each fellowship group is involved in Buddhist scriptural study, meditation and religious liturgy. The members engage themselves with the attainment of Buddhist scriptural knowledge and the practice of spiritualism through meditation and liturgy. Members also give each other social and emotional support.

In a combined effort, Reformist Buddhists from the numerous temples and lay organisations have jointly organised Buddhist activities for the public. Reformist Buddhists are pushing for a Buddhist ecumenical movement where the different groups, irrespective of their sectarian differences, come together to promote Reformist Buddhism. Since 1983, different groups have jointly organised various activities such as public exhibitions on Buddhism and public lectures. During the Vesak Day celebration, they also display Buddhist floats that paraded and travelled to the numerous housing estates in an attempt to raise their profile.

While many politicians have openly claimed themselves to be Christians in post-independence Singapore, it was only in 1997 that politicians in Singapore openly proclaimed and participated in Buddhist activities. In 1997, it was only after the then President of Singapore paid his last respects to a prominent monk after his death that many politicians began to follow suit. Since then, many highly-educated professionals and businesspeople, both English-speaking and Chinese-speaking, have also openly proclaimed themselves to be Buddhists. As a result of this move, the general public now look at Reformist Buddhism in a new light. It is now considered as a modern religion and its appeal to the younger Chinese, professionals and politicians has turned it into a force to contest Christianity's claim to modernity.

Reformist Buddhism has seen an increase in its membership since the late 1980s. In 1990, 39% of the Singapore Chinese population holds the Buddhist faith while the number of Shenists have declined from 38% in 1980 to 28% in 1990 (Department of Statistics 1994 (6): 3). In 2000, the census data shows that 54% of Chinese are Buddhists and only 11% claimed themselves to be Daoists/Shenists. Of the Buddhists, 55% are in the age group 25-49 years (Department of Statistics, 2001 (2): 110). From this it is clear that the majority of the Reformist Buddhists come from the younger age groups. Reformist Buddhism is able to state a claim to modernity, and at the same time, it is also attempting to claim a high class status but with modest success. Most of its members continue to be from the lower-middle and working-class status of the population as evidenced from the 91% of its members living in HDB flats (Department of Statistics, 2001 (2): 115). Only 7.9% of the Buddhists lived in private residential housing such as bungalow, semi-detached and terrace houses (Department of Statistics, 2001 (2): 115). In terms of education, in 1994, 2% of the Buddhists have a university education (Department of Statistics 1994 (6): 58) but in 2000, 6% of its members have a university education (Department of Statistics, 2001 (2): 122.).

CONCLUSION

The contest for membership between the Christians and the Reformist Buddhists is a very complex one. It hinges upon the perception of these two groups and how they view themselves and others. Here, the historical colonial legacy continues to play a significant role in regarding Christianity as a superior religion vis-à-vis the others in the post-colonial Singapore state. This perception is reinforced by the fact that Christianity continues to function and reinforce the modern day class structure by using English language, occupation, residential dwellings and social networks of its elite members as important criteria for defining class identity and modernity. The task of the Refomist Buddhists is to overturn this perception and restructure the social and class relationships through the introduction of its new reformist religious structure to counteract Christianity's claim to modernity and class identity. In all its activities, it has succeeded in raising the status of Buddhism and competed successfully with Christianity for membership. However, it is also important to note that while the two religious traditions compete with each other for membership, they continue to operate within the paradigm set out in the Maintenance of the Religious Harmony Act by the Singapore State.

NOTES

1. For a discussion on Chinese religion, commonly known as Shenism, see Elliot, A.J.A. (1955) *Chinese Spirit Medium Cults in Singapore*. London: LSE Monograph on Social Anthropology, no. 14.

2. For a study of the early development of Church and Christianity in Singapore, see Sng 1980, *In His Good Time: The Story of the Church in Singapore, 1819-1978*, Singapore: Graduates' Christian Fellowship.

3. Today, the HDB new towns house about 85% of the total Singapore population, from the middle and working class people of different ethnic background. Private housing in Singapore is very expensive. The average cost for a bungalow house ranges from SGD $4 million up to 10 million (approximately US$2.5 to 6 million) depending on the plot size while the cost of a terrace house ranges from SGD 1.5 million to 2.5 million (US$930,000 – 1.5 million).

4. E. Said (1978) in his work discusses on how the West orientalises the East and that the Orientalist views became a part of the discourse within the Asian societies.

5. Christians usually regard *bai-shen* as worshipping idols and thus, shenists are seen as practising "idolatry" and therefore need to be saved.

6. For a discussion on the issue of karma, merit-making and salvation, see Obeyeskere, G., 1968, "Theodicy, Sin and Salvation in a Sociology of Buddhism", in Leach, E.R. (ed.), *Dialectic in Practical Religion*, Cambridge: Cambridge University Press.

Conclusion

In this study, I have explored how traditional Chinese religion – Shenism – which is part of Chinese culture, is now subjected to a process of religious modernisation. This process of modernisation entails the Chinese moving gradually towards Reformist Buddhism. As a result of the changing needs of the Chinese community, particularly among the younger Chinese, among whom Shenist rituals seem irrelevant to modern religious needs, scripture knowledge is being popularised in its place.

The main players in the process of religious modernisation – the Singapore State, the Reformist Sangha, Reformist Buddhists and the Christians (including the Fundamentalists, Catholics and Liberation Theologists) have been influential in restructuring traditional Chinese religion from Shenism to Reformist Buddhism, offering its adherents an alternative spiritual lifestyle. The Singapore state sees religious modernisation in the Chinese religion as imperative in a variety of ways. First, there is the problem of image. Traditional Chinese religion with its magical and ritual acts is seen as irrational and outdated for a literate population of a modern metropolis. Second, religious engineering is important in order that the Singapore state can continue to maintain the ethno-religious link and that religion is severed from political involvement of any kind. The Maintenance of Religious Harmony Law ensures that each religious group polices its own religious activities and actions and so maintains religious harmony among the ethnic communities. By being involved in religious engineering, the state also ensures that the values that it wants to promote can be integrated as part of the religious discourse of the various religions found in Singapore, including welfare works.

It is possible to argue that Christian activities, especially its aggressive proselytisation serve as a catalyst for the Reformist

Buddhists to rationalise and reform existing Shenist practices into modern Reformist Buddhist practices. There has been rapid conversion of the Chinese to Christianity since the 1980s. This increase is at the expense of Shenism and Buddhism.

The state and the Christians have to a certain degree forced a re-evaluation of the Shenist belief system. At the same time, a home-grown group of Reformist Buddhists and monks has matured and readied itself to restructure Shenism and promote Reformist Buddhism. Apart from encouraging the Chinese population to embrace Reformist Buddhism and forgo Shenism, the Reformist Buddhists' other task is to encourage non Chinese to become Buddhists and to reconvert Christian converts into Reformist Buddhism. They have had some success with this.

Reformist Buddhism is being established as a modern rational religion for Chinese people. At the same time, it wants to be like Christianity and cut across the ethnic divide in Singapore. Its primary focus is on the acquisition of knowledge related to Buddhism – that is on the dharma and the understanding of the scriptural texts, the Buddhist meaning and practice of meditation and the ritual liturgy of prayers, prostration and chanting. It also invokes a commitment to the Buddhist way of life, focussing on Buddhist morality, and its members are encouraged to integrate Buddhist moral values into their daily lives. In short, Reformist Buddhism encourages the development of religious consciousness and spiritual development through its teachings and practices. This religious consciousness is an individual pursuit and not a communal one. In developing individual religious consciousness, Reformist Buddhism encourages the privatisation of religion from the ethnic communal sphere to the community of followers. It thus focuses on the individuals and the attainment of spiritual development and enlightenment. This shift from a communal Chinese syncretic religion to an individual oriented Reformist Buddhism has led to a redefinition of the meaning of religion within Chinese society. In short, Reformist Buddhism offers an alternative spiritual lifestyle to its adherents.

Today, the religious landscape within the Chinese community can be summarised into two types. The first type is religion as a ritual system – the surface structure – where the existing Chinese syncretic belief system with its regular communal religious fairs and celebrations such as the Hungry Ghost Festival and Qing-Ming Festival are practised as part of Chinese culture. At the same time, individuals continue to go to the temple and seek help from the gods and deities to help with their functional needs. The second is religion as an ideological system – the deep structure – with Reformist Buddhism focusing primarily on individual spiritual development.

Between these two systems, tension exists. In general, Shenists are suppportive of Reformist Buddhism and its activities, but Reformist Buddhists tend to be openly critical of Shenist practices. However, in very recent years, in a move to defuse tension between them, the Reformist Buddhists have now reinterpreted Shenist practices as an important part of Chinese culture.

TOWARDS A GLOBAL BUDDHISM

A factor that helps to spread Reformist Buddhism in Singapore is the role played by the global Buddhist movement today. Buddhism has gained much support in America, Australia and Europe. In a society that continues to see these countries as champions of modernisation, global Buddhist movements can only enhance the cause within Singapore. The Reformist Buddhists have been able to establish networks with these movements. In doing so, they are able to integrate the Singapore Reformist movement into the global context.

The lay Reformist Buddhist movement has been able to draw its strength from local and overseas experiences. Within the local context, it borrows ideas from other religious groups, notably the established and evangelical Christian groups, whose aggressive approach to proselytisation was rejected by the Reformist Buddhist movement but whose numerous socio-religious activities, organisational structure, fellowship schemes and economic activities set a precedent for Reformist Buddhism.

Apart from attracting the participation of the Chinese within Singapore, the Reformist Buddhist movement also hopes to attract members from other ethnic groups, and they have already had some success in doing so. However, they have been very cautious and do not proselytise in order to avoid upsetting the ethno-religious framework and antagonising other religions.

In drawing strength from the wider global Buddhist movement, the local movement attempts to remain an integrated part of it. The present thrust in the revival of religious fundamentalist and other religious revivalist movements worldwide also has ramifications on the Buddhist movements throughout the world. Like the Islamic fundamentalist movements, which often have overt political and ethnic overtones and are regarded as militant in nature, or the Christian Liberation Theology, which appeals to the oppressed and the marginal, the Reformist Buddhist movements also have their own agendas. Some are overtly political. In recent years, the Buddhist Sangha in Thailand, Burma and Korea have assumed a more politically-conscious role in their fight for social justice and religious freedom. In Singapore, any overt form of religious aggression is met with intolerance by the state. Religious militancy and attempts by religious groups to incite social and political unrest, in the eyes of the Singapore state, are dealt with swiftly. The Religious Harmony Act is a testimony to the determination of the state to stop such a move.

In some Asian countries including Singapore, Malaysia and Taiwan, the Reformist Buddhist movements are essentially religious movements oriented towards the restructuring of existing Buddhist-Shenist practices in the direction of doctrinal Buddhism, and are aimed at catering to both old and new members in a changing socio-economic environment. One consideration is to re-establish their foothold and regain membership within local communities. To this end, they are able to appeal to the Chinese sense of culture, identity and sentiments and are therefore unlikely to jeopardise their own existence through radical activities, which would find little support from their adherents, or from the state. However, many of them, insofar as they are concerned with social issues and injustices, are often seen as having political overtones.

At the international level, various Buddhist activities and events organised in different parts of the world have helped to kindle a sense of global Buddhist identity. The World Sangha Meeting has the effect of bringing monastic members from various parts of the world together. Likewise, the Vesak Day celebration is now becoming more international in outlook, with various religious activities being organised to cater to the believers across national boundaries. Communications and information technology have helped to bring these religious communities together. Buddhist organisations throughout the world now have their own homepages and disseminate information through the World Wide Web, thereby allowing messages and interaction among members and non-members regardless of where they are on the globe.

There is thus an increase in religious networking among the Buddhist groups at various levels: local, regional, national and international. These religious networks permit small groups to exchange ideas and participate in various activities. They have allowed lay Buddhist groups and members of the Sangha to go on exchange visits to different Buddhist organisations and to embark on pilgrimages to sacred Buddhist sites and temples, in various parts of the world. This has helped to build a sense of *communitas* between the Buddhists in Singapore and elsewhere. Their Buddhist world is now no longer limited to the confines of Singapore, but extends beyond to the global Buddhist community. Many consider this to be an important development in the history of Buddhism in this part of the world – that Buddhism is now able to divorce itself from Shenism and become a religion of modern Singaporeans, and to move away from a narrow parochial "Chinese" religion to become part of a global religious force. To a large extent, this can be seen as part of the growing trend towards Buddhist ecumenism. There are already some sectors within the Buddhist community in Singapore that want to do away with the sectarian labels given to them, preferring non-sectarian approaches and closer networks to further Buddhism. The extent to which Reformist Buddhist movements throughout the world are able to reshape the image of global Buddhism remains to be seen.

As a modern global religious movement, Reformist Buddhism has to fulfil the needs of modern individuals. Like members of the New Age movements, these modern individuals have differing and eclectic needs. In America and Europe, Buddhism has moved away from being associated with "oriental mystique" and towards philosophical rationalism and psychotherapy. More significantly, it is seen as an alternative to Christianity. For many, the atheistic nature of Buddhist philosophy has appealed to the sceptics and the atheists. In these developed countries, Buddhism and its various practices, including meditation, are also marketed as holistic health packages, catering to modern individuals who want an alternative health therapy. Today this image is being popularised in Asian societies, replacing the traditional Buddhist image. As a result of this changing perception, it is possible to argue that the social reconstruction of Buddhism is now underway, and has assumed various forms and is targeting different social and economic groups.

Within the globalisation process, Buddhism experiences two countervailing forces, one from developed Western countries and one from both developed and developing Asian countries. The developed countries of the Industrial West have readily embraced Buddhism as an alternative religious ideology to Christianity. Elsewhere in Asia, efforts devoted to the promotion of Reformist Buddhism mean a rationalisation, sometimes part rejection and other times, part incorporation of folk beliefs and practices as part of Reformist Buddhism.

REFORMIST BUDDHISM IN
A POST-MODERN WORLD

As the world we live is increasingly being compressed and interlaced with cultural complexities in the process of becoming globalised, we are confronted with new sets of meanings and interpretations. How will a religion like Buddhism fit into a post-modern world? Alternatively, how will a post-modern world cope with a Reformist Buddhist discourse? How does a world experiencing a rapid displacement of Western domination and hegemonic influence cope with the upsurge of Buddhism, a non-Western religion?

Reformist Buddhism has helped Asian societies to come to terms with their oppressive colonial past. Now members of these societies see themselves as having both Western knowledge and indigenous values, and therefore are in a better position to "play the game" and beat their opponents. They now use narratives based on their own cultural experiences to express their sentiments, attitudes and actions. For too long, the arguments that Asians have presented were through the narratives of the past colonial masters. Now, a number of indigenous narratives are being created. Reformist Buddhism has provided an anchorage for the perpetuation of the so-called "desirable values" in an environment where values of morality are subjected to relativism and rationalisation and are thus constantly shifting according to temporal demands. Reformist Buddhism has promoted changes to occur within a familiar framework, providing a sense of security and allowing the society and state to embrace changes in a measured and methodical fashion according to the construction of the world around them. In an ever-changing world, there is no certainty, but this allows for calculated risk-taking, with perhaps greater likelihood of success.

Reformist Buddhism therefore can become an integral ideology in post-modern Asian societies. This is especially so in Singapore, where the state and society are now taking stock of their success and failure in their path towards development and modernisation. Within the Chinese society, the same process is occurring. The extent to which shifting morality has impinged on the social fabric of the Chinese community as regards to familial discord, filial piety, wealth production, the erosion of cultural practices, language and social institutions is now being evaluated. Cultural evaluation is a recent phenomenon, and it can only intensify in scope with the maturing of the community's thoughts. Community members could either forge ahead according to the accepted dominant paradigm, or reject it and establish an alternative paradigm using acceptable indigenous values and ideas. To a large degree, what we are witnessing is the articulation of "multiple modernities" as the path towards Reformist Buddhism offers the "Asian" model of modernity that not only the Asians but also the West is increasingly embracing in their search for modern spiritualism. The excitement of Reformist Buddhism as part of the new paradigm cannot be underestimated. However, the reformers must be cautious in order not to fall into the error of re-orientalising the Orient. To do so would be a failure on their part. The challenge here is to strike a balance and create a new environment that is not narrated as a contrast of opposites such as "Oriental vs. Occidental", "West vs. East" and "Natives/Indigenous vs. Others".

Reformist Buddhism in a post-modern Asia could straddle the middle path, reuniting opposites into an integrated whole. The "East", "West", "Oriental" and "Occidental" should not be seen as polarities without complementary features. Each influences the other in an intimate manner. If they can be united as an integrated whole, where values and ideas can be communicated through modern information technology and shared by all, then the world would become more aware of itself and hopefully be a better place to live in. Reformist Buddhism can then claim itself to be truly global.

Postscript to the Second Edition: Towards a Humanist and Socially-engaged Buddhism

In the aftermath of the 9/11 incident where Islamic extremist groups under Osama Bin Laden decimated the Twin Towers of the World Trade Centre in New York, religions and religious movements have come under close scrutiny. It is unlikely that full religious freedom will be condoned in many parts of the world, including the countries that expound democratic ideals of the Western world. What one is likely is guided democracy. Many local religious groups as well as those with global networks will be subjected to either outright or discreet policing by the government and other international law enforcement agencies. Extremist religious movements, including those that champion nationalism and separatism will be regarded as high-risk religious movements capable of terrorist activities and will be monitored closely. While previously the actions of the Singapore government in religious engineering were met with cynicism and criticism by Western governments and human rights groups, such actions are now likely to be regarded as acceptable or even desirable. Furthermore, it is also likely that Asian as well as Western governments might adopt certain legislation to allow them to monitor and to intervene in certain types of religious activities. In this sense, the terrorist attacks will hasten the move towards religious engineering in both local and global contexts.

Today, as we seek to understand the role of Buddhism in modern society, an important role that is gaining currency rapidly is Buddhism's journey into humanity where apart from its role in shaping the morality of individuals and communities through its values, it is increasingly becoming socially-engaged. Socially-engaged Buddhism has witnessed a large increase in membership throughout the world where its members attempt to fight against increasing materialism and consumerism. Here, these socially-engaged Buddhists help shape a more humane local and global community through their concrete social actions for the benefit of the poorer segment of the local and global communities. Through their contributions in material form, time and actions, they are building the groundwork for the emergence of a global Buddhist philanthropic culture.

For the last three decades, socially-engaged Buddhism has gradually increased its influence on the global stage and attracted new members from various parts of the world. In particular, Buddhism has experienced rapid development in America, Europe and Australia, alongside its stronghold in the various Asian countries. Parallel to this is the rapid revival of Buddhism among the youthful population. From Japan to Southeast Asia, China and beyond, Buddhism is spreading rapidly. In Japan and Taiwan, various Buddhist groups have emerged and taken root not only within their own society, but also in the western societies. Likewise in Southeast Asia, a new reformist wave has also swept through countries such as Thailand, Vietnam, Myanmar, Malaysia and Singapore as the elites seek to reform and modernise Buddhism to suit modern needs.

On 2 May 2008, Cyclone Nagris swept through Myanmar and a great catastrophe confronted the Myanmese who lived in the Irrawaddy delta region and beyond. Where relief efforts were hampered by political resistance and inertia, Buddhist groups, small and large, were able to mobilise their members and volunteers to help the victims of this natural disaster. Likewise, the Sichuan earthquake in mid-May 2008 had also claimed a high death toll. Along with governmental and other NGO efforts, Buddhist groups too reached out to the victims both in kind and in actions. Where catastrophes have almost obliterated towns and settlements and where human lives have vanquished, what is left is the indomitable human spirit guided profoundly by their faith and belief in the continuation of human existence. In this sense, the increasingly high profile relief work of some of the Buddhist groups in reaching out rapidly to victims of natural disasters has reignited hope and faith for all and has projected Humanist Buddhism as a significant global religion.

As Buddhism has expanded its reach into the global space, it is inevitable that it will now need to cast its role further by repositioning itself to play an increasingly bigger role. Through the teachings of great Buddhist masters such as the Dalai Lama, Master Cheng Yan, Master Thich Nhat Hanh, Master Hsing Yun, Master Yin Shun, Ikeda Daisatsu and others that follow, the central tenets of Buddhism pertaining to the elimination of suffering and extension of compassion to all in the global environment have become the hallmark of what Humanist Buddhism represents. This is where the spiritual meets the social, creating a new brand of socially-engaged Buddhism.

Glossary

an-tang (庵堂) – nunnery

bai shen (拜神) – praying to gods

bai-shi (拜师) – taking on a spiritual master

bang (帮) – guild

bu-shi (布施) – alms-giving, donation

bu-xiao (不孝) – unfilial

cai-gu (菜姑) – vegetarian aunts

chi (qi) [WG] (气) – energy

Chuang-Mu (床母) – Consort of the Cot

chu-jia (出家) – renunciation

ci-tang (祠堂) – ancestral hall

Da-Bei-Fa-Hui (大悲法会) – Great Repentance Religious Service

Da-Bei-Fa-Shi (大悲法事) – Rites of Compassion

Da-Bei-Zhou (大悲咒) – Great Repentance Sutra

Da-Bo-Gong (大伯公) – Great Paternal Uncle

daimoku [J] (大题) – Sutra

dana [P] – alms-giving

dao (道) – The "Way"

Da-Shi-Ye (大士爷) – A Chinese deity

da-xi (大戏) – Chinese classical opera

dharma [P] – Buddhist scriptural knowledge

dharmacari [P] – practitioner of dharma

Di (地) – Earth

di-yu (地狱) – Underworld, Hell

Di-Zang-Wang-Jing (地藏王经) – Kistagarbha Sutra

Di-Zhang-Wang-Pu-Sa (地藏王菩萨) – Kistagarbha MahaBodhisattva

Dukkha [P] – sufferings

fa-hui (法会) – religious service

fa-ming (法名) – religious name

feng-shui (风水) – geomancy

fo-dao (佛道) – The "Buddha" way

fo-shen (佛身) – Buddha body

fu (符) – charm/amulet

fu-lu-zhu (副炉主) – deputy stove master

gen (根) – roots

gong (工) – labourers, artisans

gong (宫) – a religious place

gong-de (功德) – meritorious deeds

gong-de-tang (功德堂) – memorial hall

gong-yang (供养) – merit making

Guan-gong (关公) – another name for Guan-di

Guan-yu (关羽) – another name for Guan-di

Guan-Di (关帝) – a deified hero

Guan-Di-Miao (关帝庙) – Guan-di Temple

Guan-Shi-Yin-Pu-Sa (观世音菩萨) – Goddess of Mercy

guanxi (关系) – social connections

Guan-Yin (观音) – Goddess of Mercy

Guan-Yin-Niang-Niang (观音娘娘) – Goddess of Mercy

Guan-Yin-Pu-Sa (观音菩萨) – Guan-Yin bodhisattva

Guan-Yin-Tang (观音堂) – Guan-Yin Temple

gu-hun (孤魂) – lonely spirits

gui-jie (鬼节) – Hungry Ghost Festival

hai-qing (海青) – a black robe worn during religious services by the
    Buddhists

Hou-Bo-Gong (后伯公) – God of the Back Portion

hun (魂) – soul

jiang-jing (讲经) – expounding Buddhist sutra

Ji-Le-Shi-Jie (极乐世界) – Heavenly Western Paradise

jin-gang-jing (金刚经) – Heart Sutra

jin-zhi (金纸) – Golden joss paper

Jiu-Wang-Ye (九王爷) – Nine Emperor God

jun-zi (君子) – Gentleman

kai-shan-lao-ren (开山老人) – pioneers in opening the lands

kongsi (gongsi) (H) (公司) – trading firms

Kong-Zi (孔子) – Confucius

kow-tow (kou-tou) (H) (叩头) – prostration

Kuan-Ze-Zun-Wang (宽泽尊王) – a Chinese deity

kuei (kui) [WG] (魁) – guardian spirit

Lianhe Zaobao (联合早报)

Liu-bei (刘备) – a Chinese hero

lu-zhu (炉主) – Stove master

Ma-zu (妈祖) – another name for Tian Hou, Empress of the Heaven

miao (庙) – temple

ming-yun (命运) – life destiny, fate

mitra [P] – Buddhist friends

mu-bei (木杯) – wooden blocks

mui-tsai (mei-jie) [C] (妹姐) – sisterhood

mu-yu (木鱼) – a wooden gong

myo-ho [J] (妙法) – mystical powers

nam-mo [H] (南摩) – monks or nuns who conduct last rites of services to the dead

Namo-Guan-Shi-Yin-Pu-Sa (南无观世音菩萨) – Mantra "Namo Guan-Shi-Yin-Pu-Sa"

Namo-O-Mi-To-Fo (南无阿弥陀佛) – Mantra "Namo Amitabha"

namyo-ho-renge-kyo [J] (南无妙法莲华经) – mystical power of the Lotus Stura

nian-jing (念经) – reciting sutras

nong (农) – farmers

nu-ti-shen (女替身) – female substitute

O-Mi-To-Fa-Hui [H] (阿弥陀法会) – Amitabha religious service

O-Mi-To-Fo [H] (阿弥陀佛) – Amitabha Buddha

O-Mi-To-Jing [H] (阿弥陀经) – Amitabha Sutra

po (魄) – soul

Preta [P] – hungry ghosts

qi (气) – energies

qian (签) – destiny sticks

Qian-Shou-Qian-Yan Guan-Shi-Yin-Pu-Sa (千手千眼观世音菩萨) – Thousand Hands and Thousand Eyes Guan-Yin Bodhisattva

qian-si (签丝) – papers carrying messages of the destiny sticks

Qing-Shui-Zu-Shi-Gong (清水祖师公) – Clear Water Ancestor

ren-jian (人间) – The Human Plane of Existence

samsara [P] – cycles of suffering

Sangha [P] – Buddhist monastic order

sang-li (丧礼) – mourning rites

san-gui-yi (三皈依) – becomeing a disciple of Buddhism

San-Tai-Zi (三太子) – Third Heavenly Prince

shakubuku [J] (传教) – proaching/proselytising

shang (商) – merchants

shan-tang (善堂) – charity hall

she (社) – lay Buddhist organisation

shen (神) – gods

shi (士) – scholar

shi-ben-huo (蚀本货) – profit losing commodity

Shi-Jia-Mo-Ni-Fo (释迦摩尼佛) – Sakyamuni Buddha

Shui-Wei-Sheng-Niang (水尾圣娘) – a Chinese goddess

Taiji (太极) – Great Beginning

ta-li (他力) – Other's power

tang (堂) – a term for temple

Tian (天) – Heaven

Tian Hou (天后) – Empress of the Heaven

Tian-dao (天道) – the "Way" of Heaven

Tian-Fu-Gong (天富宫) – The name of a temple

Tian-Gong (天公) – The Heavenly God/Jade Emperor

Tian-Mu (天母) – another name for Tian hou

ting-zhu (亭主) – Chinese leader

ti-shen (替身) – a subsititute

ti-tou-di-zi (剃头弟子) – a shaven-head disciple

Tu-di-Gong (土地公) – Earth God

wang ben wang zong (忘本忘宗) – forgetting one's origin and
    ancestors

wu-gu (五谷) – the five grains category

xiang-lu (香炉) – incense urn

xiao (孝) – filial piety

xiao-zai (消灾) – purification

xiao-zai-fa-hui (消灾法会) – Rites of Purification Service

xiao-zai-fa-shi (消灾法事) – rites of purification

xiao-zai-zhang-cheng (消灾章程) – rites of purification

xin-tu (信徒) – believers

xin-yong (信用) – trust

xiu-xin (修心) – spiritual cultivation

Xuan-Tian-Shang-Di (玄天上帝) – a Chinese Deity

yang-jian (阳间) – Heavenly Plane of Existence

Yan-Luo-Wang (阎罗王) – King of Hades

yao-cai-dian (药材店) – Herbal Medicine Shop

Yao-Shi-Fo (药师佛) – Medicine Buddha

Yao-Shi-Jing (药师经) – Medicine Buddha Sutra

Yin Yang (阴阳) – Yin and Yang polarity

yin-guo (因果) – karma; cause and effect

Yin-jian (阴间) – the Netherworld

yin-yuan (因缘) – affinity

yin-zhi (银纸) – silver joss paper

you-hun (游魂) – wandering spirits

yu (狱) – hell

Yu-Huang-Da-Di (玉皇大帝) – Heavenly Emperor

Zhang-Fei (张飞) – a Chinese Hero

zhong (忠) – loyal

Zhong-Yuan-Jie (中元节) – Hungry Ghost Festival

zhuang-dao (撞到) – being hit

zi-li (自力) – one's power

zi-xiu (自修) – self-cultivation

Zu-Shi-Gong (祖师公) – Ancestor

Bibliography

Ahern, E.M., 1973, *The Cult of the Dead in a Chinese Village*, Stanford: Stanford University Press.

Ahern, E.M., 1981, *Chinese Rituals and Politics*, Cambridge: Cambridge University Press.

Anderson, B., 1986, *Imagined Communities: Reflections on the Origin and Spread of Nationalism*, London: Verso.

Alter, P., 1989, *Nationalism*, London: Edward Arnold.

Apter, D.E., 1965, *The Politics of Modernisation*, Chicago: University of Chicago Press.

Bagguley, P., et al., 1990, *Restructuring: Place, Class and Gender*, London: Sage Publications.

Bass, J.R., 1973, *Malaysian Politics 1968-1970: Crisis and Response*, University of California Berkeley, Ph.D. dissertation, Ann Arbor: UMI.

Beckford, J.A. (ed.), 1986, *New Religious Movements and Rapid Social Change*, London: Sage Publication.

Beckford, J.A., 1985, *Cult Controversies: The Societal Response to New Religious Movements*, London: Tavistock Publication.

Bedlington, S., 1978, *Malaysia and Singapore: The Building of New States*, Ithaca: Cornell University Press.

Beetham, D., 1974, *Max Weber and the Theory of Modern Politics*, Cambridge: Cambridge University Press.

Bellah, R.N. (ed.), 1965, *Religion and Progress in Modern Asia*, New York: The Free Press.

Bellah, R.N. and Hammond, P.E., 1980, *Varieties of Civil Religion*, San Francisco: Harper and Row.

Bellah, R.N., 1963, "Reflections on the Protestant Ethic Analogy in Asia". *The Journal of Social Issues*, 19: 52-60.

Bellah, R.N., 1970, *Beyond Belief: Essays on Religion in a Post-traditional World*, New York: Harper and Row.

Bellows, T.J., 1970, *The Peoples' Action Party of Singapore: Emergence of a Dominant Party System*, New Haven: Yale University Southeast Asian Studies Monograph 4.

Benjamin, G., 1976, "The Cultural Logic of Singapore's Multiculturalism" in Hassan, R. (ed.), Singapore: Society in Transition, Kuala Lumpur: Oxford University Press, pp. 115-33.

Bendix, R., 1969, *Nation-building and Citizenship*, New York: Doubleday.

Berling, J.A., 1980, *The Syncretic Religion of Lin Chao-en*, New York: Columbia University Press, IASWR Series.

Blau, P.M., 1964, *Exchange and Power in Social Life*, New York: John Wiley and Sons.

Blythe, W., 1969, *The Impact of Chinese Secret Societies in Malaysia*, London: Oxford University Press.

Bloomfield, F., 1983, *The Book of Chinese Beliefs*, London: Arrow Books.

Bosco, J., 1998, *Tin-Hou: The Heavenly Empress*, Hong Kong: Oxford University Press.

Boudon, R., 1986, *Theories of Social Change*, Cambridge: Polity Press.

Brannen, N.S., 1968, *Soka Gakkai: Japan's Militant Buddhists*, Virginia: John Knox Press.

Brown, D., 1994, "Ethnicity and Corporatism in Singapore", in Brown, D., *The State and Politics in Southeast Asia*, London: Routledge, pp. 66-111.

Buddhist Federation Free Clinic Constitution, Singapore: Singapore Buddhist Federation.

Bunnag, J., 1973, *Buddhist monks, Buddhist laymen: A Study of Urban Monastic Organisation in Central Thailand*, Cambridge: Cambridge University Press.

Caplan, L. (ed.), 1987, *Studies in Religious Fundamentalism*, London: Macmillan Press.

Carstens, S., 1975, *Chinese Associations in Singapore Society*, Singapore: ISEAS Occasional Paper: 37.

Cauquelin, J., Lim, P. and Mayer-Konig, B. (eds.), 1998, *Asian Values: An Encounter with Diversity*, Richmond: Curzon.

Chan, H.C., 1971, *Nation Building in Southeast Asia: The Singapore Case*, Singapore: ISEAS Occasional Paper: 3.

Chan, H.C., 1985, "Legislature and Legislators" in Quah, J.; Chan, H.C. and Seah, C,M. (eds.), Government and Politics of Singapore, Singapore: Oxford University Press, pp. 71-91.

Chen, K.K.S, 1964, *Buddhism in China: A Historical Survey*, New Jersey: Princeton University Press.

Chen, K.K.S., 1973, *The Chinese Transformation of Buddhism*, New Jersey: Princeton University Press.

Chen, T., 1940, *Emigrant Communities in South China*, New York: Institute of Pacific Relations.

Chesneaux, J., (ed.), 1972, *Popular Movements and Secret Societies in China 1840-1950*, Stanford: Stanford University Press.

Chiang, H.D., 1970, "Sino-British Mercantile Relations in Singapore's Entrepot Trade 1870-1915" in Chen, J. and Tarling, N. (eds.), 1970, *Studies in the Social History of China and Southeast Asia*, Cambridge: Cambridge University Press, pp. 247-266.

Chu, T.K. (trans.), 1937, *Tao-te-ching*, London: George Allen and Unwin.

Chua, B.H., 1982, "Singapore in 1981: Problems in New Beginning", *Southeast Asian Affairs*, Singapore: Institute of Southeast Asian Studies, pp. 315-335.

Chua, B.H., 1995, *Communitarian Ideology and Democracy in Singapore*, London: Routledge.

Chua, C.S., 1983-84, *Religion and Secularisation: A Study of Christainity in Singapore*, Singapore: University of Singapore, Department of Sociology, Academic Exercise, unpub.

Clammer, J., 1980, *Straits Chinese Society*, Singapore: University of Singapore Press.

Clammer, 1982, "The Institutionalization of Ethnicity: The Culture of Ethnicity in Singapore", in *Ethnic and Racial Studies*, 5(2): 127-139.

Clammer, J., 1985, *Singapore: Ideology, Society and Culture*, Singapore: Chopmen Pub.

Clammer, J., 1991, *The Sociology of Singapore Religion*, Singapore: Chopmen Publishers.

Clutterbuck, R., 1973, *Riot and Revolution in Singapore and Malaya*, London: Faber.

311

Comber, L.F., 1957, *Chinese Ancestor Worship in Malaya*, Singapore: Donald Moore.

Comber, L.F., 1959, *Chinese Secret Societies in Malaya*, New York: J.J. Augustin Pub.

Comber, L.F., 1960, *Chinese Magic and Superstitions in Malaya*, Singapore: Donald Moore.

Constitution of Singapore, 1985, Singapore: Singapore National Printers.

Coope, A.E., 1936, "The Kangchu System in Johore", *Journal of the Royal Asiatic Society, Malayan Branch*, 14(3).

Crissman, L.W., 1967, "The Segmentary Structure of Urban Overseas Chinese Communities", *Man*, 2(2): 185-204.

Curriculum Development Institute of Singapore (CDIS), *Buddhist Studies* (BS) *for Secondary Three*, 1984, Singapore: Pan Pacific Books.

Curriculum Development Institute of Singapore, *Buddhist Studies for Secondary Four*, 1984, Singapore: Pan Pacific Books.

Curriculum Development Institute of Singapore, 1984, *Confucian Ethics for Secondary Three*, 1984, Singapore: Pan Pacific Books.

Curriculum Development Institute of Singapore, 1984, *Confucian Ethics for Secondary Four*, 1984, Singapore: Pan Pacific Books.

Curriculum Development Institute of Singapore, 1984, *Buddhist Studies Teachers' Guide*, Singapore.

Dator, J.A., 1969, *Soka Gakkai, Builders of the Third Civilisation*, Seattle: University of Washington Press.

Dayal, H., 1978, *The Bodhisattva Doctrine in Buddhist Sanskrist Literature*, Delhi: Motilal Banardidass.

De Bary, W.T., 1972, *The Buddhist Tradition*, New York: Vintage Books.

De Bary, W.T., 1998, *Asian Values and Human Rights*, Cambridge, Massachusetts: Harvard University Press.

De Groot, J.J.M., 1885, *Het Kongsiwezen van Borneo*, The Hague.

De Groot, J.J.M., 1964, *The Religion of the Chinese*, Vols. 1 to 6 Taipei: Literature House.

Department of Statistics, 1994, *Singapore Census of Population 1990: Religion, Childcare and Leisure Activities*, Statistical Release 6, Singapore: Singapore National Printers.

Department of Statistics, 2001, *Singapore Census of Population 2000: Education, Language and Religion*, Statistical Release 2, Singapore: Singapore National Printers Pte Ltd.

Dewey, A., 1962, *Peasant Marketing in Java*, Illinois: The Free Press.

Dobbelaere, K., 1981, "Secularisation: A multi-dimensional concept", *Current Sociology*, 29(2).

Doolittle, J., 1865, *Social Life of the Chinese*, New York: Harper and Brothers.

Douglas, M., 1975, *Implicit Meanings*, London: Routledge and Kegan Paul, pp.249-275.

Douglas, M., 1982, "The Effects of Modernisation on Religious Change", *Daedalus*, 3(1): 1-19.

Durkheim, E., (trans.), 1957, *The Elememtary Forms of the Religious Life*, London: Allen and Unwin.

Dutt, S., 1924, *Early Buddhist Monasticism*, London: Kegan Paul, Trench and Trubner Co.

Eisenstadt, S.N., 2000, "Multiple Modernities" in *Daedalus*, 129(1), pp. 1-29.

Elliot, A.J.A., 1951, "The Significance of Religion among the Overseas Chinese", *China Society Singapore Annual*, pp. 28-32.

Elliot, A.J.A., 1955, *Chinese Spirit Medium Cults in Singapore*, London: LSE Monograph on Social Anthropology: 14.

Eno, R., 1990, *The Confucian Creation of Heaven*, Albany: State University of New York Press.

Evers, H-D., 1980, *Sociology of Southeast Asia*, Kuala Lumpur: Oxford University Press.

Evers, H-D. and Siddique, S., 1993, "Religious Revivalism in Southeast Asia: An Introduction", *Sojourn*, 8(1): 1-10.

Fallers, L.A. (ed.), 1967, *Immigrations and Associations*, The Hague: Mouton.

Fei, H.T., 1947, *Earthbound China*, Chicago: Chicago University Press.

Fei, H.T., 1939, *Peasant Life In China*, London: Routledge Kegan and Paul.

Fenn, R.K., 1969, "The Secularisation of Values: An Analytical Framework for the Study of Secularisation", *Journal for the Scientific Study of Religion*, 8(1): 112-124.

Fenn, R.K., 1970, "The Process of Secularisation: A Post-Parsonian View", *Journal for the Scientific Study of Religion*, 9(2): 117-136.

Fenn, R.K., 1972, "Towards a New Sociology of Religion," *Journal for the Scientific Study of Religion*, 11(1): 16-32.

Fenn, R.K., 1978, *Toward a Theory of Secularisation*, Connecticut: Society for the Scientific Study of Religion, monograph 1.

Feuchtwang, S.D.R., 1974, *An Anthropological Analysis of Chinese Geomancy*, Vientiane: Vithagna.

Frazer, J.G., 1960, *The Golden Bough*, London: Macmillan.

Freedman, M., (ed.), 1970, *Family and Kinship in Chinese Society*, Stanford: Stanford University Press.

Freedman, M., 1957, *Chinese Family and Marriage in Singapore*, London: Colonial Research Studies: 20.

Freedman, M., 1958, *Lineage Organisation in Southeast China*, London: LSE Monograph: 18.

Freedman, M., 1966, *Chinese Lineage and Society: Fukien and Kwangtung*, London: LSE Monograph on Social Anthropology: 33.

Furnivall, J.S., 1980, "Plural Societies", in Evers, H-D. (ed.), *Sociology of Southeaast Asia*, Kuala Lumpur: Oxford University Press, pp. 86-96.

Gaw, K., 1991, *Superior Servants*, Singapore: Oxford University Press.

Geertz, C. (ed.), 1963, *Old Societies and New States*, New York: The Free Press.

Geertz, C., 1973, *The Interpretations of Culture*, New York: Basic Books.

Gerth, H.H. and Mills, C.W. (eds. and trans.), 1970, *From Max Weber: Essays in Sociology*, London: Routledge Kegan and Paul.

Glasner, P.E., 1977, *The Sociology of Secularisation: A Critique of a Concept*, London: Routledge Kegan and Paul.

Glock, C.Y. and Stark, R., 1968, *American Piety: Patterns of Religious Commitment*, volumes 1 and 2, Berkeley: University of California Press.

Glock, C.Y. and Bellah, R.N. (eds.), 1976, *The New Religious Consciousness*, Berkeley: University of California Press.

Godley, M., 1981, *The Mandarin-Capitalists from Nanyang: Overseas Chinese Enterprise in the Modernisation of China 1893-1911*, Cambridge: Cambridge University Press.

Goh Chok Tong, 1992, *Speeches, vol. 16*.

Gosling, L.A.P. and Lim, Y.C. (eds.), 1983, *The Chinese in Southeast Asia*, vols. 1 and 2 Singapore: Maruzen Asia.

Graham, D.C., 1961, *Folk Religion in Southwest China*, Washington: Smithsonian Press.

Granet, M., 1975, *The Religion of the Chinese People*, Oxford: Oxford University Press.

Haggard, 1990, *Pathways from the Periphery: the Politics of Growth in the Newly Industrialising Countries*, Ithaca: Cornell University Press.

Hall, M.P., 1979, *Buddhism and Psychotherapy*, Los Angeles: The Philosophical Research Society.

Hammond, P.E. (ed.), 1984, *The Sacred in a Secular Age: Toward Revision in the Scientific Study of Religion*, Berkeley: University of California Press.

Hass, M., 1989, "The Politics of Singapore in the 1980s", *Journal of Contemporary Asia*, 19(1): 48-77.

Hassan, R. (ed.), 1976, *Singapore: Society in Transition*, Kuala Lumpur: Oxford University Press.

Hill, M. and Lian, K.F., 1995, *The Politics of Nation Building and Citizenship in Singapore*, London: Routledge.

Hobsbawn, E. and Ranger, T. (eds.), 1983, *The Invention of Tradition*, Cambridge: Cambridge University Press.

Hsiao, K.C., 1967, *Rural China: Imperial Control in the 19th C*, Seattle: University of Washington Press.

Hsu, F., 1949, *Under the Ancestors' Shadow*, London: Routledge Kegan and Paul.

Hsu, F., 1952, *Religion, Science and Human Crises*, London: Routledge Kegan and Paul.

Hsu, Y.T., 1951, "Great Paternal Granduncle, Second Great Paternal Granduncle and Local Paternal Granduncle" (*Da-Be-Gong, Er-Bo-Gong yu Ben-Tu-Gong*) in *Journal of the South Seas Society*, 7(2): 6-10.

Hsu, Y.T., 1952, "Discussing Again the Research on Great Paternal Granduncle" (*zai tan Da-Bo-Gong yanqiu*) in *Journal of the South Seas Society*, 8(2): 19-24.

Hu, Shih, 1969, "Religion and Philosophy in Chinese History" in Chen Zen, S.H. (ed.), *Symposium on Chinese Culture*, New York: Paragon, pp. 31-58.

Huang, P.C.C., 1985, *The Peasant Economy and Social Change in North China*, California: Stanford University Press.

Humphreys, C., 1968, *Sixty years of Buddhism in England 1907-1967*, London: The Buddhist Society.

Huntington, S.P., 1970, "Social and Institutional Dynamics of One Party Systems" in Huntington, S.P. and Moore, C.H., (ed.), *Authoritarian Politics in Modern Society*, New York: Basic Books, pp. 1-47.

Hungington, S.P., 1996. *The Clash of Civilizations and the Remarking of World Order*, New York: Simon and Schuster.

Ikeda, D., 1976, *Dialogue on Life*, vol. 1, Tokyo: Nichiren Shoshu International Centre.

Ikeda, D., 1977, *Dialogue on Life*, vol. 2, Tokyo: Nichiren Shoshu International Centre.

Jashok, M., 1988, *Concubines and Bondservants*, Hong Kong: Oxford University Press.

Jordan, D.K., 1972, *Gods, Ghosts and Ancestors: The Folk Religion of a Taiwanese Village*, Berkeley: University of California Press.

Kalupahana, D.J., 1983, *Buddhist Philosophy: A Historical Analysis*, Honolulu: University of Hawaii Press.

Katz, N., 1983, *Buddhist and Western Psychology*, Boulder: Prajna Press.

Kaye, B., 1960, *Upper Nankin Street: Singapore*, Singapore: University of Malaya Press.

Kloetzli, R., 1983, *Buddhist Cosmology*, Delhi: Motilal Banarsidass.

Kong, L., 1993, "Ideological Hegemony and the Political Symbolism of Religious Buildings in Singapore" in *Environment and Planning D: Society and Space*, 11: 23-45.

Kuah, K.E., 1988, *Protestant Buddhism in Singapore: Religious Modernisation from a Longer Perspective*, Melbourne: Monash University, unpublished Ph.D dissertation.

Kuah, K.E., 1990, "Confucian Ideology and Social Engineering in Singapore", in *Journal of Contemporary Asia*, 20(3): 371-382.

Kuah, K.E., 1991, "Buddhism, Moral Education and Nation-Building in Singapore", in *Pacific Viewpoint*, 32(1), pp. 24-42.

Kuah, K.E., 1997, "Inventing a Moral Crisis and the Singapore State", *Asian Journal of Women's Studies*, 3(1), pp. 36-70.

Kuah, K.E., 1998,"Maintaining Ethno-Religious Harmony in Singapore", *Journal of Contemporary Asia*, 28(1): 103-121.

Kuah, K.E., 2000, *Rebuilding the Ancestral Village: Singaporeans in China*, Aldershot and Vermont: Ashgate.

Kuah-Pearce, K.E., 2008, "Delivering Welfare Services in Singapore: A Strategic Partnership between Buddhism and the State" in Lai Ah Eng (ed.), *Religious Diversity in Singapore*, Singapore: Institute of Southeast Asian Studies, pp. 505-23.

Kuo, E.C.Y. and Wong, A.K. (eds.), 1979, *The Contemporary Family in Singapore: Structure and Change*, Singapore: Singapore University Press.

Kuo, E.C.Y., Quah, J.S.T. and Tong, C.K., 1988, *Religion and Religious Revivalism in Singapore*, Report prepared for the Ministry of Community Development, Singapore.

Kuo, E.C.Y., 1996, "Confucianism as Political Discourse in Singapore: The Case of an Incomplete Revitalization Movement" in Tu, W.M. (ed.), *Confucian Traditions in East Asian Modernity*, Cambridge, Mass: Harvard University Press, pp. 294-309.

Kwah, L.L., 1977-78, *A Case Study of a Mass Religious Campaign*, Singapore: University of Singapore, Department of Sociology, Academic Exercise, unpublished.

La Fontaine, J.S., 1985, *Initiation*, Harmondsworth: Penguin Books.

Lai, A.E., 1995, *Meanings of Multiethnicity: A Case-study of Ethnicity and Ethnic Relations in Singapore*, Kuala Lumpur: Oxford University Press.

Lau, P.C. (trans.), 1979, *Confucius: The Analects*, Middlesex: Penguin.

Leach, E.R. (ed.), 1968, *Dialectic in Practical Religion*, Cambridge: Cambridge University Press.

Lee Kuan Yew, 1979, *Ministry of Education, Internal Letter*.

317

Lenski, G.E., 1963, *The Religious Factor*, New York: Doubleday.

Lent, J.A., 1984, "Restructuring of Mass Media in Malaysia and Singapore - Pounding in the coffin nails?", *Bulletin of Concerned Asian Scholars*, 16(4): 26-35.

Leo, J.B., 1976-77, *Confucianism in Singapore*, Singapore: University of Singapore, Department of Sociology, Academic Exercise, unpublished.

Leong, V., 1983-84, *The Seance: The Social Function of Communication with the Dead in Chinese Spirit Mediumship*, Singapore: University of Singapore, Department of Sociology, Academic Exercise, unpub.

Lerner, D., 1958, *The Passing of Traditional Society*, London: The Free Press.

Lessing, F.D. and Wayman, A., 1968, *Introduction to the Buddhist Tantric Systems*, Delhi: Motilal Banarsidass.

Leung, Y.S., 1987, "The Uncertain Pheonix: Confucianism and Its Modern Fate", *Asian Culture*, No. 10: 85-94.

Lim, J.H., 1967, "Chinese Female Immigration into the Straits Settlement, 1860-1901", *Journal of the South Seas Society*, 22: 58-95.

Lin, Y.H., 1947, *The Golden Wing: A Sociological Study of Chinese Familism*, London, Kegan Paul, Trench, Trubner.

Ling, T., 1989, "Religion" in Sandhu, K.S. and Wheatley, P. (eds.), *Management of Success: The Moulding of Modern Singapore*, Singapore: Institute of Southeast Asian Studies, pp. 692-709.

Lo, H.L., 1937, "The Establishment of the Langfang Presidential System by Lo Fang Pak in Borneo", Canton: *Kwangchow Hsueh Pao*, 1(1): 1-38.

Lo, H.L., 1960. "A Chinese Presidential System in Kalimantan", *Sarawak Museum Journal*, 9(15-16): 670-674.

Luckmann, T., 1967, *The Invisible Religion*, New York: Macmillan.

Luckmann, T., 1977, "Theories of Religion and Social Change", *The Annual Review of the Social Sciences of Religion*, 1: 1-28.

Mak, L.F., 1981, *The Sociology of Secret Societies: A Study of Chinese Secret Societies in Singapore and Peninsular Malaysia*, Kuala Lumpur: Oxford University Press.

Malinowski, B, 1954, *Magic, Science and Religion*, New York: Doubleday.

Manan, W.A., 1999, "A Nation in Distress: Human Rights, Authoritarianism, and Asian Values in Malaysia" in *Sojourn*, Vol. 14(2): 359-81.

Marishima, M., 1982, *Why has Japan "Succeeded"?*, Tokyo: Tokyo University Press.

Martin, D.A., 1978, *A General Theory of Secularisation*, Oxford: Basil Blackwell.

Matthews, B. and Nagata, J., 1986, *Religion, Values and Development in Southeast Asia*, Singapore: Institute of Southeast Asian Studies.

Metta Welfare Association *Annual Report 2001*.

Ministry of National Development, Planning Department, 1985, *Report of Survey: Revised Master Plan 1985*, Singapore: Ministry of National Development, Planning Department.

Myers, R.J., 1986, *Religion and the State: The Struggle for Legitimacy and Power*, London: Sage Pub.

Navari, C., 1981, "The Origins of the Nation-State", in Tivey, L. (ed.), *The Nation-State: The Formation of Modern Politics*, Oxford: Martin Robertson.

New York Times, 5 November 1998.

Nyce, R., 1969, "Chinese Folk Religion in Malaysia and Singapore", *The Southeast Asia Journal of Theology*, vol.2 (81-91).

Nyce, R., 1972, *The Kingdom and the Country: A Study of Church and Society in Singapore*, Singapore: Institute for Study of Religions and Society in Singapore and Malaysia.

Obeyesekere, G., 1968, 'Theodicy, Sin and Salvation in a Sociology of Buddhism', in Leach, E.R. (ed.), *Dialectic in Practical Religion*, Cambridge: Cambridge University Press.

Ong, T.C., 1979, *Report on Moral Education, 1979*, Singapore: Ministry of Education.

Overmyer, D.L., 1976, *Folk Buddhist Religion: Dissenting Sects in late Traditional China*, Massachusetts: Harvard University Press.

Piatigorsky, A., 1984, *The Buddhist Philosophy of Thought*, London: Curzon Press and New Jersey: Noble Books.

Png, P.H., 1969, "The Straits Chinese in Singapore: A case study of local identity and socio-cultural accommodation", *Journal of SEA History*, 10(1): 95-114.

Pong, D. and Fung, E. (eds.), 1985, *Ideal and Reality*, Lanham: University Press of America.

Preservation of Monuments (Amendment) Act, 1983, Singapore.

Prebish, S.C. (ed.), 1978, *Buddhism: A Modern Perspective*, University Park and London: Pennsylvania State University Press.

Purcell, V., 1951, *The Chinese in Southeast Asia*, London: Oxford University Press.

Purcell, V., 1967, *The Chinese in Malaya*, Kuala Lumpur: Oxford University Press.

Purushotam, N., 1995, *Disciplining Differences: Race in Singapore*, Singapore: National University of Singapore, Department of Sociology, Working Paper Series: 126.

Quah, J.S.T. (ed.), 1990, *In Search of Singapore's National Values*, Singapore: Institute of Policy Studies and Times Academic Press.

Quah, J., Chan, H.C. and Seah C.M. (eds.), 1985, *Government and Politics of Singapore*, Singapore: Oxford University Press.

Rawski, E., 1988, " A Historian's Approach to Chinese Death Ritual" in Watson, J.L. and Rawski, E.S. (eds), *Death Ritual in Late Imperial and Modern China*, Berkeley: University of California Press, pp. 20-36.

Rodan, G. (ed.), 1993, *Singapore Changes Guard*, New York: St. Martin's Press.

Said, E., 1978, *Orientalism*, London: Penguin Books.

Saso, M.R., 1972, *Taoism and the Rite of Cosmic Renewal*, Seattle: Washington State University Press.

Shiner, L., 1967, "The Concept of Secularisation in Empirical Research", *Journal for the Scientific Study of Religion*, 6(2): 207-220.

Siddique, S., 1989, "Singaporean Identity" in Sandhu, K.S. and Wheatley, P (eds.), *Management of Success: The Moulding of Modern Singapore*, Singapore: Institute of Southeast Asian Studies, pp. 563-577.

Smith, B.L., 1979, *Religion and the Legitimation of Power in Southeast Asia*, Leiden: E.J. Brill.

Smith, C., 1991, *The Emergence of Liberation Theology*, Chicago: Chicago University Press.

Sng, B.E.K. and You P.S., 1982, *Religious Trends in Singapore: With Special Reference to Christianity*, Singapore: Graduates' Christian Fellowship and Fellowship of Evangelical Students.

Sng, B.E.K., 1980, *In His Good Time: The Story of the Church in Singapore 1819-1978*, Singapore: Graduates' Christian Fellowship.

Sng, B.E.K., and Choong, C.P. (eds.), 1991, *Church and Culture: Singapore Context*, Singapore: Graduates' Christian Fellowship.

Song, O.S., 1967, *One Hundred Years' History of the Chinese in Singapore*, Singapore: University of Malaya Press.

Soothill, W.E., 1973, *The Three Religions of China*, London: Curzon Press, reprint.

Spencer, R.F. (ed.), 1971, *Religion and Change in Contemporary Asia*, Minneapolis: University of Minnesota Press.

Spiro, M.E., 1970, *Buddhism and Society*, New York: Harper and Row.

Straits Times (ST), 1 November, 1990; 10 November 1990; 2 March 1991; 14 March 1991; 16 September 1991; 2 August 1992.

Subhuti, D., 1983, *Buddhism and Change in Contemporary Asia*, Minneapolis: University of Minnesota Press.

Surin, M., 1999, "Joining the Values Debate: The Peculiar Case of Thailand" in *Sojourn*, Vol. 14(2): 402-13.

Suyama, T., 1962, "Pang Societies and the Economy of the Chinese Immigrants in Southeast Asia", in Tregonning, K.G. (ed.), *Papers on Malayan History*, Singapore.

Tambiah, S.J., 2000, "Transnational Movements, Diaspora, and Multiple Modernities", in *Daedalus*, 129(1), pp. 163-194.

Tamney, J.B. and Hassan, R., 1987, *Religious Switching in Singapore: A Study of Religious Mobility*, Singapore: Select Books.

Tamney, J.B., 1996, *The Struggle Over Singapore's Soul: Western Modernisation and Asian Culture*, Berlin and New York: Walter de Gruyter.

Tan, C.B., 1995, "The Study of Chinese Religions in Southeast Asia: Some Views" in Suryadinata, L. (ed.), *Southeast Asian Chinese: The Socio-Cultural Dimension*, Singapore: Times Academic Press.

Teo, S.S., 1980-81, *Religion and Social Mobility: A Study of the Full Gospel Business Men's Fellowship International (Singapore Chapter)*, Singapore: University of Singapore, Department of Sociology, Academic Exercise, unpub.

Tivey, L. (ed.), 1985, *The Nation State: The Formation of Modern Politics*, Oxford: Martin Robertson.

Tong, C.K., 1982, *Funerals, Ancestral Halls and Graveyards: Changes and Continuities in Chinese Ancestor Worship in Singapore*, National University of Singapore, Department of Sociology, unpublished M.A. dissertation.

Topley, M., 1952, "Chinese Rites for the Repose of the Souls: With Special Reference to Cantonese Custom", *Journal of the Royal Asiatic Society, Malayan Branch*, 25(1): 149-160.

Topley, M., 1953, "Paper Charms and Prayer Sheets as Adjuncts to Chinese Worship", *JMBRAS*, 26(1): 63-80.

Topley, M., 1954, "Chinese Women's Vegetarian Houses in Singapore", *JMBRAS*, 27(1): 51-67.

Topley, M., 1956, "Chinese Religion and Religious Institutions in Singapore", *JMBRAS*, 29(1): pp. 70-118.

Topley, M., 1958, *Organisation and Social Function of Chinese Chai Tang in Singapore*, London: University of London, Ph.D. dissertation, unpublished.

Topley, M., 1961, "The Emergence and Social Function of Chinese Religious Associations in Singapore", in *Comparative Studies in Society and History*, 3(3): 289-314.

Tremewan, C., 1994, *The Political Economy of Social Control in Singapore*, New York: St. Martin's Press.

Tu, Weiming, 2000, "Implications of the Rise of 'Confucian' East Asia", in *Daedalus*, 129(1), pp. 195-218.

Turnbull, C.M., 1972, *The Straits Settlement 1926-67*, London: Athlone Press.

Turnbull, C.M., 1977, *A History of Singapore, 1819-1975*, Kuala Lumpur: Oxford University Press.

Turnbull, C.M., 1989, *A History of Singapore, 1819-1988*, Singapore: Oxford University Press.

Turner, V., 1969, *The Ritual Process*, Ithaca: Cornell University Press.

Urban Renewal Authority (URA), n.d., *A Future With A Past: Saving Our Heritage*, Singapore: URA.

Vasil, R.K., 1984, *Governing Singapore*, Singapore: Eastern University Press.

Vaughan, J.D., 1972, *The Manners and Customs of the Chinese of the Straits Settlements*, Kuala Lumpur: Oxford University Press, reprint.

Wang, G.W., 1958, "The Chinese in Search of a Base in the Nanyang", *Journal of the South Seas Society*, 14(1 and 2): 86-96.

Wang, G.W., 1991, *The Chineseness of China*, Hong Kong: Oxford University Press.

Wang, T.P., 1977, *The Origins of Chinese Kongsi with Special Reference to West Borneo*, Canberra: Australian National University, M.A. dissertation, unpublished.

Wang, T.P., 1979, "The word Kongsi", *JMBRAS*, 42(1) 102-105.

Warren, J., 1986, *The Rickshaw Coolies: A People's History of Singapore 1919-1939*, Singapore: Oxford University Press.

Ward, B., 1953, " A Hakka Kongsi in Borneo", in *Journal of Oriental Studies*.

Watson, J.L., 1988, "The Structure of Chinese Funerary Rites: Elementary Forms, Ritual Sequence, and the Primacy of Performance" in Watson, J.L. and Rawski, E.S. (eds.), *Death Rituals in Late Imperial and Modern China*, Berkeley: California University Press, pp. 3-19.

Weber, M., 1951, *The Religion of China*, New York: The Free Press.

Weber, M., 1958, *The Protestant Ethic and the Spirit of Capitalism*, New York: Charles Scribner's Sons.

Weber, M., 1966, *The Sociology of Religion*, London: Associated Book.

Weber, M., 1974, *The Theory of Social and Economic Organisation*, New York: The Free Press.

Wee, V., 1976, "'Buddhism' in Singapore" in Hassan, R. (ed.), *Singapore: Society in Transition*, Kuala Lumpur: Oxford University Press.

Wee, V., 1977, *Religion and Ritual among the Chinese of Singapore: An Ethnographic study*, Singapore: University of Singapore, Department of Sociology, M.A. dissertation, unpublished.

Wee, C.J.W.-L., 1999, "Asian Values", Singapore and the Third Way: Re-working Individualism and Collectivism" in *Sojourn*, Vol. 14(2): 332-58.

Welch, H., 1967, *The Practice of Chinese Buddhism 1900-1950*, Cambridge, Mass.: Harvard University Press.

Weller, R.P., 1986, *Unities and Diversities in Chinese Religion*, London: Macmillan.

White, J.W., 1970, *The Soka Gakkai and Mass Society*, California: Stanford University Press.

White Paper on Maintenance of Religious Harmony, presented to Parliament of Command of the President of the Republic of Singapore, 26 December 1989.

White Paper on Shared Values 1990, 1991, Singapore: Singapore Government.

Whitton, J.B., 1963, *Encyclopedia Americana*, 19: 749.

Wilson, B.R. (ed.), 1981, *The Social Impact of New Religious Movements*, New York: Rose of Sharon Press.

Wilson, B.R., 1982, *Religion in Sociological Perspective*, Oxford: Oxford University Press.

Wilson, H., 1978, *Social Engineering in Singapore*, Singapore: Singapore University Press.

Wolf, A.P. (ed.), 1974, *Religion and Ritual in Chinese Society*, California: Standford University Press.

Wong, A.K., and Ooi, G.L., 1989, "Spatial Reorganisation" in Sandhu, K.S. and Wheatley, P. (eds.), *Management of Success: The Moulding of Modern Singapore*, Singapore: Institute of Southeast Asian Studies, pp. 788-812.

Wright, A.F. (ed.), 1960, *The Confucian Persuasion*, California: Stanford University Press.

Wuthnow, R. (ed.), 1979, *The Religious Dimension*, New York: Academic Press.

Yang, C.K., 1961, *Religion in Chinese Society*, Berkeley: University of California Press.

Yeh, S.H.K. (ed.), 1975, *Public Housing in Singapore*. Singapore: Singapore University Press.

Yen, C.H., 1982, "Overseas Chinese Nationalism in Singapore and Malaya", in *Modern Asian Studies*, 16(3): 397-425.

Yen, C.H., 1985, *Coolies and Mandarins: China's Protection of Overseas Chinese During the Late Ch'ing Period 1851-1911*, Singapore: Oxford University Press.

Yen, C.H., 1986, *A Social History of the Chinese in Singapore and Malaya 1800-1911*, Singapore: Oxford University Press.

Yinger, J.M., 1957, *Religion, Society and the Individual: An Introduction to the Sociology of Religion*, New York: Macmillan.

Yinger, J.M., 1967, "Pluralism, Religion and Secularism", *Journal for the Scientific Study of Religion*, 6(1): 17-30.

Yinger, J.M., 1970, *The Scientific Study of Religion*, New York: Macmillan.

Yong, C.F., 1968, "A Preliminary Study of Chinese Leadership in Singapore 1900-1941", *Journal of Southeast Asian History*, 9(2): 258-285.

Yong, C.F., 1977, "Leadership and Power in the Chinese Community of Singapore during the 1930s", *Journal of Southeast Asian Studies*, 8(2): 195-209.

Yong, C.F., 1977, "Pang, Pang Organisations and Leadership in the Chinese Community of Singapore during the 1930s", *Journal of the South Seas Society*, 32(1 and 2): 31-52.

Zialcita, F.N., 1999, "Is Communitarianism Uniquely Asian? A Filipino's Perspective" in *Sojourn*, Vol. 14(2): 313-31.

GOVERNMENT DOCUMENTS/REPORTS

1. Singapore Statutes on Land Acquisition Acts:
   1966, pp. 153-80
   1967, pp. 427-32
   1968, pp. 239-40

2. Singapore Yearbooks: 1945-1999

3. Ministry of Education Reports:
   a. Goh Keng Swee's Education Report, 1980.
   b. Ong Teng Cheong's Moral Education Report, 1979.
   c. Letters between the Prime Minister and the Education Team February and March 1979.

4. Curriculum Development Institute of Singapore:
   a. Moral Education Manuscript for "Being and Becoming" for primary and secondary schools and teachers' guide.
   b. Religious Knowledge Programme:
      i) Minutes of Meeting for Directors,
         Edun C07-01-067, vol. 3, July 1983.
         Edun Co7-01-067, vol. 3, Sept 1983.
      ii) A list of schools offering the various Religious Knowledge subjects in English and Chinese language on pilot testing basis.
      iii) Tables on Options by School Types (Missions or government schools) with English as First Language.
      iv) Tables on Options by School Types with Chinese as First Language.
      v) Tables on Options by School Types with Malay as First Language.
      vi) Tables on Options by School Types with English and Chinese as First Languages (for the SAP schools).
      vii) Buddhist Studies Training Programme for the teachers.
      viii) Tables on Options by religions of the pupils.

5. National Archives and Oral History:
    Tape-recorded conversations with successful Singaporeans over their early life as newly arrived migrants, their religious belief, work ethics and their success. Excerpts also published in a book titled *The Pioneers* in 1985, Singapore: Ministry of Culture, Oral History Department.

6. *Speeches* – compilation of speeches given by various ministers.

NEWSPAPERS, MAGAZINES AND NEWSLETTERS

1. *Straits Times* (ST)
2. *Nanyang Siang Pao*
3. *Sin Chew Jit Pao*
4. *Far Eastern Economic Review* (FEER)
5. Peoples' Action Party newsletter, *PETIR*
6. *Lianhe Zhaobao*

PRINTED MATERIALS/PAMPHLETS ON BUDDHISM IN ENGLISH LANGUAGE IN CIRCULATION IN SINGAPORE (THE LIST IS NOT EXCLUSIVE)

Dhammananda, K.S., *Why Buddhism?*
Dhammananda, K.S., *Buddhist Attitude Towards Other Religions*
Dhammananda, K.S., *Religion in a Scientific Age*
Dhammananda, K.S., *What is this religion?*
Dhammananda, K.S., *Handbook of Buddhists*
Dhammananda, K.S., *The Duties of a Lay Buddhist*
Dhammananda, K.S., *Are Buddhists Idol Worshippers?*
Dhammananda, K.S., *Why Religion?*
Dhammanaratana, B., *Life of Gotama The Buddha*
Guruge, A., *Buddhism in Modern Life*
Lee, S.M., *Chinese Culture and Religion*
Narada, *The Meaning of Life*

Piyadassi, *Buddhist Observances and Practices*
Piyananda, *Why Meditation?*
Piyasilo, *The Total Buddhist Work*
Piyasilo, *Buddhist values on being your trueself*
Piyasilo, *Buddhist Today: Values and Identity*
Piyasilo, *Basic Buddhist Meditation Practice*
Saddhaloka (trans.), *The giving rise of the ten kinds of mind of the bodhisattva*
Saddhaloka, *The Discourse on the ten wholesome ways of action*
Santina, *Fundamentals of Buddhism*
Sarada, *Reflection on Death*
Sarada, *Meditation on Loving Kindness (Karaniya Metta Sutta)*
Subhadra, *An Introduction to the Teaching of the Buddha Gotama*
Trizin, *A Collection of Instructions on Parting from the Four Attachments*
Wijesekera, *Buddhism for Today and Tomorrow*

NEWSLETTER AND MAGAZINES OF THE FOLLOWING BUDDHIST ORGANISATIONS IN SINGAPORE

1. Singapore Buddhist Federation, Singapore Buddhist Free Clinic Magazine
2. Mangala Vihara Buddhist Temple newsletter "Echo"
3. The Buddha Sasana newsletter "White Conch"
4. National University of Singapore Buddhist Society Journal "One Wheel"
5. Ngee Ann Polytechnic Buddhist Society publication "The Golden Link"
6. Golden Pagoda Temple Newsletter and Magazine
7. Metta Buddhist Welfare Association Magazine

INTERNET WEBSITES:

1. DharmaLink <http://www.aloha.net/~horaku/dharmalink.html>
2. Singapore DharmaNet < http://www.singapore-dharmanet.per.sg>
3. Singapore Buddhist Free Clinic <http://www.sbfc.org.sg/>

Index

www.ingramcontent.com/pod-product-compliance
Lightning Source LLC
Chambersburg PA
CBHW021848020426
42334CB00013B/239